Substance and Substitution

Also by Suzanne Fraser

COSMETIC SURGERY, GENDER AND CULTURE

Also by kylie valentine

PSYCHOANALYSIS, PSYCHIATRY AND MODERNIST LITERATURE

Substance and Substitution

Methadone Subjects in Liberal Societies

Suzanne Fraser
*Centre for Women's Studies and Gender Research, School of Political and Social Inquiry,
Monash University, Australia*

kylie valentine
Social Policy Research Centre, University of New South Wales, Australia

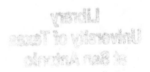

First published 2008 by
PALGRAVE MACMILLAN
Houndmills, Basingstoke, Hampshire RG21 6XS and
175 Fifth Avenue, New York, N.Y. 10010
Companies and representatives throughout the world

PALGRAVE MACMILLAN is the global academic imprint of the Palgrave
Macmillan division of St. Martin's Press, LLC and of Palgrave Macmillan Ltd.
Macmillan® is a registered trademark in the United States, United Kingdom
and other countries. Palgrave is a registered trademark in the European
Union and other countries.

ISBN-13: 978-0-230-01998-0   hardback
ISBN-10: 0-230-01998-6   hardback

This book is printed on paper suitable for recycling and made from fully
managed and sustained forest sources. Logging, pulping and manufacturing
processes are expected to conform to the environmental regulations of the
country of origin.

A catalogue record for this book is available from the British Library.

A catalog record for this book is available from the Library of Congress.

10   9   8   7   6   5   4   3   2   1
17 16 15 14 13 12 11 10 09 08

Printed and bound in Great Britain by
CPI Antony Rowe, Chippenham and Eastbourne

Contents

Acknowledgements

This book is the product of over three years of research, collaboration and consultation. Funded by the National Health and Medical Research Council of Australia, the project on which it is based was conducted at the National Centre in HIV Social Research (NCHSR) at the University of New South Wales. It is difficult to imagine undertaking a project such as this elsewhere in Australia. Staffed by a broad range of highly expert and unfailingly generous researchers, the NCHSR provided a wonderful environment in which to pursue an unusual project: one that combined policy-oriented research (on which a report has also been produced) with theoretically informed sociological work of a feminist bent. For fostering this environment we must first thank the NCHSR's recently retired director and chief investigator on the study, Susan Kippax. Profound thanks must also go to the head of the NCHSR's hepatitis C and illicit drugs program, Carla Treloar, also a chief investigator on the study. Her expertise, unflappable calm and unerring decency made our three years' work a real pleasure. And here the study's third chief investigator, Alex Wodak, must also receive thanks. Without his knowledge and professional standing the study might never have eventuated. Likewise, Paul Van de Ven, originally also a chief investigator, deserves our gratitude. He too was instrumental in the study's birth.

The study was also lucky enough to be guided by a reference group of generous and committed experts: Andrew Byrne, Max Hopwood (a co-designer of the study as well), Anne Lawrance, Denis Leahy, Sarah Lord, Susan McGuckin and Catherine Waldby. Their input not only informed the analysis in invaluable ways, it expedited many of the practical aspects of the study, including the sometimes arduous task of recruiting interview participants. Regular well-attended meetings and frank discussion meant the group never allowed us to oversimplify the issues – a tendency all too common in discussions of drug treatment – and for that, and many other contributions, we are extremely grateful.

Peter Muhleisen in Melbourne and Irvine Newton in Sydney provided practical assistance and advice on the day-to-day practices of methadone treatment, and the assistance of doctors, pharmacists and clinic staff (whose anonymity we need to preserve) in New South Wales and Victoria was vital in recruiting.

Of course, the study would not have been possible without the 87 in-depth interviews that provided the basis for our analysis. We are, therefore, very much obliged to the clients, service providers and policymakers who generously gave their time to talk to us about their experiences. Recruiting these participants and conducting so many interviews was very time-consuming, and was only possible with the help of two research assistants, Nadine Krejci and Anna Olsen. Both worked extremely hard to find participants, and both often conducted challenging interviews with impressive sensitivity and insight. Some of the most moving stories we have drawn on in the book were collected by these two researchers, and we owe them a debt of gratitude for their skill and effort.

It is also important to acknowledge here the very generous and illuminating contributions of David Moore and Helen Keane, who read and made valuable comments on the manuscript for this book.

Of course, each of us also drew support and inspiration from different friends and colleagues. Accordingly, Suzanne would like to express her gratitude to the following people.

My thanks must first go to kylie valentine of course – I could have wished for no better collaborator. For much appreciated companionship and advice at the NCHSR, I thank Joanne Bryant, Sarah Fitzherbert, Martin Holt, Christy Newman, Kane Race and Robert Reynolds. For wonderfully reliable professional guidance and assistance, as well as some of the most rewarding friendships I have known, I also thank Jeanne Ellard and Asha Persson. Beyond the NCHSR, I am very grateful for the friendship and support offered by the following people: Dean Murphy, Celia Roberts, Fiona Rummery and Gina Thomson. Louise Fraser, Jason Fraser, Michelle Fraser and Jane Caldwell have given all the best things family can, and more, especially in Louise's case. And last there is John Jacobs. Well, any good wishes and thanks – heartfelt though they might be – that lines such as these can offer, fall absurdly short of capturing the gratitude I owe John. I can only leave it at that.

kylie would like to thank: Suzanne; colleagues at the NCHSR, especially Max Hopwood and Joanne Bryant, who shared their office; colleagues at the Social Policy Research Centre, especially Cathy Thomson, Trish Hill, Karen Fisher and Melissa Roughley; Celia Roberts; Elizabeth Wilson and Gill Straker; friends and family, especially Nikki Potent, Gina Laurie, Jam Dickson and Vivienne Laurie-Dickson, Gilly Dempsey, Paul Martin and Rose Dempsey-Martin; and

my closest loves, Richard Short and Pax Valentine, who make everything so complexly wonderful.

* * *

Parts of the following chapters have already appeared in print, albeit
in different forms. Sections of Chapter 3 appeared in 'The chronotope
of the queue: Methadone maintenance treatment and the production of
time, space and subjects', *International Journal of Drug Policy*, 17, 2006:
192–202 (reprinted by permission of Elsevier). Sections of Chapter 4
appeared in 'Methadone maintenance treatment and making up people',
Sociology, 41(3), 2007. Sections of Chapter 5 appeared in 'Speaking
addictions: Substitution, metaphor and authenticity in newspaper representations of methadone treatment', *Contemporary Drug Problems*,
33, 2006: 669–698 (copyright Federal Legal Publications). The extract
from *Junky* by William Burroughs is Copyright 2003 the Estate of
William S. Burroughs, reprinted with permission of The Wylie Agency.

Collaborations take a range of forms, and ours involved a planning
process followed by the largely independent authoring of chapters. This
writing stage was then combined with discussion and further writing as
we worked towards bringing the chapters together. Both authors co-wrote
the Introduction. Suzanne wrote Chapters 1, 3, 5 and the Conclusion,
while kylie wrote Chapters 2 and 4.

Introduction

Methadone just allows us to be normal, that's all. It's no
different from a diabetic taking insulin. No different.
Best analogy. Or [...] a vampire taking his blood every
night, or, or a lion getting his meat [...] We need it just
to stay normal, and that's it, we're poisoned, so we
need the poison, and that's all it does, it's just the same
as heroin. Except the only difference is you don't get a
rush [...] you're just normal.

(Cameron, Melbourne, Victoria,
client, 42 years old)

Like many other areas of medicine, methadone maintenance treatment
(MMT) inspires feelings of intense ambivalence among its consumers. As
one of the participants in the study that forms the basis of this book
makes clear, methadone is both meat and poison; it is *pharmakon* in
Derrida's fullest sense in that it combines remedy, toxin and is 'a means
of producing something'.[1] Yet methadone also differs from almost all
other areas of medicine in at least one devastatingly important way: it
treats a condition widely seen as mainly social in significance. For heroin
addiction, accompanied though it is by physical symptoms, and reframed
though it has been in recent decades as a medical rather than moral issue,
is not considered primarily physical in the sense that diabetes or cancer
or heart disease usually are. If it were, it would undoubtedly enjoy more
acceptance. Instead, it continues to register in Western discourse firstly as
a political, cultural and social problem, a form of 'deviance', and, policing aside, methadone is Western liberal society's main response to it.

Illicit drug use occupies a uniquely stigmatised position in contemporary society. Terrorism and child abuse (to which it is often linked in

1

political and media discourse [Dawn Moore, 2004]) are perhaps the only social phenomena currently more vilified. Treatment responses to illicit drug use, therefore, emerge out of and themselves generate intense political and social pressures, both disrupting and reproducing conventional understandings of what it means to be human, citizen, woman or man. MMT – the sprawling, heavily regulating treatment for heroin dependence – is an especially powerful example of this. To date, however, methadone has attracted comparatively little attention from social sciences and humanities scholars. A thorough literature search spanning last two decades turns up a relatively small number of journal articles that use social and cultural theory to analyse MMT, and only one book-length work (a sociological account of women on methadone treatment in the US by Friedman and Alicea published in 2001). Eclipsed, perhaps, by the relatively sensational or spectacular aspects of heroin, MMT functions, it might be said, as Western liberal society's 'suburban dream/nightmare' of illicit drug use. Representing neither the (sometimes romanticised) outlaw lifestyle of unfettered heroin addiction, nor the fully-fledged respectability of a drug-free existence, MMT offers a uniquely marginal social location for its consumers. Indeed, in its role as oft-maligned substitute for a similar yet highly illicit substance, and in its co-enactment of pharmacological, social, medical and legal objects and interests, MMT offers fascinating insights into the contemporary tensions and contradictions entailed in the production of the proper law-abiding, autonomous, responsibilised, 'stable' subject of liberal society. Alan Petersen, among others, has analysed the rise of this subject in the context of medicine and public heath in Western liberal societies, arguing that 'Being a "healthy", responsible citizen entails new kinds of detailed work on the self and new interpersonal demands and responsibilities' (1997: 204). He links this shift with particular changes in the West towards neo-liberal models that focus on, among other things, 'the tendency for individuals to be evaluated according to their abilities to effectively regulate themselves and others in line with prescribed norms of conduct for "healthy living"' (203). This emphasis on self-regulation and the choosing of particular norms of health entails a complex, sometimes contradictory set of implications and effects for those individuals considered 'addicts', and perhaps especially, those undertaking MMT.

This book combines in-depth interviews with analyses of the media and with contemporary theory to examine a form of treatment used by hundreds of thousands of people across Australia, the United States (US), the United Kingdom (UK), Canada and Western Europe.[2] Drawing on recent science and technology studies and feminist science studies theory, we reframe MMT as a 'phenomenon' – as an assemblage of human and non-human actors made in its encounter with politics, culture and research such as ours – and we use this framework to explore treatment and its social and political implications through a broad range of actors and relationships. MMT addresses the physical, the social and the cultural, and our task in this book is to find ways of thinking treatment that hold both the physical (or material) and the social-cultural in view without collapsing one into the other. Later we turn to Karen Barad's feminist ontology to begin this task. We interview MMT clients along with prescribing doctors, dosing nurses, dispensing pharmacists and policymakers in two states in Australia (New South Wales and Victoria) in the view that the treatment program, and the substance of methadone itself, are materialised in specific ways through the perspectives of, and encounters among, all these groups.

In turn, we use MMT to explore and elaborate on recent theoretical insights into the nature of materiality. We argue that, in attempting to understand both the role of MMT in the production of individual lives, and its broader social and political effects, methadone must be reconceptualised. An analysis that recognises methadone's co-construction with interlocking medical, social, legal and political forces changes the usual focus. Instead of viewing it as a fixed, pre-defined system that treats similarly pre-existing subjects in order to nurture a beneficial change, we analyse it in terms of the powers it exercises and responsibilities it carries in generating particular subjectivities, while constraining or disallowing others. As Isabelle Stengers and Oliver Ralet (1997: 222) have pointed out in relation to drugs: '[E]ach proposed solution anticipates and suggests, through the way it addresses the individual, what this individual is, and what he or she can do.' In part, we ask, how does MMT address individuals, and how does it define and delineate what individuals involved in the program can do. These questions allow much needed, and newly conceived, consideration of the political and ethical issues intrinsic to drug treatment.

Methadone maintenance treatment in Western liberal societies

Methadone is a synthetic opioid developed mainly for the treatment of pain. It is an opioid receptor agonist, which means it occupies the receptor sites in the brain which otherwise take up heroin. Methadone is one of a group of medications used in the treatment of opioid dependence.

Hostility to MMT from advocates of abstinence stems in large part from the similarity between methadone and heroin: although methadone has a simpler chemical composition than heroin, they both bind to the opioid receptors and are understood to produce similar effects. The other medications comprise the partial agonist buprenorphine, the antagonist naltrexone and the recently developed buprenorphine/naloxone combination, which combines the partial agonist with an antagonist to produce a substance effective when absorbed under the tongue, but ineffective, even harmful, when injected. Among Australian drug users and service providers, the best known of the opioid antagonists probably remains naloxone (marketed as Narcan), which is administered by paramedics and other health workers to counteract the effects of opioid overdose. Each of these medications is distinguished within pharmacology and medicine by different properties and effects (see Fiellin, Friedland and Gourevitch, 2006). They also therefore have different social and political implications, many of which will be discussed in the chapters that follow. Methadone, for example, is considered stronger (to use a rather crude term) than buprenorphine, so is thought by some to better discourage some clients from returning to heroin use. Buprenorphine is considered longer-acting than methadone, so is thought by some to allow some clients to dose every second day rather than daily. Buprenorphine/naloxone is understood to produce withdrawal symptoms when injected, so is thought by some to discourage illicit sale of treatment medication. Naltrexone is considered 'non-euphoric', so is thought by some to more effectively break the 'cycle' of drug addiction than do the full and partial agonists. Medical opinion on these medications, their effects and their relative merits is by no means consistent, but there is little doubt that opioid pharmacotherapy is the most effective treatment for opioid dependence (Ward, Mattick and Hall, 1998). What these terms mean – what we might understand by words such as 'dependence' and 'treatment', and what it means to take for granted pharmacological effects on the body, to treat the material as prior to the social – remains contested. Investigating these concepts and these assumptions is part of the purpose of this book.

It is possible to give only approximate figures for the numbers of people enrolled in MMT in Australia and the two countries with which Australia is often compared, the UK and the US. Even approximations, however, indicate that large numbers of people are directly and indirectly affected in each jurisdiction. According to the Australian Institute of Health and Welfare (2005) there are around 34,000 registered clients who receive either methadone or buprenorphine in Australia, a country with a total population of about 20 million people. In England about 70,000 people receive methadone or another opiate substitute from a total population of around 60 million (Great Britain, 2006). In the US, which has a population of about 300 million, there are around 236,000 methadone clients (Drug and Alcohol Services Information System, 2006). In all these jurisdictions, methadone is the most commonly used medication among the available opioid pharmacotherapies. Australia thus services the highest proportion of pharmacotherapy clients per capita (0.017 per cent) with the UK placed second (0.011 per cent), and the US third (0.008 per cent). Drug addiction is sometimes represented as the fate of only the most reckless fringe dwellers, at other times as a lurking danger imperilling everyone. These figures give the lie to both representations. Diabetes affects far more people: up to 7 per cent of the Australian population (Australian Institute of Health and Welfare, 2006a: 70). In contrast, the number of people living with HIV/AIDS in Australia (around 15,500 people) totals less than half those on phar-macotherapies (National Centre in HIV Epidemiology and Clinical Research, 2006b).

Comparisons with HIV and diabetes are useful to discussions of methadone treatment because of what they reveal about the social and cultural meanings of diagnosis, identity and treatment, not because of incidence rates. Diabetes is sometimes discussed alongside MMT as a comparable daily treatment for a physical condition. Indeed, methadone treatment pioneers Vincent Dole and Marie Nyswander were among the first to develop a metabolic model of addiction (Dole and Nyswander, 1967). Yet, despite attracting increasing scrutiny as an indicator of both the perils of affluence and intra-country inequalities, diabetes is not constituted as a political condition in the sense that addiction and drug treatment always is. Debates around the validity of treating addiction as analogous to diabetes continue to inflect both the organisation of drug treatment and the social recognition of illicit drug use. HIV incidence in Australia is much lower than in many comparable countries, especially the US, where around 1.2 million people are living with HIV/AIDS (UNAIDS, 2007). This is in part because of the adoption of harm reduc-tion strategies, such as the introduction of needle and syringe programs and the expansion of methadone maintenance programs, early in the pandemic (Gibson, Flynn and McCarthy, 1999; Wodak and Cooney, 2006). The politics of HIV articulate through global biopolitics, homo-phobia, stigma, racism, new social movements, political identity and biological citizenship. The history of HIV is recognised as inextricably, and ironically, bound up with the constitution of 'gay community'

(Altman, 1994; Patton, 1990; Race, 2003; Rofes, 1998; Watney, 1994). Drug addiction and treatment echo these themes, but opportunities to reorganise society to better reflect the interests of drug users in terms of the politics of both recognition (societal patterns of representation, interpretation and communication) and redistribution (political and economic structures) (N. Fraser, 1997) have not yet been subject to similar scrutiny and analysis.

There are a number of similarities between methadone treatment programs in Australia and the UK, along with differences between both and the US. Treatment in the UK and Australia combines general practitioner and specialist services. This means some clients receive treatment by obtaining a prescription from their doctor. This is then filled at a community pharmacy.[3] Others attend a clinic, the exclusive business of which is opioid pharmacotherapy treatment. In the US almost all clients receive their methadone from clinics: in 2005 more than 80 per cent of clients were dosed at facilities whose sole business was opioid pharmacotherapy prescription and dosing. The median number of clients in these facilities was around 200 (Drug and Alcohol Services Information System, 2006). Prescribing and dosing arrangements, as will become clear, are hugely important to the experience of treatment, and the US experience of large, publicly visible and heavily stigmatising clinics is not shared by all Australian clients. It is, however, the experience of many clients: one survey of Australian treatment services found the median number of clients per pharmacotherapy service to be 150, and clinic dosing is common in some states (Bryant et al., forthcoming[a]). Similarly, blind dosing, a practice whereby clients are not informed of the amount of methadone they are being prescribed, rarely if ever happens in Australia and the UK. In contrast, it is estimated that blind dosing happens in up to half of all clinics in the US (Bleich et al., 2001). The importance to clients of dosing levels, communication and respectful relationships cannot, as we will see throughout this book, be underestimated.

Broadly speaking, treatment rules in Australia and the UK can be described as more liberal than in the US. Australia and the UK are not identical, however. While the treatment guidelines produced by the UK Department of Health are similar in many respects to those of the Australian states of NSW and Victoria, there are two important differences. The UK guidelines are explicit about their defined legal position: they do not have a position, except insofar as they are subject to legal obligations relating to the prescribing of controlled drugs. The status of the Australian states' guidelines is less clear, and causes some confusion, as our study shows. The UK guidelines also mention, albeit with many cautions and caveats as to the limitations of their use, two drugs that are never prescribed in Australia and the US: first, heroin (diamorphine), and second, methadone intended to be injected rather than swallowed (Department of Health, Scottish Office Department of Health, Welsh Office and Department of Health and Social Services Northern Ireland, 1999). By contrast, injectable methadone cannot be prescribed in Australia (indeed, it cannot be prescribed in tablet form, unless in exceptional circumstances) and nor can heroin in any form.

While the regulations governing methadone vary between and within countries, research on client experiences and views of treatment reveal many basic similarities. In all jurisdictions the operational cultures of clinics and pharmacies vary, as do the philosophies of individual workers, and both have an enormous impact on clients' experiences. Treatment often involves daily pick up and can entail conflict, humiliation, long periods of waiting and regular intrusions on privacy. Equally, when respect and care are present and providers are adequately resourced, treatment is often valued by clients. This has been shown to be the case in the US (J. Fraser, 1997; Lovejoy et al., 1995; Rosenbaum, 1985; Stancliff et al., 2002), in the UK (Lilly et al., 2000; Neale, 1998, 1999) and in Australia (Mitchell, Dyer and Peay, 2006). As we argue throughout this book, the particularities of methadone treatment within and between countries are important, but the experiences of Australian clients share much with those of clients elsewhere. Our observations and recommendations should thus be taken into account in any jurisdictions operating similar treatment regimes.

Methadone as a problem for social research

As we noted at the outset, pharmacotherapies for opioid addiction, of which MMT is the oldest and best known, have been the subject of little sustained social research. The clinical dimensions of treatment, effectiveness evaluations, patient compliance and client views of treatment are analysed in the pages of public health and clinical journals. The logic and principles of substitution therapies, which prescribe a synthetic opiate to heroin-dependent people, have been subject to much debate between advocates of harm reduction and advocates of abstinence. These are relatively narrow fields, however, and the broader social meanings of methadone treatment have received little attention. Drug addiction in general, and the politics of illicit dealing and consumption in particular, have received much more attention (Brodie and Redfield, 2002; Denton, 2001; Keane, 2002; Maher, 1997; Valverde, 1998). Pharmacotherapy clients sometimes describe the experience of treatment as one of leaving an outlaw culture and entering a passively dependent one, and a similar logic seems to underpin the relative academic neglect of treatment. Addiction and crime have long been core to sociology and remain so, whether or not reports of the 'death' of the sociology of deviance are accurate. Treatment complicates the figuring of the 'addict' as deviant or resistant and despite this, or perhaps because of it, has not proved as productive a source of study. Yet the importance of biomedicine and the biological self to contemporary sociology indicates other ways in which drug treatment can illuminate power and subjectivity. For example, Jennifer Friedman and Marixsa Alicea's *Surviving Heroin*, the only full-length work on methadone treatment to be published in the last two decades, deploys binaries of resistance and conformity in its representation of heroin and methadone. Heroin is destructive but also an avenue for empowerment: it 'provides a sense of freedom from traditional race-class-gender constraints' and breaks down 'the confining walls of objectification' (Friedman & Alicea, 2001: 88–9). Methadone treatment, in contrast, tames these refusals and rebellions. It makes the lives of clients legible, generates rules and norms, and renders those bodies that have previously 'transcended' passivity docile (91, 147). Resistance to control can still be found, the authors argue, in women who use methadone clinics strategically rather than obediently, but essentially methadone treatment represents capitulation:

> With methadone they can function, they can work, they can save money and possessions, they can take care of themselves and others, they can have a life. But there is a trade-off. To have this life, they must realign themselves to the historical times. Their bodies and minds must become colonised by the language of medical 'experts', for within these institutions, there is little place for a discourse of resistance.
>
> (205)

Resistance is also central to Philippe Bourgois's *In Search of Respect*, an ethnography of crack dealing in New York (Bourgois, 1995). The book focuses on two main characters, Primo and Caesar, and its central argument is conveyed in its title. Rather than accepting their 'structural victimisation', Primo and Caesar 'embroil' themselves in the underground economy, 'proudly embracing street culture [and] seeking an alternative to social marginalisation'. This type of resistance is not heroic in any uncomplicated sense, however: 'they become the actual agents administering their own destruction and the community's suffering' (143). Methadone is not covered in the book, but in an article published in 2000, Bourgois recounts that Primo is now on methadone and has been for three years. Characteristically provocative on epidemiological and other clinical research, Bourgois provides this summary of what methadone is and how it works:

> Researchers are so uncritically immersed in the disciplining parameters of their biomedical framework that they fail to recognise that it is the painfully physiologically addictive properties of methadone that reduce even the most oppositional outlaw street addicts [...] into stable patients once their bodies have built up a large enough physical dependence on methadone to make it too physically painful for them to misbehave.
>
> (Bourgois, 2000: 183)

Similarly, methadone is metaphorised by clients and health care workers internationally as 'liquid handcuffs', and what research there is on methadone seems to accept this description. On this view, heroin addiction is dangerous and destructive, but also represents resistance to the victimisation instated by late capitalism and patriarchy. Methadone treatment allows some of the privileges of patriarchal late capitalism, but the cost is surrender and domination.

Such binaries work to reinforce, and are reinforced by, cultural stereotypes. The drug taker is a pathologised deviant and also a countercultural hero, as evidenced by the paroxysms of angst regularly enacted by politicians and media commentators over any putative 'glamourisation' of drugs. As Chapter 1 argues, methadone's place in popular culture is distinct from both these stereotypes. It represents a brief, unsatisfying episode for Renton in *Trainspotting* (1996) and for the two protagonists in *Sid and Nancy* (1986), and barely appears elsewhere. It may be that these stereotypes are part of the reason for the sociological neglect of methadone treatment. In any case, the academic reinscription of drug treatment as capitulation to neo-liberalism does little to recognise the dignity of those who are in treatment. It is surely possible to recognise the resistant or rebellious possibilities of 'drug addiction' without casting treatment as its opposite or forgetting the limits of the figuring of drugs as subversive. Moreover, as we show in this book, scholarly neglect of treatment also entails missing the insights that can be gained from a sustained consideration of the related materialities of biomedicine, prescription drugs, illicit drugs and social identities.

This book attempts to move beyond the opposition of outlaw and victim and focuses instead on the implications and effects of MMT as biomedical treatment, and of addiction as a chronic condition. In doing so, we also attempt to dismantle other binaries, most particularly, those that present addiction as either a vice or a disease; treatment paradigms as centred on the body or the mind; and drug addiction itself as either a 'social' or 'individual' concern. Pairings such as these animate many of the extant histories of methadone treatment. For example, an account of the life and work of Marie Nyswander includes this characteristic summary of the 'metabolic' theory of addiction she championed with Vincent Dole:

> [It] dispensed with sin and personality, relying instead on the action of narcotics on the user's body [and] emphasised the permanency of the metabolic change, which meant that addiction was a chronic, relapsing disorder.
>
> (Courtwright, 1997: 259)

The emergence of pharmacotherapies for addiction was 'a key step in the partial remedicalisation and somaticovisceralisation of narcotic' addiction, replacing the dominance of mid-century psychodynamic models of sociopathy (260). MMT, then, moved away from judging the personalities and morals of addicts and relocated the site of addiction to drugs in the body. This type of whiggish account is useful in some respects, particularly in its recognition that addiction has been produced as a chronic medical condition through the development of pharmacotherapies. However, the separation of medicine from morality, and body from mind, that drives these histories have serious conceptual limitations. Arguments that medicine liberated drug addicts from social prejudice are at best naïve about the social worlds of drug treatment. More fundamentally, they neglect the mutual constitution of the social and the medical. Just as critiques of drug treatment sometimes represent biomedicine only as political repression, heroic accounts of medicine doing battle with the social also misrepresent the nature of each.

As contemporary studies of science and technology emphasise, the social and scientific are not distinct in this way. Adrian Mackenzie, for example, presents an alternative to the two contesting principles that are often used to explain contemporary technology:

> that of 'technology' as an empty, metaphysical-ideological abstraction disguising social processes, and that of technology as an ahistorical hand colonising human cultures with its material structures and logic.
>
> (Mackenzie, 2002: 205)

Explaining technical practices as either 'forming' culture or 'formed by' it presupposes some separation of the two. Mackenzie instead analyses divergent realities and the productive tension in the 'folding' of human collectives and non-human forces in technical practices. Our aim, in this book, is to investigate methadone maintenance as necessarily enfolding the human and the non-human, the social and the scientific, the discursive and the material.

The political economies of methadone

In taking this approach to the object of our study, we are drawn to conceptualise it in the broadest terms – to think of MMT as always social, individual, political, medical and economic – as always already the (paradoxical) product of Western liberal governance. In this way, we depart from the existing literature by redrawing MMT as what we will call a 'phenomenon'. This term will be explained later when we describe in more detail the theoretical approach the study takes. First, however, we draw on existing studies of MMT that emphasise the importance of poverty and social marginalisation to treatment, and on contemporary feminist theory that emphasises the importance of disrupting conventional points of view, to consider the social and political organisation of methadone treatment in Australia.

Critical ethnographic studies of illicit drugs, such as those undertaken by Philippe Bourgois in the US (Bourgois, 1995), Lisa Maher in the US, South East Asia and Australia (Maher, 1997, 2002) and David Moore in Australia (Moore, 1992, 2004), draw attention to the importance of physical and political environments and the systems of meaning relevant to drug users. We take our lead from these studies, and from contemporary feminist theory that animates in new ways the (by now fairly well known) insight that 'reality' is always contingent, partial and mediated. Through investigations of science and technology in particular, this scholarship brings into view the activities of apparatuses often understood to be passive or mere background. Donna Haraway's argument in 'Situated Knowledges', for instance, uses the example of scientific accounts of bodies and machines, arguing that there can be 'no unmediated photograph or passive camera obscura', only 'highly specific visual possibilities, each with a wonderfully detailed, active, partial way of organising worlds' (Haraway, 1991b: 190). This insight has been used by Valerie Hartouni, Barbara Duden and Karen Barad (of whom more below) among other feminist scholars to contest the meanings given to the pregnant body and foetus as a result of ultrasound technologies (Barad, 1998; Duden, 1993; Hartouni, 1997). Images of the foetus that erase the maternal body, that represent an autonomous being floating free, are both useful to anti-choice propaganda and so pervasive that thinking the foetus 'otherwise' is increasingly difficult. That pregnancy happens in women's bodies; that ultrasound technologies construct (not simply present) the foetal body; that in most respects it is simply bizarre to think of foetal life as 'independent': all of this is potentially obscured by conservative uses of technology, but made clear through feminist insistence on the partial vision that 'objective' vision necessarily is.

Similarly, feminist qualitative researchers such as Donelda Cook and Michelle Fine argue for a shift in vision when considering the question of 'problem' populations. Indebted to critical traditions in anthropology (Rosaldo, 1989) and elsewhere, they emphasise the need to 'shift [our] kaleidoscopic lens from a critical look at the behaviours' of individuals to 'a critical look at the contexts' in which individuals live: 'Research which fetishises the individual as if she were the problem or the solution occludes and protects obscene contexts of economic inequity, racism, and social despair' (Cook and Fine, 1995: 138). Cook and Fine argue that researchers need to invent strategies that tell stories but do not romanticise individuals, and this argument applies to drugs research.[4] Most of our understanding of those who use drugs comes from individualist accounts, despite a fairly long critical tradition against them (Moore, 1990; Mugford and O'Malley, 1991), and this is as true of research as of other discourses. Lip service is often paid to the political and social constitution of 'addiction', but this is mostly then lost in a focus on individual deficits and problems. Our project, like those of the feminist scholars of science cited above, is to argue for a political revisioning of reality that is also more empirically robust than conventional visions and to tell individual stories that do not neglect the political environments, in this case, liberal societies, which co-produce them.

Australia is a wealthy country, and public expenditure on health and social services is relatively high (Marston and Watts, 2004). As a liberal regime in Esping-Anderson's typology of welfare capitalism (Esping-Andersen, 1990), it has a tradition of Keynesian policies of macro-economic management and the welfare state (Castles, 2001). Since the 1980s, however, Australia has shared with other liberal democracies a marked shift in the role of the state in providing basic services, and a marked upswing in the rhetorical and political organisation of certain kinds of people as 'dependent'. MMT clients are recipients of health services and, as such, very much affected by changes to health policy and the provision of public services. They are also classified, by definition, as 'dependent' and so occupy an invidious relationship to the normative 'participating' worker citizen and proper liberal subject. Treatment clients often spend some time out of the formal labour force and so their status as dependent is multiple: both welfare dependent and drug dependent, they are doubly excluded from the imaginary communities of the 'reformed' welfare state. Changes to the organisation of health and welfare services, and to the figuring of who belongs in them, contribute to the political imagining of methadone clients. Just two of the most significant of these changes will be briefly summarised here: mutual obligation and privatisation. The purpose of this discussion is to unmoor some of the most common, and ideologically distorting, narratives of treatment that focus on the individual client (or doctor, or clinic) to the exclusion of the broad social forces that make the phenomenon of MMT possible.

The term 'mutual obligation' is endogenous to Australia, but its equivalent can be found elsewhere, especially in the UK's 'Third Way' prescriptions around responsibility (Giddens, 2001). It was generated to describe a 'new' system of reciprocity between welfare recipients and the state, as though the social contract did not already exist. Contemporaneous welfare reform in the US, such as the replacement of the Aid to Families with Dependent Children program with the Temporary Assistance for Needy Families program, deployed a similar rhetoric of an end to 'welfare as we know it', although the US had never had a welfare state on the same scale as that of Australia or the UK to dismantle (Quint et al., 1999). Recipients of income support and other welfare payments have always been subject to obligations and codes in Australia and elsewhere, but the germinal text of 'mutual obligation' signalled important rhetorical and material shifts (Howard and Newman, 2000; Reference Group on Welfare Reform, 2000). *Participation Support for a More Equitable Society*, otherwise known as the McClure

Report, outlined new rules increasing the burdens on those receiving unemployment benefits, child support payments and disability payments (Reference Group on Welfare Reform, 2000). Since then, further impositions and penalties have been introduced, the most recent associated with the passing of the Welfare to Work Bill in 2005. This introduced lower payments for people with disabilities and single parents; stringent 'activity tests' around applying for jobs; a compulsion to accept almost any job; and a compliance and penalty regime that includes the suspension of all payments for up to eight weeks. Penalties are applied after either 'three strikes' or, in the case of failure to take a job or join a 'work for the dole [unemployment benefits]' scheme, 'one strike' (Australian Council of Social Services, 2006; Australian Government, 2006). Mutual obligation underpins these 'reforms', presented, as they are, as encouraging active, participating citizens obliged to avoid the trap of 'welfare dependence'. Dependence here is a pathological condition tied to passivity: 'passive welfare recipients' justify 'administrative incentives to maximise their participation' (Reference Group on Welfare Reform cited in Bessant, 2002: 17). In 1999 the then Minister for Employment, later Minister for Health, Tony Abbott, described the unemployed as 'work-shy' and 'job snobs' in a widely reported newspaper interview, arguing that high unemployment results from 'a culture of welfare dependency' (cited in Bessant, 2002: 18).

The problem of dependency, here, is restricted to those who receive income support payments; those dependent on family income and those who receive income from sources such as shares and property portfolios are exempt from the category (Cass and Brennan, 2002). Corporate welfare is only barely considered dependence (Olsen and Champlin, 1998; van Dyke, 2003). The rhetorical constitution of dependent, passive non-contributors not only ignores the contributions that those on income support make, but reconfigures the role of the state in addressing unemployment. Rather than being responsible for employment, industry and education and training policies, governments become responsible for dismantling a 'culture' of 'dependency' (for which, it should be noted, no evidence exists) (Bessant, 2002; Cass and Brennan, 2002). Australian governments are doing little that is really original here.[5] In their genealogical survey of 'dependency' in the US, Nancy Fraser and Linda Gordon argue:

> The contention is that poor, dependent people have something more than lack of money wrong with them. The flaws can be located in

biology, psychology, upbringing, neighbourhood influence; they can
be cast as cause or effect of poverty, or even as both simultaneously.
(Fraser and Gordon, 1997: 139)

In Britain, Ruth Levitas's analysis of New Labour detects a 'moral underclass'
discourse as one influence driving policy, characterised by a focus on
'the behaviours of the poor rather than the structures of the whole
society' and the argument that 'benefits are bad, rather than good,
for their recipients, and encourage "dependency"' (Levitas, 1998: 21).
Those who receive income support are no longer classed as citizens with
entitlements from the state to meet their needs, but supplicants in need
of charity and psychological intervention. Similarly, the policies effected
by mutual obligation have in common a stripping away of existing social
supports and increasingly punitive regulations. Thus, for example, the
Australian Commonwealth Employment Service was abolished in 1998,
and replaced with a tendered system of charity-sector job brokering
services. The state no longer had a responsibility in providing employment services, and non-government organisations with a tradition of
advocating for the unemployed and impoverished became charged with
the responsibility of providing both services and surveillance (Cass and
Brennan, 2002). Other basic services have also been reformed almost out
of existence. Public housing agencies have sold significant percentages of
stock, meaning access is denied to all but the most deprived. Public
health and education are increasingly treated not as generalist and universal resources but as residual systems, used only by those who cannot
afford those provided by the market. Such structural changes to the provision of health and other services are often not considered in drugs
research, which tends to focus on the characteristics of individuals. As
we will argue in later chapters, the representation of pharmacotherapy
clients as dependent, passive and otherwise problematic illuminates
these critical analyses of welfare reform in new ways.

Privatisation is also integral to changes in the welfare state, and
although all states and, especially, the Australian Commonwealth have
been active in driving it, the paradigmatic instance is still that of Victoria
under the Liberal government headed by Premier Jeff Kennett between
1992 and 1999. Prisons, electricity, public transport and health services
were privatised and public assets sold. The public sector was reduced by
over 25 per cent or 70,000 staff through a combination of outsourcing,
privatisation and 'downsizing'. Industrial relations were transformed
through the abolition of state awards, the encouragement of individual

labour contracts and the abolition of compulsory arbitration and conciliation. In health and elsewhere, policy was separated from provision through purchaser/provider arrangements and services contracted out to a mix of public and private agencies through compulsory competitive tendering (O'Neill, 2000; Russell, 2000; Stanton, Young and Willis, 2003). Funding was allocated on the basis of accountability for outputs and efficiency measured in terms of cost reduction (Brown, 2000). In many cases privatisation did considerable damage to both service provision and the workforce, so it is perhaps unsurprising that, seven years into the Labor government that succeeded Kennett's tenure as premier, our Victorian interview participants are still talking about him. Service providers and policymakers talk about the organisation of services while Jeff, a Melbourne treatment client, describes a much more direct effect. The closure of a well-resourced agency with multiple services led to increased heroin use and an increase in his methadone dose.

> **Jeff**: There were staff around, there were groups happening, and ... it was a good, a well operated program that just sort of kept me occupied (laughs). I just, yeah, I just wasn't using at the time, I sort of put that down to the program and the structure of it, yeah.
>
> *Interviewer: Yep. And then, when [your methadone dose] went back up again, was that when you were, when you stopped being on that program?*
>
> **Jeff**: Yeah, they closed it. It was, um, the Kennett Government axed a lot of those programs. Um, and that's when I had to find my own pharmacy then. And things, (laughs), and things changed. The lifestyle changed a bit, I started using again, and the dose started creeping up.
>
> (Jeff, Melbourne, Victoria, client, 47)

All of this has had, of course, an enormous effect on MMT. Methadone services in NSW are provided through public clinics, private clinics and a combination of GP prescription and pharmacy dispensing. In Victoria, provision of methadone services occurs almost entirely through a GP–pharmacy mix. The optimistic view of the latter arrangement is that it enables the normalisation of treatment provision: while large clinics are visible and thus potentially stigmatising, doctors' surgeries and pharmacies are discreet – a large number of prescribers and pharmacies service a small number of clients each. Methadone provision, in this view, becomes no more notable than the provision of contraceptive pills or cholesterol medication. The invisible hand of the market ensures quality of service and client demand drives supply. In practice, methadone clients attending general practitioners and pharmacies remain a highly stigmatised population and the market provides insufficient incentives for many prescribers or pharmacists to become involved in the program. A small number of prescribers and pharmacies have a large number of clients each and the state bears no real responsibility for ensuring that standards are adequate for provider or client. A consequence of this is that clients have very little choice of prescriber or pharmacist, and standards of care widely recognised as inadequate persist unchecked.

It is important to note here that while in NSW there has historically been less reliance on the logic of the market in ensuring provision of treatment, things are not necessarily any better. The experience of treatment for clients depends to a large extent on location and to some degree on luck: in Victoria, for example, clients who live in metropolitan Melbourne may have more choice and better access to a range of public health services than those who live in some parts of metropolitan Sydney. In NSW a moratorium has been declared on the opening of any new private clinics, manufactured outrage at the operations of existing clinics often seems to take priority over legitimate needs, and both private and public clinics are, in fact, visible and stigmatising. We take up these points in more detail in Chapters 2 and 4.

Pharmacotherapy treatment is, then, a specific example of a wider trend. As the welfare state has been progressively dismantled so too have traditional models of human service delivery been replaced with market-driven ones. What are the outcomes of this retreat by the state from the provision of health and welfare services, of the fragmentation and under-resourcing of urgently needed care? One result is a decline in the quality of services to meet basic needs such as housing and employment, and much more work for those services left. Health care and policy workers report in our interviews that clients often require counselling, financial assistance, training, legal support and other social services that are simply unavailable. Many take a holistic view of clients and their needs, and would like to provide that kind of support. They rarely have the training, time and other resources to do so, however, and while a much-touted benefit of treatment is the increased chance of access to other services, this cannot happen when other services are unavailable.

A second result is the significant unmet demand for treatment places. Treatment for opioid dependence is funded primarily by individual states but also by the Commonwealth through the Pharmaceutical Benefits Scheme (PBS) (Australian Government, 2003). While it is true that more resources are available for more kinds of treatment than in some countries such as the US (D'Aunno and Pollack, 2002), resource allocations do not tell the whole story about demand and availability of treatment places for people who want them. Healthcare workers, policymakers and clients in NSW and Victoria all report unmet demand, under-staffing and depleted equipment and spaces. There are some modes of treatment, such as rehabilitation, that require a commitment and moral decision: you have to want to get better. This requirement is one of the paradoxes of the disease model of addiction: biochemical explanations do not dispense with moral judgements around will (May, 2001). Yet clients and service providers alike report that an important benefit of pharmacotherapy treatment is that zealotry around changing behaviour and achieving total abstinence is not required. There are many barriers to treatment, and treatment commencement is an especially fraught time,[6] but it is possible for people to undergo treatment without upending their lives and abstaining from other drugs entirely. In this sense, MMT is a pragmatic and attractive proposition to clients, and it is partly for this reason that there is unmet demand for places (Agar et al., 2001).[7]

A third effect of changes to the organisation of services is the impact of under-resourcing on service providers. Because our interviews were undertaken with prescribers, pharmacists and nurses working in a range of settings, it is possible to compare the effects of the different environments in which people work. For example, Stuart, a prescriber in regional NSW, experienced the death of one of his patients by methadone overdose. He found this experience very distressing, and made extensive unsuccessful efforts to get advice and guidance, with new supervision arrangements only made two years after the event.

> I found it was fairly confusing when I first started prescribing, and it took me a while to really establish a sense of, that I was part of a bigger system. It felt, it was a fairly isolating experience actually [...] I think when you first start prescribing you think, 'no-one's really watching what I'm doing at all, and no-one really cares'. It's only when something goes wrong that everyone suddenly gets interested. I think it's a terrible way to approach it.
>
> (Stuart, regional NSW, prescriber, 45)

In contrast Patrick, who prescribes in Melbourne, reports access to enough support to enable him to overcome work-related stress and anxiety:

> I've been through some really good training about how to manage people who can get aggro and stuff like that, and I think that having

had that, that framework makes all that stuff a lot easier. Had one, I guess, one sort of pivotal moment when I thought somebody was going to pull a knife on me. And I got really stressed and took some time off work and all that sort of stuff. And that affected what, I didn't know if I could go back to that sort of work after that, but yeah, did a bit of counselling and got my head around it, and don't get stressed by that sort of stuff now.

(Patrick, Melbourne, Victoria, prescriber/policy, 40)

Given the disadvantage and trauma experienced by many methadone clients, it may seem discordant to describe very privileged professionals as traumatised by their experience of methadone. But it is also clear that some professionals have been subject to serious anxiety, possible danger, isolation and neglect in the course of their work. Others have not. It is important that these differences are not attributed to chance: the particular clients, or policy bureaucrats, with whom Stuart and Patrick had contact. Instead, a systemic view of the intra-activity of individuals, policies and environments is needed. For some professionals, resources including support and a sense of safety are inherent in their work, while others experience instead the worst instances of contemporary governance: surveillance and mechanistic risk management in the place of care (we take up this point again in Chapter 2).

Mutual obligation and the dismantling/privatising of public services are generally characterised as either liberal or neo-liberal. As Marston and Watts (2004) argue, though, in effect they barely meet the criterion of 'freedom from' injury and excessive state interference set out by Isaiah Berlin as a principle of liberalism, let alone the principle of 'freedom to' promote the capacities that allow people to do what they would like:

There is a strong case to be made that the actual practices that unemployed and low-income Australians have to put up with when negotiating access to the 'mutual obligation' income support constitute an abuse of this 'negative freedom'.

(Marston and Watts, 2004: 38)

As we will see, the accounts of methadone clients tend to confirm this view. Methadone clients, of course, are an abused and stigmatised group within this abused and stigmatised group of impoverished people. Forces that are apparently remote from the lives of marginalised individuals, such as political decisions to tender out service provision, in fact have daily, intimate impact. Describing methadone clients as stigmatised or socially excluded is accurate, but the means by which this stigma is lived and reproduced is missed if it is understood only to be an effect. Mary Douglas writes:

> Stigma is interesting as a self-fulfilling prophecy. Prejudiced and exclusionary behaviour validates itself. The urban poor are housed in crime-infested districts with unpoliced subways, ill-lit streets, damp walls, and malodorous drains. They are more infectious in their bodies, more exposed to disease and mutilating accidents at work, with a shorter life expectancy. The stigma is not a false symbol of contamination: the sign is true.
>
> (Douglas, 1990: 15)

Similarly, the stigma and social exclusion of methadone are more than descriptors of the current state of affairs. The political constitution of methadone clients happens not only through their rhetorical figuring as passive and dependent, although that is crucial, as we will see in Chapters 1, 3 and 5. It happens more broadly in the transfiguring of charity and NGO services into job brokers and financial managers, so that agencies that have always been advocates for the marginalised are now proxies for the surveillance, regulation and punishment of the state. It happens through the abrogation of state responsibility to provide services, and faith in the market to deliver them. It happens in the depletion of resources to services and the absence of measures to correct or regulate the poor standards that result. Methadone clients are in many cases stigmatised as denuded and marginal, and their treatment works to confirm their status. 'Socially excluded' seems not so much what methadone clients *are* as what MMT at its worst *does*: 'socially excluding' seems as good a way as any to describe the submission to scrutiny and testing; the time waiting in run-down clinics; the resources spent on getting to the same pharmacy every day to be treated shabbily by the people who work there. The political economies of methadone may appear in traditional models of public health as 'distal', but, as we will see, they fold into everyday lives and they work as both cause and effect of client marginalisation (Malins, Fitzgerald and Threadgold, 2006).

Making substance matter

How to produce an account of MMT capable of embracing the material, political and social complexities we describe here? How, indeed, to fold in elements usually relegated to the status of context or the distal, and to do so without – as we note earlier – obscuring the role either of politics and culture in shaping, even provoking, methadone treatment, or of the materiality of dependence and of methadone as substance itself? To begin, we turn to the work of Karen Barad. Emerging simultaneously from the feminist science studies tradition and from the discipline of physics, Barad's work synthesises and builds on aspects of recent feminist theory and science and technology studies to formulate theoretical tools with which we can sketch our object of study broadly (that is, beyond the individual enacted in treatment), and in so doing, take account of both the social/cultural/discursive and the material.[8] In part, our intention is to open up consideration of MMT in a way that recognises the constitutive role of the (intensely productive, intensely controversial) materiality of methadone as substance, without characterising that role as determining.

In a 2003 article entitled 'Posthumanist performativity: Toward an understanding of how matter comes to matter', Barad criticises the tendency to accord language a determining role in the production of culture and material objects in the following way:

> Language has been granted too much power. The linguistic turn, the semiotic turn, the interpretive turn, the cultural turn: it seems that at every turn lately every 'thing' – even materiality – is turned into a matter of language or some other form of cultural representation ... Language matters. Discourse matters. Culture matters. There is an important sense in which the only thing that does not seem to matter any more is matter.
>
> (2003: 801)

The essence of Barad's complaint is that in the humanities and social sciences, that which is conventionally understood as the material has been divested of all agency or influence in understanding how realities become. There is certainly something in this. However, in the interests of keeping in mind both the political tightrope any critical account of the role of materiality must negotiate (elucidated in Fraser and valentine, 2006) and the important considerations that led feminists to formulate social constructionist positions in the first place, it is worth recognising at least one contrary (and intensely productive) recent development within medicine and popular culture. This development accords an unsettlingly large amount of agency to materiality in the form of genetics[9] (Haraway, 1992; Hubbard, 1995; Nelkin and Lindee, 1995; Lewontin, 2000). In other words, and to state the obvious, in some highly influential contexts, the linguistic turn has never happened. Within these contexts, the careful dismantling of binary distinctions between language and the material is simply absent: bioscientific instances of material determinism continue to reinscribe the split between discourse and material, and to privilege the material (defining it as prior to discourse and as immutable in its characteristics and action). It follows that in formulating concepts that take account of both discourse and material objects such as bodies, and substances such as methadone, it is important to remember that there are reasons why feminists among many have turned to the possibilities offered by language and discourse, and why any return to the material must be navigated carefully. Of course, despite the rhetorical tone Barad strikes in the comments above, there can be no doubt that she is well aware of this tension. Indeed, the complex and intriguing work which follows her complaint attests to this.

Barad's aim in 'Posthumanist Performativity' is to refine Judith Butler's theory of performativity to allow for due consideration of the role of matter in the production of realities. Some of the concepts she draws on resonate strongly with aspects of science studies theory such as actor network theory (ANT). For example, she notes that notions of performativity have previously been used in the work of strong adherents of ANT such as Bruno Latour, as well as in that of scholars who indicate a degree of indebtedness to ANT, such as Andrew Pickering, but she suggests that these formulations differ from poststructuralist and feminist uses, with which she more closely identifies. Her approach differs from ANT in its particular formulation of performativity – its interest (in keeping with the term's links with queer theory) in the performativity of gender, sexuality and sexual practices, and in its aim to reconsider matter in its materiality.

Barad begins with a discussion of the critique of representationalism that highlights the problems with treating the process of representation as separate and distinguishable from that which is represented. Her focus in this paper is on the practices of science, and in pursuing this, she directs our attention to questions of the nature of measurement. She argues that

A performative understanding of discursive practices challenges the representationalist belief in the power of words to represent pre-existing things.

(802)

Similarly, this understanding challenges the representationalist distinction between the process of measurement and the 'thing' being measured. For the purposes of the argument being made here, it is enough to note that her critique functions to blur the ontological boundary between observation and object (language and referent, representation and entity). Following Rouse, she identifies this boundary as the product of Cartesian thinking which contains a commitment to an inside/outside binary delineated at the junction that is the knowing subject.

Barad goes on to identify her argument as part of a desire to pursue a particular approach to performative accounts of the nature and production of matter. This approach, which has figured in her work for some years, is termed 'agential realism'. In 1998 she used the work of physicist Niels Bohr and Judith Butler to elaborate the concept, making in the process a point very similar to that argued above. In this paper she argues that contrary to much thinking:

> 'Subjects' and 'objects' do not preexist as such, but are constituted through and within particular practices.
>
> (106)

One such example of the habit of thought she challenges is the distinction assumed between words and things. In her later article (2003) she rejects this distinction. Specifically, she argues against the existence of 'relata' (pre-existing components of relations). Following Bohr again, she counters the notion of relata by positing the 'phenomenon', defined as comprising 'ontologically primitive relations – relations without pre-existing relata'. In her model, the phenomenon replaces the notion of the independent object which possesses inherent boundaries and properties (815), and in so doing, it scrambles conventional formulations of causality. That is, it questions the assumed causal chain running from the object via its subsequent relations to meaning, and substitutes it with the 'intra-action' of phenomena which themselves are produced through the inseparability of object and observer. Here, intra-action is defined as distinct from 'interaction', which 'presumes the prior existence of independent entities/relata' (815).

Pursuing her interest in the practices of science, she mobilises this theory to discuss the status of scientific apparatuses, which she argues are all too often seen as stable, pre-formed objects that 'sit atop a shelf' (2003: 816), employed to produce stable, objective measurements of a pre-existing reality. On the contrary, in her view, they are 'neither neutral probes of the natural world nor structures that deterministically impose some particular outcome' (816). Barad uses the example of the apparatus here quite specifically in relation to scientific practices, but it is interesting to consider the apparently pre-formed, ontologically stable subjects, objects and practices of MMT in light of her arguments. What emerges when we do not assume any of these elements to be either neutral or determining? What are the effects of treating them as phenomenon? These questions form part of the theoretical project of this book.

Barad's summary of her agential-realist model is a particularly dense starting point for thinking about the interview material collected for this study. She reiterates that

> The primary ontological units [of the world] are not 'things' but phenomena – dynamic topological reconfigurings/entanglements/ relationalities/(re)articulations. And the primary semantic units are not words but material-discursive practices through which boundaries are constituted. This dynamism is agency. Agency is not an attribute but the ongoing reconfigurings of the world.
>
> (818)

Here, agency is reformulated as emerging from the intra-action of phenomena, rather than simply from the intentionality of the Cartesian subject. This Barad calls, following Butler, 'iterative intra-activity' (822). From this point of view, agency is not a quality or characteristic of humans, it is an enactment, inhering in the moment of intra-action and iteration. In a related move, Barad poses the 'human' as phenomenon, thus reconstituting the boundary between human and non-human (including inanimate matter) as itself indeterminate and unstable. This is a useful means of undermining the distinction between discourse (as product of human agency) and materiality (as its inanimate opposite). As a result, deliberations about the relative merits of according determining agency *either* to 'humans' *or* to 'matter' are rendered redundant.

Barad's theory challenges conventional assumptions about the ontological and epistemological autonomy of three elements: the knowing subject, discourse and matter. In doing so, it opens up ways of understanding the co-construction – the intermingling and fluid intra-action – of all kinds of material/semiotic subjects, objects and practices, for example, that of methadone as substance, media representations of methadone, treatment regulations, the dosing point, client identities and prevailing social and political values. The chapters that follow explore this co-construction as a means of generating understandings of MMT that do justice to the tense, contradictory and highly productive series of relations it enacts within Western liberal societies.

After all, for Barad, a concern with materialisation is a concern with how the world 'kicks back', expanding the field of critical analysis to include the natural sciences and non-human bodies: the recognition of 'a need to understand the laws of nature as well as the law of the father' (Barad, 1998). As Joseph Rouse writes, Barad's distinct philosophical contribution is 'integrating feminist philosophy of science with a feminist ontology' (Rouse, 2004). Aside from the insights offered by Barad's attention to the 'ontological there-ness' of apparatuses and the dynamic intra-activity of discourse and matter, what else is brought to bear on the study of MMT when reading Barad 'through' the qualitative research methodologies employed here? (Or rather, how does Barad's work assist in delineating the 'cut' that marks MMT, which is the object of study, and the apparatuses of its observation, for this study? (Barad, 1998))

One answer, useful to this book, is the second part of the aphorism cited above: the law of the father. Barad's work both disrupts and advances Judith Butler's work on gender and performativity, and cites Marxist, poststructuralist and postcolonial scholarship. Broadly, then, Barad's work is concerned with power, and resistance to hegemonic power, enacted across social domains. It is indebted to and contributes to Foucauldian scholarship on the regulatory and disciplinary exercise of power through individual bodies and through populations. Famously, Foucault argued that the end of the eighteenth century saw the emergence of a new form of power, a 'biopolitics' of the human race, in which new apparatuses of observation and production were applied to the population treated as a political problem. In this way, political problems became biological problems (Foucault, 2003; Rose, 2001b). Medicine is also formed as a regime of power, producing discourses on sexual perversion, delinquency, 'unreason' and criminality – and Butler's work has been instrumental in elaborating the possibilities for other political subjects, especially gender and sexual minority subjects, which also emerge from these discourses (Butler, 1990; Deveaux, 1994).

In Foucault's account, sovereign power, or disciplinary power, which is addressed to bodies, characterises the eras prior to the nineteenth century; after this time sovereign power co-exists with a new regulatory power that applies to man-as-living-being. Regulatory power does not supplant disciplinary power, however, and the field of medicine exemplifies the operations of both:

> Medicine is a power-knowledge that can be applied to both the body and the population, both the organism and biological processes, and it will therefore have both disciplinary effects and regulatory effects.
>   (Foucault, 2003: 252)

Also at the level of individual and population, circulating between regulatory and disciplinary power, the 'norm' becomes crucial (Foucault, 1973, 2003). Foucault argues that the 'normal' replaced the 'healthy' as organising principles of modern medicine: the lives of individuals and races become intelligible not in terms of their own internal structures but through the 'medical polarity of the normal and the pathological' (Foucault, 1973: 35). As Nikolas Rose notes: 'the idea of the norm involved an overlaying of social and vital ways of thinking. More precisely, the term "normal" condensed a statistical, a social, a moral and a medical judgement' (Rose, 2001a: 21). Medicine then is crucial to understanding power: acting on individuals and populations, and constituting the apparatuses of measurement and observation that materialise norms. All of these questions are explored throughout our book, especially individual norms of independence (Chapter 1), gender norms (Chapter 5) and the organisation of populations according to contemporary technologies of measurement and management (Chapter 2). Methadone clients are constituted through a range of discourses as deviant or lacking and these illuminate much about the social, political and cultural imperatives behind contemporary norms of health and social functioning within liberal regimes.

Of course, separating the law of the father and the laws of nature is useful for heuristic purposes (and for the organisation of our middle chapters: Chapter 2 focuses on the regulatory power applied to methadone and other populations; Chapters 3 and 4 focus more closely on the operations of power through individuals and the formation of new selves through the exercise of power). Questions of law, however, are also questions of responsibility. Barad's account of agential realism incorporates responsibility, especially 'recognising one's own participation in the reproduction of power relations, acknowledging its consequences, and holding oneself accountable to those for whom one's actions are consequential' (Rouse, 2004: 156). Elaborating on the example of ultrasound technologies used to envision the foetus, Barad argues that ultrasonography is not merely a physical instrument but instead 'designates specific material-discursive practices, limiting what is seen and produced in accordance with its own iteratively intra-active techno-scientific, medical, economic, political, biological, and cultural etc development as an ever-changing phenomenon' (Barad, 1998). Technoscientific, medical, economic, political, biological and cultural concerns are critical to this book, and we argue throughout that the phenomena/apparatuses that constitute MMT incorporate all of them.

Assembling method

Interviewer: What in your view does methadone do?

Patrick: What does it do?

Interviewer: Yep.

Patrick: Um, to who? To the punters? To clients? Or to society? Or me?
(Patrick, Melbourne, Victoria, policy, 40)

A theoretical project such as ours requires a sympathetic approach to method, one that recognises that observation (in this case research) co-constitutes the object of study, that this object, this phenomenon, is made up of a range of other phenomena. Further, it must recognise that the action of methadone as substance, of MMT as program and of addiction as material-discursive object, is best described/constituted through attention both to the local and specific – to those in treatment, to the action of daily doses and so on – and to formulations of the object of study that go beyond traditional boundary-making to include constructions of the subject within liberalism, and the performative relation between these and other phenomena such as medicine, the media, the law and the action of matter itself. As Patrick's questions above make clear, methadone, and the program that administers it, reaches well beyond the client in its relevance and effects.

John Law's recent book, *After Method: Mess in social science research* (2004), offers a range of insights into social science research such as ours that can help us formulate a method and object of study in keeping with Barad's ontology. Emerging, as does Barad's work, from the generative encounter between feminist science studies and science and technology studies, Law's book takes as its aim the development of a new vocabulary for method, one that embraces rather than ignores or suppresses the elusive, the disorderly and the chaotic in research, which thoroughly recognises the constitutive role of research in realities, and which places politics at the centre of knowledge production. Law insists, rather like Barad, that materiality is not destiny, but that the (contingent) agency of objects must not be neglected when understanding the ways in which realities materialise. In making this case Law challenges the traditional approach to research taken by the natural and social sciences. This approach treats nature and material objects as (24–5)

1. independent of the processes of study,
2. anterior to the processes of study,
3. definite in terms of attributes and characteristics, and
4. singular in form.

In so doing, it assumes that good research method always produces an orderly picture of reality, and that research methods that find mess or the multiple or the elusive, must be intrinsically flawed. As Barad's theories would suggest, there are ways of thinking about matter and about the processes of research that move beyond these assumptions, recognising instead that objects are constituted in the processes of research, that they do not exist independently of, or prior to, observation, that their attributes and characteristics are far from definite, and that they do not necessarily take, or maintain, a singular form. Law is attracted to this approach in that he is concerned with the politics of research as much as with the truth-making possibilities of it. Indeed, he sees these two as inseparable, noting that adopting these insights into research allows us to acknowledge, following Latour, that 'the future of reality is always at risk in a sea of uncertainty'. The future of reality? By this he means that while traditional research methods might seek to pin down the actions and attributes of objects then draw conclusions from that knowledge to specify the future of the objects and thus the future of reality, an 'ontological politics' of matter recognises that such futures are contingent. Where objects are phenomena, in Barad's terms, where they have no independence, anteriority, singularity or definiteness, in Law's, they cannot dictate the future. In this respect, research helps constitute the future: it is deeply political. As he argues, 'collectively and in the longer run ... particular realities are brought into being with and through the array of inscription devices and disciplinary practices of natural and social sciences' (31).

This leaves research with a particular responsibility. But Law is quick to emphasise that this responsibility is not a matter of making simple 'choices' about which realities to bring into being. He introduces the term 'hinterland' to describe all the accumulated knowledge practices, techniques, inscription devices and other objects, discourses, and other factors that make up, but become largely invisible within, the research process. While research can do otherwise – can work towards either new or traditional realities – it cannot do this lightly, and it carries with it the hinterland of objects, practices and concepts that exert their own force in producing and adjudicating truths. Because this notion of the hinterland entails a legion of machines, people, concepts, texts and so on, it clarifies method's hidden life: the degree to which method can be seen to extend infinitely beyond the bounds conventionally ascribed to it. To capture this hidden life, this 'missing seven-eighths of the iceberg of method', Law reframes method as 'method assemblage'. He uses words such as 'bundling', 'gathering', 'entangling' here, words that resonate with Barad's emphasis on performing materiality through intra-action, and he settles on a definition of method assemblage as

> a bundle of ramifying relations that generates presence, manifest absence and Otherness, where it is the crafting of presence that distinguishes it as *method* assemblage (emphasis in the original).
>
> (42)

This, then, is precisely what distinguishes method: it creates presence. In the process, it also creates manifest absence (those things manifestly excluded) and Otherness (those things excluded and suppressed so that their absence is invisible, unimagined, unthought). This, too, is what our research project does. Yet, following Barad and Law, the aim is to bring to presence those things routinely Othered in studies of addiction and drug treatment, those things so excluded by the hinterland of research and the politics entailed in it, that they usually remain unthought. Such phenomena emerge when the ontological politics of matter shift, when objects are ascribed agency, but agency as contingent, objects as phenomena. Thus, our method can be described as follows.

The study was based on a semi-structured interviewing method assemblage. A total of 87 interviews were conducted,[10] and participants comprised MMT policymakers, service users, prescribing doctors, dosing nurses and dispensing pharmacists.[11] These interviews were gathered via an inscription device (digital recorder) and rendered through an inscription practice (verbatim transcription).[12] These inscription processes, combined with the intra-actions of the interviewers and participants, produce traces not of an anterior, definite, singular and independent reality, but of an 'out-thereness' (Law's word) more appropriately considered itself phenomenon. This phenomenon or these phenomena (as Law reminds us, there is no single reality, only multiple, partially overlapping realities) are co-produced by the research process in a range of other ways as well, for example, each participant was given an information sheet and asked to sign a prepared consent form. A semi-structured interview technique was used, and questions were devised which covered experiences of and attitudes towards MMT, takeaway dosing (the consumption of doses away from clinic or pharmacy premises) and illicit sale and consumption of methadone. Interviews brought together researchers with unique cultural and linguistic resources and participants with other, unique cultural and linguistic resources. The interviews were discursive events, supported by audio recording equipment and other technologies, that generated new textual and experiential phenomena. The interviews were approximately one hour in duration. The semi-structured interview format permitted a balance between some degree of consistency of topics, and flexibility in capturing or 'gathering' the elusive, the multiple or the indefinite in participants' stories. In all these respects, the research process co-constituted the data.

Further, participants were recruited via specific methods. Approached through fliers, snowballing and professional contacts in public and private treatment programs, rural and urban needle and syringe exchange programs and methadone clinics, state health departments and professional bodies in NSW and Victoria, the recruitment methods captured some potential service user participants and not others. Likewise, doctors, nurses and pharmacists were recruited through professional organisations. MMT policymakers were contacted through state health departments. The sample of participants spanned the range of methadone prescribing and dispensing models (general practitioners, pharmacy, public and private clinics) and included regional sites as well so as to capture a greater diversity of narratives.[13] This breadth of recruitment allowed us to generate range in our data, but in keeping with our theoretical and methodological approach, was not undertaken in the view that the data would allow us to reconstitute a singular, reliable, exhaustive reflection of reality. Instead, the decision to interview service providers and policymakers as well as clients was an initial means of recognising some of the hinterland, some of the submerged seven-eighths of method, by reframing those usually treated as outside the 'problem' of drugs – those sometimes manifestly absented, at other times Othered – as always already entangled in it. Again, our aim has been to redraw the research boundaries – to draw in more than the usual range of elements understood to comprise MMT, and to go beyond the usual focus on the individual drug user as the primary 'problem' of research, or object of study.

The interview data were then organised using the qualitative data software program NVivo. This inscription device allowed us to produce the necessary patterns of presence, absence and Otherness that Law identifies as central to all method assemblages, traditional or innovative – to gather or 'craft' a reality from the 'mess' that is our object of study. It aided us in generating and cross-referencing patterns in the interviews, in making present metaphors, concepts and devices usually Othered in drugs research. These include, as we will see in the chapters that follow, the social role of the treatment regulations, the co-constitution of space and time in daily dosing, and metaphors of authenticity and repetition in treatment. At the same time, it could not avoid the creation of otherness – of those themes excluded as beyond our awareness, and this othering is also part of the political legacy of this book.

Put simply, this approach to method allows us to acknowledge the ontological politics of our knowledge production (and not just our own – all research, including those studies that have come before, are equally implicated, and their knowledge equally partial). This emphasis on politics is central to our project in that methadone treatment, in our view, could be otherwise. We cannot simply choose to produce alternative realities for drug users any more than we can choose the realities our research co-constitutes, but we can work from the conviction that methadone as substance and addiction as idea and as embodied condition are contingently produced. Their relation to liberal values is not foregone; it is contingent and thus open. Their materialities, intensively politicised, deeply invested as they are within Western liberal societies, are not destinies. They too can be otherwise, and in this, of course, research has a role.

Crafting order

In keeping with Barad's agential-realist ontology of materiality, and with Law's methodology of partial realities, then, the five chapters that follow are designed to trace the co-production of a range of phenomena (the liberal subject and its Others, methadone as substance(s), technologies of regulation and assessment, social identities, political discourses, the space-time manifold of treatment, the gender of agency and so on) in MMT, rather than to provide an exhaustive account of the program as a stable reality 'out there' awaiting investigation through objective method. Each chapter focuses on a specific theme generated through the interview material we collected, and each builds on, bundles with, the others, although the result is not structured in a strictly linear fashion. As we have already suggested, the 'mess' this study aims to capture – the ways in which methadone, itself the product of a range of overlapping social, material and political forces, acts as the commonplace through which identity, matter and politics are made and remade – would not be adequately served through such an approach.

The book begins by examining some of the ways in which methadone treatment appears in the mainstream press. The first chapter focuses on three respected daily newspapers, *The Times* (London), the *New York Times* and the *Sydney Morning Herald*, to explore the use of metaphor in relation to methadone and addiction. It draws out some of the effects of the use of particular metaphors in discussing methadone, and of the use of methadone as metaphor to figure other phenomena. In doing so, it identifies a link to methadone's own status as a kind of metaphor for heroin, arguing that this link is one of the reasons for methadone treatment's derogated location in Western liberal discourse. By placing this chapter first we do not mean to suggest that the attitudes about and approaches to methadone and addiction documented in the chapters that follow simply *emerge from* the discursive environment mapped out here. Representation and reality, we argue following Barad, are not so straightforwardly separable as this, and attributing the origins of particular viewpoints on these issues to the media would only beg the question of what might have prompted the formation of media viewpoints in this way in the first place. Rather, we present this analysis at the outset as a means of gesturing towards some of the broadest concepts at work in Western liberal societies' discussions of methadone, in order to provide a sense of the discursive environment that both provokes and is provoked by the medical, social and regulatory forces also in play. This is not a question of *context*, however. This term tends to suggest the use of preconceptions to treat some aspects of an assemblage or phenomenon as the 'background', and in making such prior judgements, risks obscuring the role of important elements in generating the phenomena. Instead, we open the book in this way as a means of stepping into the 'middle' of our method assemblage for exploring methadone treatment as phenomenon.

In the second chapter we take another broad approach to methadone treatment, this time looking at its regulation, and the intertwining of this regulation with contemporary notions of risk. In keeping with our expansive method assemblage, our intention in the book is to define the subjects of methadone broadly. Here, this is reflected in a move away from a focus on clients alone to one that connects service providers and their experiences of treatment with clients and theirs. Thus the chapter investigates the different modalities service providers use to interpret the treatment guidelines and, in particular, the regulation of methadone treatment through the governance of clients as 'risky' populations. These different modalities have direct effects for the experiences of clients: they materialise treatment in quite different ways. This chapter's aim, in addition to elaborating these effects and problematising the relations each interpretation helps give rise to, is to familiarise readers with the regulatory aspects of treatment in NSW and Victoria, and offer a sense of the kind of work service providers are expected to do in this idiosyncratic area of medicine. This work, it will become evident, is informed by (and informs) the stigmatisation and marginalisation mapped in the newspaper stories discussed in Chapter 1.

Building on the broad explorations undertaken in Chapters 1 and 2, the third chapter moves to an analysis of the day-to-day experiences of treatment as described by clients. It looks at a common feature of the program in Australia and elsewhere, the queue, to think further about the co-production of subjects and identities through treatment. Using Barad's work on the relationship between space and time, the chapter conceptualises the queue as a spatio-temporal phenomenon, and draws out in detail the ways in which the design and layout of clinics co-produce the very subjects treatment seeks to 'cure'. Enjoined to approximate the autonomous, responsibilised liberal subject, yet simultaneously addressed as less than this – indeed co-produced as such by the treatment system itself – clients find themselves pulled between powerful competing forces, subject to strictures and expectations as much informed by the judgements and stigma identified in Chapter 1 as by therapeutic considerations or scientific evidence (and of course, none of these are straightforwardly separable from the others).

In Chapter 4 we turn to the identities that methadone treatment produces through the regulations described in Chapter 2 and the spatio-temporal phenomena described in Chapter 3. The chapter is concerned with the agency of the human and non-human actors of treatment in producing treatment identities. As we argue, the 'making up' of people occurs both from 'above' and from 'below' and reveals the multiplicity of material-discursive practices that constitute treatment. Making up people involves contestation and negotiation and demonstrates the distributed relations of power between medicine, the state and individuals. We show how the regulations discussed in Chapter 2 help co-produce subjects and their identities. These identities, informed also by broad social and cultural enactments of addiction and its related concepts, trouble some of the assumptions at work in treatment as well as reinforce them.

Our last chapter investigates another area in which subjects and identities are produced in treatment: that of gender. The chapter takes up some of the observations made at the outset (in Chapter 1) about the links that can be drawn between cultural and social understandings of addiction and related notions such as dependence, femininity and the non-rational, to argue that the common conceptualisation of MMT as repetition operates to doubly disadvantage women in treatment. It turns to Simone de Beauvoir's analysis of femininity, reproduction and housework as mere repetition to establish the denigrated location of repetition in Western culture, and demonstrates the links that are made between this denigration, and that of femininity. Exploring the interview material through repetition's companion concept, agency, the chapter shows how traditional understandings of gender materialise treatment in particular ways, materialising male and female clients along troublingly asymmetrical lines.

As this outline makes clear, *Substance and Substitution* takes a critical look at MMT. Its aim is to consider some of the ways in which the program intra-actively co-produces its constituents: notions of addiction and of the proper liberal subject, norms of health and sociality, understandings of medication and of the matter of drugs, and 'drug addicts' themselves. In so doing, the book traces some of the ways this process also co-produces life in specific ways for those involved in treatment. This critical approach ought not be understood as a call to abolish or even reduce MMT. As will become clear, the complexity of life for people who regularly consume opioid drugs should not be underestimated or trivialised. The ways in which methadone acts as *pharmakon* – as both meat and poison together, as a means of 'producing something' of substance and of intensity – render such calls where they exist simplistic. What, then, does MMT produce exactly? If we are to follow Barad and Law, we must ask this question carefully. In short, we must formulate all our questions with the phenomenon in mind. It is the phenomenon alone we can know (rather than the independent, anterior, definite, singular object taken for granted in conventional research). It is *agential* reality alone we can investigate, understand and realise – yes, realise in both senses of the word: to conceive of and to enact.

1
Substitution, Metaphor and Authenticity

> As figure, metaphor constitutes a displacement and an
> extension of the meaning of words; its explanation is
> grounded in a theory of substitution.
>
> (Ricoeur, 1978: 3)

Press coverage of addiction tends to be prolific, if not always accurate or considered. We begin our investigation of MMT by examining the ways in which it is reported in three respected daily newspapers, the *New York Times* (US), *The Times* (London, UK) and the *Sydney Morning Herald* (Australia). What place does methadone occupy in Western liberal discourse? What does this place offer to policy and practice in terms of scope for the development of treatment? What does it tell us about clients in terms of their status either as liberal subjects or as Others of liberalism? To conduct this analysis we have chosen to focus on the role of *metaphor* in articles on MMT. As will become evident, the use of metaphor is a primary way in which methadone treatment is given meaning in these texts. This is not to say that coverage of methadone treatment per se in the three papers under examination is voluminous; in fact, as we will be arguing, there is a particular kind of silence around the basics of the programs operating in each country. In part we ask what this silence means, and what effects the use of metaphor – both to figure methadone and to mobilise it as a figure for other phenomena – has in a context where addiction, including heroin addiction, is by contrast extensively discussed. In the process we consider the status of metaphor within Western liberal discourse, and trace the (in some respects damaging) ways in which methadone treatment can be seen not only as a resource for, and object of, metaphorical description and production, but itself as a kind of metaphor – *a metaphor for heroin*.

Why is it important to map and analyse media accounts of methadone? A commonsense response might be: because these representations reflect specific understandings of it, influencing, by disseminating those understandings, the formation of policy and practice around it and the esteem in which those who participate are held in society (McArthur, 1999). As Isabelle Stengers and Olivier Ralet (1997) have pointed out, public debate on drugs and drug treatment is regularly characterised in terms of a putative moral consensus: 'don't take drugs'. Related to this, perceived public opposition to methadone treatment is frequently cited as grounds for timidity or reserve in policymaking (Treloar and Fraser, 2007). The literature examining representations of drug use and drug treatments in the press tends to take this approach, with some very useful results. It finds, for example, that coverage of drug use and drug services is often poorly informed, unbalanced and inclined to reproduce stereotypes (Orcutt and Turner, 1993; Elliott and Chapman, 2000; Coomber, Morris and Dunn, 2000; Treloar and Körner, 2005; Körner and Treloar, 2004). Thus, Orcutt and Turner look at the ways in which particular research findings on student drug use were distorted in the US press, and explore the creative choices, organisational circumstances and other factors that drove the distortions. Other literature on drugs and the media argues that policy is shaped in the context of, and even by, media reports (McArthur, 1999; Elliott and Chapman, 2000; Rowe, 2002). Elliott and Chapman, for instance, explore media treatment of a proposed trial of prescribed heroin in the Australian Capital Territory and the federal government's withdrawal of support for the trial. They argue that it is important to analyse the ways in which drug use is presented in the media because (to paraphrase the work of Ericson et al., whom they quote) the media provide commonsense understandings of deviance and societal options for, and limits on, managing deviance. McArthur also investigates the coverage of the proposed heroin trial, concluding that 'sections of the media had a hand in its demise' (153). Rowe examines a different period in press coverage of drug use, focusing on a flurry of reports in 1995 on a supposed heroin epidemic in Melbourne. He asserts that '"public opinion" and what the policy-making apparatus of governments understand to be real depend heavily on the mass media' (38).

This literature resembles in some respects our own approach to the relationship between the media, policy, the views of members of the public and drugs as material objects. We do, however, think it important to question this framing in that it tends to echo an unexamined inclination within Western thought to take for granted the ontological separateness of representation and reality, in this case, media discourse and drug use and drug treatment. For example, Elliott and Chapman (2000: 193) ask, 'What was it about the nature of heroin users as portrayed in the press by supporters and opponents of the trial that may have contributed to a lack of political support for [the trial]?' Terms such as portrayal imply prior categories, in this case, the 'nature of heroin users'. While it is absolutely necessary to think about the ways in which media representations co-produce policy, daily life and politics, it is important not to reify 'representation' and 'reality' by treating them as separate entities with a priori attributes. In the Introduction we argued that to account better for the role of material objects such as drugs in producing realities, a theorisation of materiality is necessary that sees it as neither passive in the face of culture or discursivity, nor determining of it. In making these arguments we use Karen Barad's work to formulate perspectives on the agency of objects that best express the co-constitutive nature of the relation between humans, objects and discourse. This relation is nowhere more usefully elaborated than in the discussion of the media, and Barad's theories apply directly to the central issue structuring discussions of the media: the question, as noted above, of the relation between 'representation' and 'reality'.

Along with this different approach to the ontology of representation, our analysis departs significantly from the existing literature in two main ways. First, it is based on an international corpus of newspaper articles, and second, it focuses on the role of metaphor in generating meaning. As a result, the analysis takes a more abstract view of the production of meaning, looking at, for example, the role of images such as that of the silver bullet and its association with the occult. At the same time, it shares with its forerunners a conviction that representation matters for the world and for individuals, even if this mattering of representation is conceived in rather different terms.

Theorising representation

How might we best understand the action of the media in 'representing' phenomena such as methadone? Here, we will look a little more closely at one aspect of the ideas elaborated in the Introduction. As we know, one of Barad's aims is to highlight the problems inherent in treating the process of representation as separate and distinguishable from that which is represented. The argument she develops resonates with contemporary cultural studies approaches to the media, within which the thinking of this chapter is largely situated. In short, Barad's theory offers a way to refine the current formulation of one of cultural studies' central issues (an issue related directly to the representation/reality connection): the question of polysemy. It is a truism of contemporary cultural studies that cultural representations such as newspaper texts are neither able to guarantee meaning (that is, the ways in which they are interpreted by their readers) nor be entirely 'polysemous' (open to any kind of meaning making). In this respect, the relationship between text and meaning, in particular the causal relationship between the two, is understood to be a complex one. In thinking through the implications of polysemy, however, the debate tends to find itself limited to a choice between an emphasis on the power of texts and an emphasis on the power of readers, often settling for a formulation somewhere between the two. Thus, in describing the contribution of the idea of hybridity to cultural studies, Simon During (1993: 7) says:

> Concepts like hybridisation, as they develop out of the notion of 'polysemy', return us to a new culturalism because they enable us to see how particular individuals and communities can actively create new meanings from signs and cultural products which come from afar. Yet a concept like 'hybridisation' still does not account for the way that the meanings of particular signifiers or texts in a particular situation are, in part, ordered by material interests and power relations.

Karen Barad's rethinking of ontology offers an approach that lifts the debate beyond this continuum model. Because Barad's background is in particle physics, her consideration of representation focuses on the representational role of the experiment. Our interest here is in a different representational role: that of the media, but her insights are nevertheless of value to understanding this different role. As Barad has argued, the linguistic turn has tended to position materiality as the product of discourse (in a process that is largely figured as one-way). Cultural studies has tended to focus on the production of meaning and experience for individuals and groups through culture, understanding materiality as either prior to, or the effect of, these moments of meaning making. This approach tends to see reading as a sequential, causal process in which a kind of struggle between the forces of a dominant culture and the resources of the individual takes place. In doing so it treats materiality as indubitably crucial to, but nevertheless one step removed from, this process. Barad's formulation of the phenomenon allows for the consideration of the contribution of materiality to reading that presents it as immediate rather than in some sense distanced from the specific encounter of reading. In this model, meaning making is the product of the intra-action between texts, readers and material conditions, and meaning, rather than being the effect of *pre-constituted* agents – the text and the reader – is understood as a highly contingent phenomenon co-constituted by other highly contingent phenomena. This model shifts the focus from a choice between two agents (the text and the reader) whose prior attributes are assumed to emerge out of political, social and material conditions, to the constitution of all agents (including materiality) and their attributes in the moment of reading.

It must be said that this chapter does not focus on the making of specific meanings by readers based on the texts under consideration. Rather, its aim is to look at the texts themselves and reserve judgement on how meaning is negotiated by readers. This approach is rather different from that taken in the next chapter, which looks explicitly at the different ways readers negotiate clinical guideline texts. This does not mean, however, that the content of these news texts is of no scholarly or political interest. As the model elaborated above makes clear, all readings depend in part on the *phenomenon* of the text.

Compiling texts

The material we analyse here was drawn from three newspapers, the *New York Times*, *The Times* and the *Sydney Morning Herald*. The articles were gathered by searching the online database Factiva using the search term 'methadone' and limiting the search to a two-year period: 2004 –2005.[1] All resulting citations (a total of 135) were retrieved in the first instance and examined for the purposes of our analysis. Those that made only isolated references to methadone in pieces of one paragraph or less, or were devoted to unrelated topics, were noted, and greater focus was placed on those articles that made more substantive references to methadone. This latter group included articles containing more than one reference to methadone, articles in which methadone was central to the overall story and articles in which the reference to methadone was especially vivid, suggestive or idiosyncratic (a total of 77 – *SMH*: 29, *Times*: 27 and *NYT*: 21).

All three newspapers examined enjoy relatively high circulation and readership. The *New York Times* was the third-highest daily circulation paper in the US for the six months ending 30 September 2005 (1,682,644).[2] *The Times* enjoyed the second-highest daily circulation among 'quality' newspapers in the UK for the period ending 30 November 2005 (671,666).[3] The *Sydney Morning Herald* had the highest daily circulation among quality newspapers in Australia during the six months ending 31 March 2006 (211,700).[4] Each one is a longstanding and generally well-respected daily journal, representing, for some, the liberal democratic ideals of journalistic independence and reasoned debate. In selecting these newspapers we leave unexplored representations of methadone in tabloid or 'populist' journalism. There is no doubt that an interesting study could be made of the material found in tabloids, but, being obliged to limit the scale of our search for practical purposes, we chose to explore the ideas and assumptions operating in relatively sober newspaper discourse. It seems to us that there is a great deal to be learnt from the limits of some of Western liberal democracy's most trusted reporting.

Metaphor

There are a number of different ways in which an analysis of newspaper coverage of methadone could be undertaken. In this chapter we focus on the operation of metaphor because the ways in which it appears in the texts gathered is both striking and, we think, revealing. As Helen Keane (2002: 9) has noted,

> As one reads about addiction in both popular and specialist texts one soon notices the reliance on metaphor, and the use of different metaphors to support different understandings of the phenomena. Is addiction like diabetes or high blood pressure (a chronic disease)? Is it like hunger or thirst (a visceral drive)? Is it like enjoying opera (an acquired taste incomprehensible to non-enthusiasts)? Is it like watching TV in the evening (a routine habit)? Is it like falling in love (an irrational attachment)?

A similar emphasis on metaphor, and a similar range of metaphorical figuration, can be identified in texts dealing specifically with methadone. More will be said later about the content of the texts gathered for this study. Before this, however, it is important to consider the meaning of the term 'metaphor'. The status of metaphor as a specific, unique part of language has been under debate for many years. Aristotle provided Western philosophy's first authoritative definition of metaphor, arguing that although in some respects nothing more than an ornament or accoutrement to language, it can also create a change in perspective and, therefore, yield new insights (Miller, 2006: 63). Aristotle's formulation implies a distinction between metaphor and other forms of language. This view has been challenged in recent decades by theorists such as Ricoeur and Derrida. In *The Rule of Metaphor*, Ricoeur argued that if metaphor 'displaces a certain logical order', it must be

> the same as that from which all classifications proceed. The idea of an initial metaphoric impulse destroys these oppositions between proper and figurative, ordinary and strange, order and transgression.
> (Ricoeur, 1978: 22–3)

This argument has led others to conclude that metaphor characterises all thought and language. As Don Miller says, 'Most metaphors are old; some others are new and these shape the next wave of knowledge and action in the world' (2006: 64).

In making reference to 'old' metaphors, Miller invokes the work of Derrida, among others, on metaphor. In 'White Mythology' (1974) Derrida sets about deconstructing the literal/metaphorical binary, arguing that all concepts contain 'worn-out' metaphors that are no longer evident to speakers or listeners, appearing instead as literal language. These worn-out metaphors nevertheless help shape the trajectory of our thinking. While he takes a tack rather different from Ricoeur's, Derrida also concludes that metaphor is at the centre of all literal language, that there is, in fact, no clear separation between the two. As James Seitz puts it, 'It is tempting to say that metaphor "creeps into" language when we are not looking; but in fact it is metaphor that allows us to look – to speak our looking – in the first place' (1991: 292). This formulation emphasises not only the role of metaphor in expressing ideas, but, by bringing otherwise unrelated things together, in generating new ideas. Again, as does Ricoeur, Derrida sees metaphor as important not least because it is at the centre of the production of new concepts. How do the metaphors operating around methadone create new concepts, or shape the trajectory of our thinking? This will be explored in the next section.

Metaphor has also attracted feminist critique, some of which is highly pertinent to the subject under consideration in this chapter. Meryl Altman (1990), for example, notes that feminists have tended to be suspicious of metaphor for several reasons. The appropriation of femininity as metaphor (for terrain, the passive, the ornamental, the duplicitous and so on) has been shown to be widespread within literary and political texts, with significant implications for meaning making around gender. In this respect, some feminists have argued that metaphor has been traditionally used against women's interests. Others, however, have embraced metaphor as a means of imagining new relations, including those of gender, the work of feminists writing in the genre of *Écriture féminine* (for example, Cixous, 1976; Irigaray, 1985) being an important example of this. As Cixous (1976: 875) puts it, 'Woman must write her self: must write about women and bring women to writing, from which they have been driven away as violently as from their bodies'. This writing must be done by breaking up the 'arid millennial' (875) textual ground of masculine dominance, the primacy of reason and the suppression of women's unconscious. Her classic article 'The laugh of the Medusa' offers an example of such writing, replete, as the title exemplifies, with figurative language of all kinds.

How might this use of metaphor for feminist purposes operate? Altman (1990: 496) describes the function of metaphor in the following way: 'what begins as an interesting analogy spills over into a proposition about how something "is". This blurring is the source of a tremendous discursive power'. Clearly, such 'spilling' can have both positive and negative effects. Altman notes, for instance, that gender hierarchy is itself a pervasive metaphor for other phenomena (499). For some feminists, and other critics, however, metaphor is not only potentially subversive, it is *inherently* so. Where Enlightenment thinking – reason, univocality, linearity and the concrete – dominates, metaphor, in its fluidity, suggestiveness and liminality necessarily occupies an oppositional domain (Janusz, 1994). Of course, feminists can be as guilty as others of using metaphor in dominating ways – the once-famous expression 'women are the niggers of the world' is the example Altman offers here. She identifies the expression's appropriation of racist oppression to feminist politics as distinctly colonising. Also concerned with the politics of metaphor, geographer Neil Smith makes a rather different observation, but one nevertheless linked to Altman's in its attunement to the dynamics of the centre and the margin. He points out that part of the function of metaphor is to establish the object as unknown and the phenomenon being used as the metaphor as self-evident: 'To the extent that metaphor continually appeals to some other assumed reality as known, it systematically disguises the need to investigate the known' (1992: 64). Later we will consider the implications of this dynamic for those surprisingly common textual cases where methadone is mobilised as a metaphor for other phenomena.

These critical issues are important for thinking about the status and action of metaphor, though in taking them on board it would be a mistake to lose sight of what is perhaps the twentieth century's most significant observation about metaphor – that (as noted earlier) the literal and the metaphorical cannot be separated.[5] Indeed, amid the debate among feminists over the merits of metaphor is the recognition that, in any case, metaphor is both ubiquitous and indispensable. Michelle Le Doeuff, for instance, identifies the operation of metaphor in philosophical texts, arguing that metaphor cannot be excised even from these works, which, after all, often aspire to being purely rational discourse. Instead, the appearance of metaphor in such texts demonstrates the impossibility of operating entirely in the rational, and more specifically, of the places within the text where there is something 'the system itself cannot justify, but which is nevertheless needed for its proper working' (Le Doeuff, 1989: 3).

If this is the case, if metaphor is everywhere, what is it about metaphor that can be identified as the object of investigation in this chapter? How should it be read when it appears? Here, we return to Barad's take on representation: her recognition that all phenomena always already incorporate the very process of observation that identifies them, in other words, that all phenomena are made in relation to the observer and to other phenomena. Likewise, metaphor is always already produced through the process of observation (such as through our reading of it), and through its relationship to other concepts such as the 'literal'. Any ambition to isolate and reify the metaphorical as an autonomous object of study would not only be misguided, but would occlude valuable interpretive tasks. Indeed, as Seitz (1991: 291) points out, while it is tempting to think of metaphor as something that is 'chosen' or 'used', such formulations tend only to reinstate an erroneous construction of the subject and agency as *prior to* metaphor rather than produced within it, and of metaphor itself as somehow dotted throughout language, rather than as co-constitutive of it in various ways. For these reasons, we want to mobilise a broad concept of metaphor, albeit one that can also take account of the different senses in which metaphor operates within texts.

In keeping with this interest, we structure the next section of this chapter according to the different ways in which metaphors work in the newspaper texts gathered for this study. We begin by discussing an instance of the 'worn-out metaphor' described by Derrida, that is, an expression that has so long been used as to have lost its obvious metaphorical function. As we will argue, expressions such as this are nonetheless active in co-constructing their object. Indeed, in their invisibility, they can be especially powerful generators of meaning. Following this we will look at some overt examples of metaphorical language used in relation to methadone and consider the implications of their use. Third, we will conduct a close reading of an extended metaphor found among the texts and ask how methadone, those who take it, and the social, cultural and political conditions under which the treatment is deemed to make sense are co-produced through this metaphor.

Tracing metaphor

The 'worn-out' metaphor of addiction

In examining the metaphors used in references to methadone in the *New York Times*, *The Times* and the *Sydney Morning Herald* during 2004 and 2005, it is important to emphasise that such references were relatively uncommon in all three, and that where they did occur, they were most often isolated instances, surrounded by little or no explanatory detail. Contexts for these references varied enormously, from stories about the use of sniffer dogs on New South Wales railway stations (Gibbs, *SMH*, 2 July 2004) and the gentrification of New York neighbourhoods (Mooney, *NYT*, 25 January 2004), to the development of iris recognition technology (Chessell, *SMH*, 19 March 2004), and a court case surrounding an aged pensioner charged with supplying heroin (N.A., *Times*, 16 October 2004). The consistent absence of explanatory detail accompanying these references suggests that authors take for granted reader familiarity with methadone, and its implications. In this respect, these references recall Smith's observation on metaphor in that they produce some elements in a text as known, and others as unknown.

What does it mean that methadone is regularly referenced as if it were widely understood – as 'known'? Little or no research exists on public awareness or understanding of methadone programs, though there is some literature on public opinion on needle and syringe programs and other harm-reduction measures (see Treloar and Fraser, 2007, for an overview of this literature). In one sense, then, it is difficult to evaluate this assumption. However, given the stigma associated with methadone treatment and illicit drug use (Murphy and Irwin, 1992; Gourlay, Ricciardelli and Ridge, 2005) and the relative silence around drug treatment in most communities, it is doubtful that readers are indeed well informed about it. The implications of the assumption of familiarity and understanding depend very much on the nature of the references themselves. Perhaps the only consistent effect we might identify is the suggestion that methadone treatment is so established that it needs no explanation. Yet, in tension with this, the references perform quite different notions of methadone. As such, each would need to be examined individually to draw conclusions about its impact. It must be said, however, that most of the references mentioned above carry negative implications in that they are articulated with other textual references to crime, poverty and ill health.

What of the specific use of metaphor in references such as these? One of the most 'worn-out' metaphors associated with methadone must be that of 'addiction' itself. A *Times* article, for example, describes filmmaker David Graham Scott as having been 'addicted to heroin and methadone for 20 years' (Chater, *Times*, 8 June 2004). Likewise, a *Sydney Morning Herald* article on drug treatments states that 'depending on the level of addiction, either methadone, buprenorphine or abstinence will be prescribed' (Pelly, *SMH*, 26 February 2004).[6] There is no doubt that in contemporary English the term addiction is understood to have a literal rather than metaphorical function. Literary critic David Lenson (1995: 35) notes, however, that the origin of the word 'addiction' relates to the Latin *addicere*, meaning to say or pronounce, to decree or bind. In his view, this etymology references drug users' loss of control over language and of consciousness, that is, the notion that they are already 'spoken for', bound and decreed. Instead of *saying*, one is *said* (35).

Given the centrality of language to Western liberal formulations of the subject, this metaphor – and its contemporary identification as literal expression – has significant implications for the status of drug users in liberal societies. Our argument is not that this etymology is known to those who use the term, rather, that the term's early meanings helped shape notions of addiction from their inception. Where regular drug use is designated by a term that implies the inability to agentially generate or enact speech, where, indeed, the drug user is designated by the ontological state of being defined rather than by the ontological act of defining (that is, of passivity rather than activity) there is little room for surprise that drug users are commonly presented as other than, or less than, fully fledged liberal subjects (that is, full citizens). As Lenson notes, through the metaphorical figuration of regular drug use as a kind of surrender to (and of) the powers of speech, 'the addict is changed from a subject to an object' (35). This change can have significant implications for the materiality of treatment programs such as methadone treatment; for example, pharmacotherapy clients are often excluded as stakeholders from policy development around treatment provision (Treloar, Fraser and valentine, 2007). This exclusion points in part to the perception of addicts as most appropriately spoken rather than speaking. In turn, it co-produces treatment conditions (such as those around the regulation of takeaway doses or the physical conditions under which clients can access treatment in clinics and pharmacies) specific to the interests and concerns of the stakeholders consulted, materialising programs in particular ways. In the next section we look at metaphors of methadone itself.

Bullets, handcuffs and strangleholds

As Helen Keane (2002: 3) observes, 'there is a view that addiction is intrinsically bad because it destroys the addict's freedom'. Indeed, the basis for this preoccupation with freedom is indicated in the etymology of addiction. Yet it is not only through worn-out metaphors like that described above that issues of freedom and entrapment inform discussions of methadone and drug use. For example, overt military, policing and pugilistic metaphors are commonplace in the newspaper material. In an article on the negative effects of crystal methamphetamine, for example, methadone is identified as the 'silver bullet' for heroin: 'Drug experts say there is no methadone, no silver bullet, to treat methamphetamine addicts' (Jacobs, *NYT*, 12 January 2004). This reference is interesting for a number of reasons. First, as with other references described above, it occurs in isolation in the text. No further information on what might be meant by the comparison is provided. This is particularly significant in that methadone treatment is rarely, if ever, described as a silver bullet – indeed, its risks, costs and shortcomings are regularly revisited in almost any relevant discursive context (medical articles, consumer newsletters, sociological commentaries and policy materials are some examples). Evidently, it is worth considering what effect the discussion of a new drug thought to be even more destructive and addictive than heroin (crystal meth) may have on the discursive construction of opiates in the future. In this instance, methadone, at least, appears to fare well by comparison. Of significance is the way in which a sequential metaphorical move is made in this reference. Not only is the 'silver bullet' used as a metaphor for methadone, but methadone itself is used as a metaphor. In this sense, methadone is both signified (expressed by the idea of the 'silver bullet') and signifier (expresses a concept something like 'perfect solution', although of course the analogy refers in turn to, of all things, werewolves, and to the notion of the ideal or singularly efficacious kind of ammunition). Understood in Smith's terms, this metaphorical instance sets up two relationships of the known to the unknown. In the first, methadone is presented as unknown, as somehow inadequately elaborated, and our understanding of it as thus expanded by reference to the 'silver bullet'. In the second, it operates as the known; the poorly articulated generic 'perfect solution' is clarified by reference to a known perfect solution – methadone. In both cases, methadone is co-constructed through association with ideas of conflict and danger. Heroin addiction operates as the 'werewolf', as it were, and methadone as the mythical, almost sacred, ammunition.

While the 'silver bullet' metaphor is a familiar one – especially in relation to illness – it is particularly suggestive in the context of addiction. Otten (1986: 8) describes changing formulations of the werewolf, noting that

> While the ancient myths are powerful warnings to humans to abstain from indulging bestial appetites and from obeying irrational promptings, and the ecclesiastical and Scriptural werewolves are to be feared because of the wily stratagems of the Devil who goes about 'seeking whom he may devour' (1 Peter 5: 8 AV), the werewolf in the medieval narratives evokes pity and sympathy for the werewolf, who, banished by fellow humans, was barbarised by his shape and excluded from human fellowship and love.

The power of bestial appetites and irrational influences, the threat of corruption, the devastating effect of stigma and discrimination, all these aspects of the werewolf reproduce familiar understandings of the addict.

Also implied in this metaphor, of course, is the view that methadone does indeed annihilate heroin addiction. In some respects, then, this metaphorical reference to methadone presents it in positive terms; as ideal solution, the sole answer, able to slay the monster. In other respects, such references to monsters and to slaying – to images of danger, death and the 'unnatural' – can be seen to do methadone no favours. In some contexts dependence on methadone is seen as little better than dependence on heroin. The state of addiction is identified in these instances as an evil in itself, inevitably leading to further evil (Hall, Ward and Mattick, 1998a: 7–9). For these reasons, it is unlikely that metaphorical constructions that demonise heroin will ultimately benefit methadone treatment.

For some, methadone does not slay the monster, it merely shackles it. One *New York Times* article (Kilgannon, 6 October 2005) discusses the documentary film 'Methadonia', focusing on one of its subjects, Mario Belfiore, saying he 'has been using methadone – sometimes known as liquid handcuffs – for thirty years, but still suffers relapses with pill addictions'. In this example, reference is made to a metaphor for methadone perhaps not familiar to the general public, but widely known among heroin users and methadone clients (see Stancliff et al., 2002). The view of methadone as liquid handcuffs has international currency among drug users, referring in part to the perceived role of methadone treatment as a form of incarceration, a convenient method of controlling the behaviour and limiting the freedom of those who would otherwise use heroin. We will return to this point throughout the book – the force of this metaphor in co-producing experiences of treatment is discussed in Chapter 4, and alternatives to common understandings of treatment as constrained repetition are considered in Chapter 5. Indeed, the metaphor carries a range of implications, perhaps the most obvious being that methadone treatment constitutes an imposition of controls and constraints where none existed before. Clearly, regular heroin use entails a range of obligations and constraints even for the most wealthy of users, yet these are overlooked in this analogy. This is perhaps because the objection to methadone implied in this metaphor (or, more specifically, to the social and political economy in which methadone treatment becomes a 'solution') is its nominal status as legal, and the convoluted circumstances under which the biochemically similar drug that clients otherwise prefer (heroin) is not legal. In this respect, the metaphor refers to the somewhat arbitrary introduction of an element of criminality to – of the injunction to police – drug use that renders methadone treatment a meaningful solution (and heroin a meaningful problem) in the first place.

This metaphor also operates in intra-action with others found in the material, not least with the metaphor of the silver bullet described above. In speaking of technologies of shackling, it rather clearsightedly identifies Western culture's 'fallback' response to addiction where slaying the monster proves impossible. In the process of constructing the metaphor of the shackle, however, the monster itself is reframed as a victim of overzealous policing rather than as a perpetrator of terror and destruction. Coined by clients to describe the process by which they, as heroin users, are inserted into a kind of carceral economy, it criticises the tendency of methadone treatment to exert control over clients in limiting travel and the ability to work, and in requiring submission to techniques of surveillance such as urine testing for the presence of illicit drugs.

The sense in which the metaphor appears in Kilgannon's article is, of course, rather different from that intended when it is invoked by clients (that is, criticism of the program's effects and rationale). In citing methadone's putative shackling role when describing Mario's history and his continued, if intermittent, consumption of prescription medications, the article tends to indict *him* as evidently in need of constraint, rather than the substance or the program as excessively controlling. Clearly, the ways in which metaphors signify are specific to their context, even as it is possible to trace meanings in these metaphors which help to shape the phenomena to which they refer. The impact of particular metaphors always rests on the operations of other metaphors and of the accompanying text (that which is not overtly metaphorical). In this sense too, metaphor and literal speech cannot be separated. As Barad might put it, these phenomena are made only in their intra-action with other phenomena.

The image of the handcuff is not the only figure of constraint that appears in the newspaper coverage examined here. A different example is that of methadone as exercising a 'stranglehold' on clients. In an article in the *New York Times* (O'Connor, 3 August 2004) on recent developments in pharmacotherapy treatment for opioid dependence, the field is described in the following terms:

> Methadone's limitations prompted experts to look for medications that were less likely to place recovering addicts in a stranglehold.

The way in which methadone is thought to exercise a stranglehold is not clarified in the article, yet the article's commitment to the idea of a kind of wrestling match goes further. A similar metaphor is used to figure addiction itself in the article's title: 'New ways to loosen addiction's grip'. In both these metaphors, an intense, highly corporeal, even visceral, struggle is invoked. Both heroin and methadone emerge as in some sense personified: ruthless and entrapping 'dirty' fighters. Other examples of this type of metaphor are common; thus, it is possible to 'combat' (*Times*, Bird, 31 January 2004) or 'beat' (*Times*, Lister, 1 April 2004) addiction using methadone.

While these pugilistic metaphors vary in how they position methadone (some present it as an illegitimate aggressor, others as a legitimate, necessarily tough, response to the aggression of heroin), they all present addiction as a battleground, as necessarily involving violent struggle (see also Kaufman, 2004; Warren, 2005; English, 2005). In these images, the stakes for those involved are extremely high, and the possibility of a peaceable co-existence with addiction is obscured (see also Tong, 2004). This last effect not only renders obscure other ways of living addiction, it also tends to instate a mythical proper subject untouched by dependence – an unimpeachably autonomous agent, innocent of compulsion or the processes of engaging it.

Elsewhere, Fraser has identified and critiqued binary thinking related to health and illness, in particular to the formulation of appropriate prevention responses to hepatitis C infection rates, focusing on untenable but commonplace binaries such as clean/contaminated, closed/open and well/sick (Fraser and Treloar, 2006). The metaphors at work in the literature examined here point to another salient binary for health research, especially that relating to addiction treatment: autonomous/dependent (see Charmaz, 1997).

How might the construction of addiction as battleground, and the subject as characterised by the binary autonomous/dependent, co-constitute MMT? Perhaps most obviously, the battleground image finds echoes in the design of some methadone treatment clinics such as those in New South Wales, Australia, in which, as we describe in Chapter 3, security measures are felt by some to eclipse the development and maintenance of humane relationships between staff and clients. The binary model of the subject finds resonances, for instance, in blanket disapproval among some practitioners and others of maintenance treatment in general, or in the view that methadone treatment should, at least, be short term, leading quickly to abstinence from drug use. The latter view entails specific approaches to program funding and delivery, materialising in, for example, dosing regimes based on progressive reduction. Further, as Émilie Gomart (2002) has argued via the notion of the *dispositif*, the different ways in which programs are delivered constitute not just different treatment regimes or different views on and experiences of treatment, but different 'methadones' with different effects. In other words, the substance itself can be understood to be co-constituted through processes of representation. The 'battle' to overcome addiction to heroin or methadone, the action of methadone as shackling: these metaphors have significant implications for the materialisation of methadone as substance, especially in relation to questions of withdrawal.[7]

Charm, appeal and authenticity

Occasionally newspaper articles make use of extended metaphors relating to methadone. Here, we examine one example of this. Referencing a recent feature film dealing with issues of memory, identity and fidelity, this *New York Times* piece is entitled 'Eternal sunshine of an addicted mind' (Erian, 27 March 2005). Intended as a light-hearted look at modern dating in New York, and classified as a product of the newspaper's 'magazine desk', the article of some 1000 words describes a newly single woman's dalliance with a charming but somehow inauthentic romantic partner. The article begins by locating love and romance squarely in the domain of addiction, and by identifying a commonly formulated dilemma associated with methadone:

> Two years ago, at 35, I met the Methadone Man. My husband of eight years had just moved out, and I was on my own. I didn't know that he was the Methadone Man at the time, that I'd come to depend on him to wean me from my romantic addictions.

Neatly condensed here are several phenomena popularly associated with drugs: emotional vulnerability (in author Alicia Erian's newly single state), naivety (in her failure to understand the likely trajectory of the relationship and the real effects of the Methadone Man) and entrapment (in that her 'solution' to dependence becomes another instance of it). The article goes on to develop an account in which Erian establishes a relationship with the Methadone Man, despite recognising that he is not 'serious'; that he should not be mistaken for the real thing. This absence of integrity or authenticity in both the Man and the relationship troubles Erian, yet she finds he is useful when her dependence on love leads her into two 'lousy relationships' (presumably these, or love itself, could be figured as 'heroin' in this extended metaphor). Each time Erian recognises that she has become unable to 'shake free' of a bad relationship, she encounters the Methadone Man again, and his charm and attention are enough to replace the 'lousy' partner, and therefore enable her to end the relationship. As she explains:

> I was in a lousy relationship [when the Methadone Man asked me out for dinner]. It was in that instant that the Methadone Man earned his name. Because it was also in that instant that, miraculously, the other man I'd become involved with was erased from my mind.

Again, as Smith has pointed out, metaphor is about the designation of the known and the unknown. In this extract, while the particular emotional dynamic described by Erian (what might perhaps be called, following the popular idiom, 'co-dependence') is accompanied by a substantial amount of explanatory detail, implying its status as unfamiliar – as worthy of investigation and elaboration – the phenomenon used metaphorically to furnish this detail goes entirely unexplained.

Its meaning, in other words, is treated as self-evident. Implied in this reference to methadone are several assumptions:

1. That heroin use is akin to a 'lousy relationship': that is, useless and destructive, in need of discarding
2. That heroin use is difficult, if not impossible, to stop
3. That methadone is able to 'erase' the thought of heroin from the mind, and presumably, its influence on behaviour
4. That this action is in one respect or another 'miraculous'.

While heroin accumulates a range of negative associations through the use of this metaphor, as with some of the previous examples, methadone emerges in a relatively positive light. Yet, as we argued in the previous section, the meaning of metaphor is not made in isolation. All metaphors also construct meanings for the objects that surround them, that is, in Barad's terms, for the other elements that constitute the phenomenon of methadone beyond the commonplace understanding of the boundaries of the material object itself. To rehearse a point made earlier, where heroin is represented in terms of compulsion, desperation and entrapment, methadone too is liable to materialise in the same ways. Indeed, as Erian concludes, the Methadone Man himself becomes the object of compulsion for her, something she must, in turn, free herself from: 'Now though,' she says, 'I have to get off the Methadone Man'. As with the metaphors described in the previous section, the focus is on a dynamic of struggle or battle.

This odd extended metaphor (patently not 'worn-out') is surprising not least because it appears to take for granted the audience's familiarity with the role, functions and pitfalls of methadone treatment, while the relatively prosaic vagaries of dating are thought to warrant spelling out. Why would methadone present as an appropriate and effective literary device to explain a romantic phenomenon? Why would this otherwise largely stigmatised substance, associated as it often is with regimentation, urine tests, security guards and barred dispensing counters (see Chapter 3), be thought to evoke, in a meaningful way, a charming and attractive man? Admittedly the Methadone Man's very charm and attractiveness could be seen to approximate methadone's positive effects, and its appeal. But considering that methadone is understood to be the (relatively) non-euphoric alternative to heroin (Bourgois, 2000) – its workaday cousin – the analogy would appear to be better suited to heroin. Then again, the shallowness of the relationship with the Methadone Man, the fact that it does not ever register as 'the real thing' for Erian could be seen to bear some similarity to methadone's status as replacement for the genuine, the more satisfying, the real, experience of heroin.

Nevertheless, the appropriation of methadone to elaborate Erian's account of dating and love strikes an incongruous note, raising with it questions about the politics of metaphor. Erian's mobilisation of methadone as a metaphor for mainstream concepts of love and romance would seem to deny the controversy surrounding it, even to obscure or ignore the severity of stigma and discrimination faced by those on methadone treatment. There is a sense in which Altman's concern about the colonising reflex of some metaphors can be identified here. However, a reverse argument could also be made that in domesticating methadone as something akin to the commonplace experience of romantic love, Erian's piece counters the stigmatisation of methadone, materialising it as rather more banal. No doubt both these interpretations have some validity, and in any case, readings such as these rely on the perspectives brought by the reader and the context of the reading. They are themselves phenomena.

The ontology of methadone

How is Erian's apparent inclination to take for granted methadone's lack of authenticity, its lack of substance, its infidelity, read by its audience? In the absence of empirical research, we cannot say. Other observations, however, can be made. Striking in this example is the connection that can be drawn between methadone and metaphor as both exemplars of inauthenticity. We have already noted that metaphor has long been linked to the feminine via its definition as seductive, (merely) ornamental, untrustworthy and non-rational. Questions of authenticity pertain to all but perhaps the last of these. Ricoeur's (1978: 11) account of Plato's approach to rhetoric is especially evocative here. For Plato,

> [r]hetoric is to justice, the political virtue *par excellence*, what sophistry is to legislation; and these are, for the soul, what cooking in relation to medicine and cosmetics in relation to gymnastics are for the body – that is, arts of illusion and deception. We must not lose sight of this condemnation of rhetoric, which sees it as belonging to the world of the lie, of the 'pseudo'. Metaphor will also have its enemies, who, giving it what one might call a 'cosmetic' as well as a 'culinary' interpretation, will look upon metaphor merely as simple decoration and as pure delectation.

Central to Plato's formulation are gendered taxonomies of the real and the meritorious. Where cooking and cosmetics are framed as lesser, even false, versions of medicine and gymnastics, femininity is, by association, framed equally disadvantageously in relation to masculinity. Likewise, femininity and metaphor are sites of inauthenticity, while masculinity and literal speech are sites of authenticity.

It is similarly possible to identify the aligning of notions of addiction with femininity in Western culture (and this is explored further in Chapter 5), in that both are understood to involve the dominance of the emotions, a lack of control, irrationality and untrustworthiness. Thus, a series of connections can be drawn between metaphor, femininity and addiction. All occupy the same side of a series of well-known dualisms at the centre of Western thought. These, as Fraser has noted elsewhere (Fraser and Treloar, 2006), operate in a hierarchical way to establish legitimate and illegitimate practices, forms of experience and lives.[8] However, the case of methadone is more complex than this. In the metaphors described above and elsewhere, methadone is doubly materialised in relation to addiction and all it entails in terms of inauthenticity and untrustworthiness, but also as inauthentic in relation to *heroin itself*. As noted earlier, methadone is often understood in policy and practice as the non-euphoric, 'synthetic' alternative to heroin (Bourgois, 2000): the legal alternative that replaces what some consider a desperate, others an outlaw, lifestyle with a domesticated, relatively regimented existence in which participation in crime is minimised. (Its impact on crime is widely documented: see Digiusto et al., 2006; Hall, Ward and Mattick, 1998b. Other effects and uses of methadone, such as its place in new ethics of care, have received less attention, as we explain in Chapter 4.)

In this respect, methadone's designation as 'replacement' (see Ward, Mattick and Hall, 1998: 1, for example) is as important to our argument as the specific elements it is understood to replace. This chapter opened with Ricoeur's observation on metaphor:

> As figure, metaphor constitutes a displacement and an extension of the meaning of words; its explanation is grounded in a theory of substitution.
>
> (Ricoeur, 1978: 3)

Likewise, methadone, in operating as a 'substitute' for heroin, can be seen to constitute a displacement and extension of the meaning of heroin. By registering, for example, as domesticating and regimenting, it extends and displaces other meanings of heroin, reformulating it as undomesticated, outlaw, even chaotic (Fraser and Moore, in press).

This sense of methadone as itself a 'metaphor for heroin' carries with it all the implications of metaphor explicated above. Where metaphor is considered secondary to the literal, where it is associated with the feminine, with inauthenticity, with artifice and untrustworthiness, it can offer only a stigmatised, marginalised location for those undertaking methadone treatment – indeed, the stigmatisation of those who take methadone is well documented (Murphy and Irwin, 1992; Gourlay, Ricciardelli and Ridge, 2005). This observation is, however, complicated by the fact that the acknowledged alternative to methadone use, heroin use, is also denigrated and stigmatised, but in rather different ways. To put it more specifically, then, *both* in the particular ways in which methadone is metaphorised within the public realm, such as in newspaper articles, *and* in the sense in which methadone itself operates as a metaphor for heroin, it occupies a doubly problematic relation to mainstream liberal values. As Ricoeur says,

> the 'place' of metaphor, its most intimate and ultimate abode, is neither the name, nor the sentence, nor even discourse, but the copula of the verb *to be*. The metaphorical 'is' at once signifies both 'is not' and 'is like'. If this is really so, we are allowed to speak of metaphorical truth, but in an equally 'tensive' sense of the word 'truth'.
>
> (7)

Herein lies the motor of methadone's double marginalisation. Methadone is both *not* heroin and *like* heroin – this is the ontological dilemma that informs its liminality, its struggle for legitimacy. In being *not* heroin, it is inauthentic. In being *like* heroin, it is dangerous, defiling, disordering. This double meaning is rather prosaically condensed in one newspaper's reportage of comments made by Australian federal Health Minister Tony Abbott:

> 'Methadone is an important part of our response to the drug problem, but in the end it's just a substitution of a legal for an illegal product,' Mr Abbott said. 'It doesn't stop people being addicts ... This Government would like to see people off drugs.'
>
> (*SMH*, Robotham, 3 December 2005)

In this extract methadone is represented as a replacement for heroin rather than a real solution: a replacement that is not different enough from heroin to leave those consuming it without the (negatively valued) addiction that prompted treatment in the first place. Given that methadone operates ontologically as a metaphor for heroin, it is unlikely that its status will improve unless that of metaphor (and of heroin) also improves.

Conclusion

In making the particular argument we have made here, we take for granted that the accounts of methadone given in the press are not straightforwardly separable from methadone as it operates in reality. To restate our approach, there is no methadone except that which is represented, and the differing ways in which methadone is represented produce not different 'aspects' of methadone, rather, different 'methadones' (Gomart, 2002, and in a different context, Willems, 1998). On this argument, matter such as methadone is not seen in terms of a priori attributes, rather as a phenomenon produced in specific intra-actions with other phenomena, including particular media accounts. It is in this sense that media accounts of methadone can be said to matter: they are profoundly implicated in methadone's material becoming, and this constitutes their ethical action. Given that many of the references to methadone in the newspapers examined here are either isolated and poorly elaborated, or whimsical or comical in intent, this ethical burden may seem incongruous. Yet it is the spectre of 'public opinion' (partly revealed, it is often assumed, through press coverage) that politicians, legislators, policymakers and service providers regularly cite in formulating the legal and material conditions for harm-reduction strategies such as methadone provision (see Treloar and Fraser, 2007). At present, methadone is materialised in part through its representation in the print media as aligned with inauthenticity, disorder and the feminine, as well as, in an ontological sense, always already metaphor. All these alignments, indeed, all these 'Others' of liberalism (Moore and Fraser, 2006) may need to shift together if the standing of methadone and those who take it is to change to any significant degree. Yet policy may have a small role here. Perhaps most straightforwardly, there is a role for policy in reconsidering the framing of methadone treatment as 'replacement' or 'substitute'. These terms are always likely to invoke the inauthentic, and alternatives should be found. Different ways of naming and framing methadone will bear on how it is represented elsewhere – indeed, this reframing will remake methadone in its materiality. This is, of course, no simple process (indeed, what follows in this book is as implicated in the remaking of methadone as are the texts analysed above). As Miller (2006: 65) has declared: 'The world needs a multitude of new metaphors ... but metaphor, like life, is full of risks.' Because methadone is co-constituted in the media, it is here that some of these new metaphors must be performed, as well as in works such as this book (here we also return to Cixous's conviction that representation is an opportunity for remaking). And this – the need to remain open to media coverage rather than to hope for, or act to, minimise it as do some politicians, policymakers and providers – constitutes one of the many productive risks methadone and those who support it must take.[9] The next chapter extends this observation by considering the ways in which other texts, and the risks they entail, work to co-constitute methadone treatment.

2
Governing Treatment

In the last chapter we argued that MMT and those enrolled in it are defined in some liberal contexts as inauthentic, untrustworthy and irrational. This chapter shifts focus to the explicit governance of those clients and the rules and regulations that define and manage them. The regulation of clients, we argue, shares much with the metaphors, images and figuring found in media texts. Clients are constituted in treatment, as they are in other public discourses, as unreliable and deficient, and this is materialised in regulatory practices through risk management.

We will begin the chapter with examples of the regulations of clients in practice. If you were to be a pharmacotherapy client in Australia, here are some of the things that may happen to you:

- You may have to sign a contract with the pharmacist who dispenses your dose, in which you undertake not to dress 'scruffily'.
- You may have to undertake to attend the pharmacist unaccompanied.
- You may not be allowed to wait in the pharmacy for your dose if there are other customers.
- You may not be allowed to wait on the footpath just outside the pharmacy either.
- If you are allowed to wait in the pharmacy, you may be required to queue behind yellow tape on the floor.
- On the other hand, you may be forced to queue at a dosing window exterior to the chemist, because you are not meant to enter the pharmacy at all.
- Your treatment may be stopped if your doctor hears that you have misused your dose, even if there is no other evidence than hearsay.
- You may be required to give urine samples regularly, in toilets that are inadequately protected from view.

Humiliations of methadone clients are often reported in academic research, professional literature and interviews. Philippe Bourgois (2000), for example, writes of the arguments and denigrations that clients are forced to undergo because of the physically addictive properties of methadone. Friedman and Alicea argue that methadone is a form of discipline that produces what Foucault refers to as 'docile' bodies (2001: 147). As with the clinics they study, the above list is produced through treatment contracts and clinic rules, that is, through the regulatory management of MMT. Unlike their studies, seven of the eight items in the list above refer to the regulation of clients who receive their dose in the retail environment of the pharmacy, where they are ostensibly being treated the same as any other customer.

Governmentality and regulation have informed scholarship of an extraordinary breadth and depth after Foucault, and this scholarship is particularly rich in the field of biomedicine (see, for example, Clarke et al., 2003; Rose, 2001b; Squier, 2004; Turner, 1992; Waldby, 1996). Yet there is something in the treatment of drug addicts that seems to render our most supple critical approaches inadequate. At first glance, descriptions of the responsibilised biological citizen seem otiose. What could analyses of obligation and choice add to our understanding of the methadone client compelled, as a condition of treatment, to urinate behind a shower curtain instead of a door?

Bourgois considers concluding that Foucauldian biopower is omnipresent before moving to argue for the role of another Foucauldian model, that of the 'specific intellectual' (Bourgois, 2000: 188). In a similarly schematic but more provocative argument, Nancy Fraser has proposed that post-Fordism has brought about new regimes of regulation and governmentality that depart from the Foucauldian framework in a range of ways (N. Fraser, 2003: 15). These include changes to the external regulation of individuals. Alongside the transformation of citizens into consumers who are made to bear responsibility for their own lives, post-Fordism also brings *desocialisation*: changes to the role of the state in regulation and redistribution. State responses to the increased inequality and social stratification brought about by these changes are more likely to take the form of 'outright repression' than responsibilisation – the example given here is the brutalising treatment meted out to millions of indigent Americans via the prison-industrial complex. Modernity, or Fordism, was operationalised through individual self-regulation, fostering rational, activating and self-governing individuals. Post-Fordism strips away the welfare functions of the state and brings about pronounced but contradictory changes to individual regulation. For those consumer-citizens who fit these new arrangements, the self-regulation of Fordism is heightened and developed, and the logics of competition, accountability and risk management have increasing purchase. These individuals are required to be reflexive and autonomous, and to make choices for their own and the public good. For those who do not fit, the self-regulation of Fordism retreats and is replaced with the imposition of regulation through external means. Following Robert Castel (1991), Fraser points to a bifurcation in post-Fordist regulation. This is the emergence of a 'segmented governmentality: responsibilised self-regulation for some, brute repression for others' (N. Fraser, 2003: 169).

When it comes to lists of those who do not fit into models of citizenship, almost all include 'the drug addict'. Some of the operations of MMT lend themselves readily to the typologies proposed by Fraser and Castel, as does the treatment in general of those identified as addicts. Methadone clients, as drug addicts, do not meet the criteria required of them to function as autonomous bio-citizens, so they are subject to the repression and subjugation of a post-Fordism that reanimates *pre*-Fordism. Modern biomedicine obliges citizens to be well, to be reflexive, to make active choices, to be self-governing, but methadone clients are outside this frame, so other things are imposed on them, most notably restriction, infantilisation and punishment.

Yet things are not so simple. For MMT is also an example of biomedicine, and exerts the same power and follows the same rules as other biomedical arenas. It invokes obligations, communicative exchanges, clinical encounters and therapeutic relationships. It is a technology of care and operationalises care of the self. Clients are subject to responsibilisation and feel obligations to be well, to make choices, to conform to prescribed norms. Opioid substitution regimes such as MMT meet more of the criteria for 'evidence-based' medicine and policy than any other treatment for opioid dependence, especially the abstinence models so favoured by anti-drugs populism (Gibson, Flynn and McCarthy, 1999; Wodak, 2002). Many of the insights of studies into modern biomedicine are relevant to studies of methadone.

Moreover, clients who undergo treatment often experience benefits, in the manner that treatment can bring. Participation in the paid workforce, abstention from crime, improved 'social functioning' and so on bring benefits to the state, but they can also improve the quality of people's lives and make them happier. Nancy Fraser is among those who chide Foucault for missing the emancipatory effects of liberalism, and while this criticism is probably unfair, there is something to be said for recognising the potential of some regimes of governance. For our purposes, there is not much to be gained in deliberating over whether these benefits are analogous to medical treatment or to social welfare services, if MMT is best compared to treatment with insulin or to treatment through an integrated case management model of therapy. This implies a split between the social and the medical, between the 'chemical' and 'psychological' facets of addiction that are often enmeshed in the experience of clients and service providers. Better, without making this split, to agree that arguments about repression and responsibilisation are both pertinent but that neither fully capture the possibilities of treatment. It is not possible then to say that MMT represents either the 'rump' of Castel and Fraser's two-tiered society or its hypercompetitive and wholly integrated 'top' tier. Neither is it possible to say that treatment follows the logic of either Fordist self-care and surveillance, or the post-Fordist logic of outright repression. It does both, and it does other things as well.

This chapter, which proceeds from the insights of Fraser and Castel, considers the dual regulation of methadone clients, conforming to both Foucauldian/Fordist modes of regulation and later, which is to say earlier, modes too. Building on the previous chapter's analysis of media constructions of methadone as an inauthentic substitute, our aim is to consider in some detail the practices and effects of rules governing clients. These include the role of both the state and the market in managing marginalised populations, the politics of inequality and distribution, risk management, and the medicalisation of welfare. The regulations that will be described here belong to a range of categories: policies (clinical and professional), guidelines (governing supervision of dosing, discipline, complaints) and contracts (between clients and doctors, between clients and pharmacists). These regulations are also to be found in areas less directly connected to drug use and treatment: such as in the effects of privatisation and changes to the welfare state, as we have seen in the Introduction. That is, the regulations governing MMT operate through health and economic policies; the organisation of professions; and at the capillary level of everyday transactions in the clinic, pharmacy and doctor's surgery (we examine these sites in detail in later chapters). As this suggests, clients are not the only people subject to regulation, as doctors, pharmacists and policymakers also come under their domain. The impact on service providers is distinct in many ways from the impact on clients, but also reveals much about the manifestations of contemporary governance.

MMT is a highly regulated regime within a broader field of medicine that is itself subject to high levels of regulation and complex governance. However, there are other levels of policy and regulation pertinent to methadone; and a deficit of many analyses of treatment and drug use is that they do not consider the complex social worlds in which affected people live. Critical engagements with the clinical encounter draw attention to often-neglected questions of power and ethics and to the political, economic and institutional forces at work (Anderson et al., 2003; Mykhalovskiy, McCoy and Bresalier, 2004; Wright and Morgan, 1990). As an attempt to correct this, and to produce a more comprehensive analysis of the governance of methadone than a narrow focus on clinical rules alone would allow, this chapter considers governance and regulation as questions of risk and risk management. This allows connections to be made between the regulation of MMT and neo-liberal regimes of governance more broadly. The second section, on interpretation, deals with the specific uses to which the clinical guidelines and policies governing MMT are put. The discussion moves, then, from what is normally considered the macro (risk and the state) to the micro (relationships between individuals) but it is important to emphasise that this does not translate to a hierarchy of rules or an organisation of factors into 'proximate' and 'distal'. Rather than understanding individual treatment contracts as more directly connected to personal experience than economic forces, our approach is guided by the feminist scholarship of Karen Barad and others, who direct our attention to the embodied subjectivity of individuals (see Fraser and valentine, 2006, for a summary). A focus on the individual as an embodied subject emphasises the political constitution of individuals and the multiple forces that perform them intra-actively.

We are also indebted in this chapter to critical traditions in social welfare and policy, and so need to acknowledge that these traditions are not universally relevant to drug treatment clients. As important as poverty and stigma are to MMT, clients are not always poor and not always stigmatised. It is important to emphasise that clients often conform in most respects to normative figurings of the liberal subject as consumer-citizen, prevented only from meeting these requirements by the fact that dependence or addiction to drugs is incompatible with these norms. People who take methadone have jobs in the market economy, raise their children according to prevailing standards and behave themselves. We need to emphasise this to correct the inaccuracies of the anti-drugs hysteria that often circulates through media texts, as we argued in the previous chapter, and contest the moral verities of anti-drugs doxa. It is also necessary because of the emphasis placed by many, including practitioners and advocates for treatment, on the social disadvantages and marginalisation associated with heroin addiction. In the course of this study we interviewed clients in their workplaces and in houses that they owned. We spoke to clients keen to emphasise the absence of abuse and trauma in their childhood, and the continuing presence of support and social connections in their lives. Service providers spoke about 'hidden' populations of drug-dependent professionals. A number of clients do not bear the stigma of the methadone user and some of those we spoke to were very concerned to pass as 'straight' and protect their privacy (we take up this point in the next Chapter). Emphasising social marginalisation is a necessary counter to anti-drugs rhetoric, and serves strategic purposes: effective lobbying for greater resources to be available for treatment, recognition of the multiple domains of problematic drug use and the political dimensions of 'addiction'. But greater awareness of the heterogeneity of methadone clients, including their diverse needs in relation to welfare and social services, is sorely needed. For this reason, the relevance of discourses around 'welfare' to methadone clients should not be assumed.

Nevertheless, critical approaches to social work and social welfare offer useful insights, for two reasons. Many methadone clients are not impoverished, 'high risk' or especially 'vulnerable'. That said, many are identified as all of these things, and much of the regulation of treatment is organised around this latter group of clients. Second, MMT shares with child protection a regulatory dominance of risk. Critiques of the dominance of risk management in domains of social care are pertinent here. Moreover, child protection, which has been subject to sustained criticism on these grounds, shares considerable overlap with methadone treatment.

Risk

A great deal of analysis of the operations of contemporary liberal states has been mobilised around the question of risk. Risk has been argued to transform the relationships between individuals, and between individuals and the state. As we will argue shortly, methadone clients, who are understood to occupy a doubled relationship to risk (at risk of harm, and posing risk to others), are especially vulnerable to the dominance of risk in policy discourse and individual clinical encounters. Before then, a brief review of the manifestations of risk in scholarship and policy can illustrate the extent to which individuals, collectives and states are organised under its rubric.

The best-known example of this manifestation is probably Ulrich Beck's individualising 'risk society'. For Beck, awareness of the risk of environmental catastrophe is the basis of the risk society and strategies to confront this risk are a new means of framing modernity and globalisation (Beck, 1992). Beck argues that the prospect of catastrophic risk has transformed social relations and identities. In this schema class, race and gender are no longer the primary means by which social relations are organised, and the political potential of alliances and activities based on these identities and their relation to the state is also gone. Developing Beck's framework in a conceptualisation of contemporary subjectivity and social identity, Anthony Giddens links reflexivity and future-orientation to the need to identify and manage the risks posed to the unfettered action of human agency. Giddens has also been responsible for the articulation of Beck's risk society through the UK's Third Way program (Giddens, 2001) and for a brief moment it seemed as though one-time Federal Labor leader Mark Latham would try something similar in Australia:

> [G]overnment ... needs to be able to help people with the management of economic risk. This means assessing the risks of disadvantage and poverty ... and then devising the services and reciprocal responsibilities by which each individual might avert these risks. The public sector needs to replicate the success of the financial sector in developing sophisticated systems of risk assessment and risk aversion.
>
> (Latham, 2001: 31)

Risible as this is, risk is useful to many discussions of governance because it is encountered by both individuals and state regimes and because a key concern in many areas, including health and aged care and welfare, is the devolution or dispersal of risk from the state to the individual. Thus, Braithwaite, Gatens and Mitchell argue that the question of how to manage social risk is an urgent contemporary question, with the major changes to Australia's welfare system over the 1990s representing a shift 'away from publicly funded risk reduction policies towards privately funded risk mitigation (insurance) supported by social security benefits of "last resort"' (Braithwaite, Gatens and Mitchell, 2002: 232). As we argued in the Introduction, MMT is one particular instance of changes to the welfare state and the political constitution of individuals and collectives, and the devolving of risk from state to individual is a critical component of this.

The notion that contemporary states and contemporary individuals are united under the rubric of managing various risks has become commonplace. Within the space of the clinical encounter, responsibility and the burden of risk moves between medical practitioners and patients: no longer, if it ever was, the sole responsibility of professionals to make assessments and decisions, patients are expected to act as rational and informed decision makers, and choose courses of treatment based on likely outcomes and cost effectiveness.

Beck's individualising thesis has been subject to strong criticism. Celia Roberts (2006), Sean Scalmer (2006) and Lisa Adkins (2002) are among those who argue that reflexivity and agency are articulated through class and gender, Beck's 'zombie' categories of social identity, whether risk is the object of study or not. Beck argues that risk society replaces class society, which is to say that social categories such as class are no longer relevant. In constituting society as individuals joined together in collectivities of risk, Beck rejects race, class and gender as social identities and in doing so distorts these and other differences between individuals (the question of identity is central to chapter 4). Moreover, the deployment of risk in domains such as MMT can obscure important distinctions between the self at risk and the self who puts others at risk (Brownlie, 2001). This inflection is pertinent to MMT in ways that it is not in other medical relationships. It is also pertinent to child protection, the sexual practices of gay men and some heterosexual men, licit drug use by pregnant women and illicit drug use in general. In these domains 'risk' obtains not only through its meaning of risk *to* the patient or client but also the risk *of* the client (Adkins, 2001). To speak of some kinds of people in terms of risk – those identified as addicted to drugs, or with a certain kind of psychiatric diagnosis, or a certain kind of family arrangement, or belonging to certain categories of epidemiological or demographic criteria – is to claim that what is at stake in decisions around these people is not only the risks they may be subject to, but what kinds of risk they may be subjecting others to. 'At risk' parents are conceived of as both endangered and a danger to their children; 'at risk' pregnant women seen as a threat to their foetus; and drug addicts who are not managed properly put themselves, their family, their neighbourhood and broader society in peril. These different meanings of risk suggest alternative means of approaching it than those proposed by Giddens and Beck. Rather than accepting exposure to risk as an experience that unites individuals and does away with traditional social divisions, it is productive to look to the effects of co-constituting individuals through risk, in particular, the technologies of surveillance and monitoring provoked (Ogden, 1995).

Risk, then, organises MMT along two axes: first, the place of risk and responsibility in contemporary health care and, second, the constitution of risky selves who may endanger themselves and others. This maps roughly, again, onto the two tiers proposed by Castel. On the one hand, methadone clients are subject to shifting responsibilities for the management of risk and treatment decisions, a key move in the biopolitics of neo-liberalism (Helén, 2004). On the other hand, regulation of methadone is also organised to govern and contain danger, that is, the methadone subject who is not only at risk but who places others at risk. The following analysis concentrates on the latter meaning, that is, the governing of danger. This is in no way meant to imply that risk is insignificant for service providers or clients. Methadone is a potent drug, and misuse of it can have severe consequences. Mary Douglas argues that the use of 'risk' in public discourses does not have much to do with probability or the scientific calculation of likelihood, this original meaning 'only indicated by an arm waving in the direction of possible science: the word *risk* now means danger; *high risk* means a lot of danger' (Douglas, 1990: 3). This does not mean, however, that perils are imagined: 'the reality of the dangers is not at issue. The dangers are only too horribly real, in both cases, modern and pre-modern' (8). It is similarly possible to question the regulation of methadone clients through a framework of risk management while recognising the risks that MMT can bring.

Regulatory documents organising MMT explicitly frame in terms of risk management, and are noticeably more emphatic in 2006 than 1999.[1] In Australia, state government departments produce clinical guidelines for prescribers and pharmacists, with detailed sections on most aspects of treatment, including assessment, dosage, supervision of dosing, labelling of bottles and reporting requirements. The Victorian 2006 clinical guidelines describe risks and strategies that could be described as *program-level* (including, for example, complicated pharmacokinetics, injury and psychiatric co-morbidity) (p. 9) and a check-list for risk assessment of *individual* clients (that require information on domains such as drug use, mental state, medical co-morbidity, housing and recent injecting) (p. 49). In 1999 the NSW guidelines mentions risk 76 times in 106 pages; the 2006 document is about 70 pages longer and 'risk' occurs 202 times. The documents are similar in many respects when describing the risks of treatment, especially takeaways.[2]

NSW:	Victoria:
• 'Patient may deliberately administer the dose to another person. Ingestion of methadone can be particularly dangerous for children. Even the smallest amount can be fatal. • Patient may divert the dose to another person. • Another person, such as a child, may inadvertently consume the dose [...] • Patient may attempt to inject the dose. Injecting methadone syrup or buprenorphine tablets can cause venous damage, emboli and tissue necrosis and (if needles are shared) transmission of infectious diseases including HIV, hepatitis B and hepatitis C [...] • Patient may combine the dose with other drugs, increasing the risk of overdose. • Patient may not take the dose at the specified time, perhaps choosing to combine doses for an enhanced effect (risking overdose). • Patients seen less frequently may be less likely to seek help if they experience problems, or may present later' (NSW Health, 2006: 47).	'Despite the proven success of pharmacotherapy, there are some risks. Methadone, in particular, is a potentially toxic drug with a low therapeutic index (the therapeutic dose is relatively close to the toxic dose) [...] Some patients have psychiatric and social problems. Using a potentially toxic drug to treat a patient whose behavioural history may put them at special risk warrants a cautious approach. Patients treated for heroin dependence have often been involved with a complex culture of drug use. Much of their social network may have been associated with this culture, and many have been involved in illegal activities to support their habit. These factors can create a risk of diversion of prescribed doses for illicit or unsanctioned use' (Drugs and Poisons Regulations Group, 2006: 8).

The 'risks' associated with methadone are well known: diversion, overdose and injection. Very rarely mentioned in policy or clinical documents, or in our interviews, is the fact that these are program-level rather than individual-level risks, and that clients who inject their methadone are not therefore likely to sell or administer it to someone else.

Our interviews suggest that one effect of this may be a conflation of these risks, such that the likelihood of one type of illicit use makes another type of illicit use likely as well:

> **Pamela:** [I]t's not because we want to differentiate you between other people in society, it's because we, we, it's an unsafe drug to be, to be out there on the streets.
>
> *Interviewer: Yep.*
>
> **Pamela:** Especially when there's children involved, and, um, yeah, I mean, we don't give methadone out so you go and sell it to somebody else. That's not the idea of it.
>
> (Pamela, regional NSW, nurse, 46)

There are serious consequences associated with a number of the risks associated with diversion: children accidentally (or not) being given methadone, an opioid naïve adult accidentally (or not) taking methadone, accidental client overdose when methadone is used with other drugs, blood-borne virus transmission through unsafe injection, venous injury and abscesses acquired through injection. These consequences are often discussed in the same context as trafficking and illicit sale. This tends to obscure the fact that much diversion takes place between clients or heroin users, is unremunerated, takes place between clients, and carries none of these consequences (we take up this point in chapter 4). The differences between these risks are also obscured: diversion is a crime, which makes it a risk of a different order than that of death through overdose. Also obscured is the fact that one risk factor at an individual level does not suggest the presence of another. A number of clients we interviewed, for example, inject their methadone, but there is nothing to suggest that these clients are more likely to sell or mismanage their doses than anyone else.

Many of the service providers interviewed were pragmatic about these points, and realised the benefits of MMT even to 'risky' clients. Yet the impact of risk management as a technology of governing methadone was also evident. Deaths from methadone are relatively rare and happen in most cases to clients (not children) in the early days of treatment[3]: but the imagined coroner's court loom in a number of our interviews:

> I don't care what you tell me, you could tell me you've been abducted by aliens. But you need to demonstrate to me in a particular way, where if reviewed by my peers or by the coroner's

court, I am confident that I can say, in my best judgement [why] I have done this.

(Barry, Sydney, NSW, policy/prescriber, 40)

And the risk for our program is, the more diversion there is, the more children die of overdoses, or if people get found with methadone in their system when the coroner does a post mortem, the more criticism we have of the state program.

(Lawrence, Sydney, NSW, policy, 61)

So, um, that seems to be a real issue, and we really are sticklers for the, the rules, because it's on our head if, I don't want to end up in the coroner's court over it.

(Sandra, regional Victoria, pharmacist, 37)

Nigel Parton's analysis of child welfare in advanced liberalism argues that systems of child welfare and child protection operate within severe resource constraints and pressures of responsibilisation on practitioners. Both of these are also found in MMT. At the heart of this system is the notion of risk, governed through technologies of audit:

Audit responds to failure and insecurity by the managerialisation of risk ... the entities to be audited – social workers and other professionals – are themselves transformed in order to make them auditable. Where the key concern is risk, the focus becomes, not making the *right* decision, but making a *defensible* decision, where the processes and procedures have been followed.

(Parton, 1998: 20–1)

As Castel argues that governance of risky populations is now managed through a calculus of risk factors and autonomised management, Parton points to practices of social care becoming increasingly dominated by the gathering of data to calculate risk and prioritise resources. Calculation of risk is also about 'dividing and sifting the prudent from the imprudent, the self able to manage itself and high risk situations, and those who must be managed' (Parton, 1998: 19), and rationing the provision of care according to those categories. Critical social work scholars such as Parton, Dorothy Scott (2006) and David Thorpe (Thorpe and Bilson, 1998) argue that this combination of resource scarcity and governance through risk management means that the provision of quality care in child welfare has been supplanted by surveillance. Within MMT, similar technologies of governance, resource scarcity and the categorisation of clients according to risk have had similar effects on the provision of care.

This is illustrated in the ways practitioners chafe against systems of audit and risk calculation. In Victoria, for example, prior to the introduction of new guidelines in June 2006, a permit system was in place whereby takeaways prescribed 'over the guidelines', that is, more than one per week, were authorised through the issue of a permit from the Department of Human Services. Permits were given after an assessment. In practice it seems that in many cases the assessing consultant would defer to the doctor on the basis that doctors were in the best position to judge the stability of their clients. Some doctors reported this system being nominal and having no real effect on their practice, either because they rarely if ever prescribed more takeaways than the guidelines allowed or because the process of permit acquisition was streamlined for them. Others, however, report a burden of work and irritation:

> The whole thing's bullshit [...] I go back to the department, write down that I spoke to [name of consultant] you know, and he said that it was perfectly all right for me to do that for my client, um, you know, well what do you know, 'cause he's just got what I'm telling him. So as I said, the whole thing's a bit ridiculous, but it, it means then that the people authorising the takeaways feel that, well, they are protected because the consultant said it was all right [...] You know, and I'm thinking, well, you know, doesn't anyone take any responsibility around here for anything. You know, it is a bit silly.
>
> (Aaron, Melbourne, Victoria, prescriber, 59)

The impact of risk on the provision of care is also illustrated by our interview respondents' consciousness of the defensible rather than the correct decision:

> When senior experienced people talk to me about, about takeaway stuff [...] or I might have been overly generous, ah, their teaching point is to do with me being at risk in regard to, you know, a dead child, then court. 'Where did this come from, how can you, here's the guideline saying, you know, no more than "x", and you've given them "y", and, you know, how can you explain that to them.' You know (laughs), and whether your insurance company will stick by you. I try not to think of my practice in those terms.
>
> (Terence, regional NSW, prescriber, 59)

As we have already seen in the Introduction, the organisation of health care provision in Australia is such that there is unmet demand for services for impoverished and socially marginalised populations such as methadone clients. In addition, inconsistency of service provision has a significant impact on the experience of treatment, a point that will be taken up in the following section. Given both of these circumstances, systems of risk management that are interpreted by practitioners as bureaucratic risk mitigation rather than meaningful assessment could have an adverse effect on retaining service providers in MMT. This is a very practical consideration, materialising the program in specific ways and clients as dangerous populations. Nigel Parton calls for the revalorising of ambiguity and judgement in the management of risk:

> Rather than seeing a commitment to uncertainty as undermining and lying at the margins of practice, I would suggest it lies at its heart, and that its recognition provides an opportunity for valuing practice, practitioners and the people with whom they work.
>
> (Parton, 1998: 23)

Moira, a client in Victoria, makes this connection explicit:

> So there's no legislation, so consumers have got, kind of, almost no rights, um, you know, everything is only guidelines and if the doctors and the pharmacists don't follow the guidelines, and the person dies, then they could find themselves in the coroner's court, but, um, you know, it's ... for the patient to really benefit from the program you kind of have to have doctors who are prepared to take risks.
>
> (Moira, Melbourne, Victoria, client, 38)

Moira argues not for recklessness or disregard for the dangers of methadone but for practices that are organised around care rather than the procedural minimisation of risk. Clinical judgement is recognised as important in even the most stringent definitions of evidence-based medicine, and the responsibility for risk in treatment decisions is increasingly held by patients. Moira's call for doctors to take risks echoes Parton's point about the need for judgement and uncertainty. This would also involve separating the *impact* of a possible event, such as the death of a child, from its *likelihood*. Both are components of risk but tend to get elided in the practical management of methadone risk.

The reasons for this elision, and for the apparent will to make every decision defensible in an imagined coroner's court, are connected to the constitution of methadone clients as a dangerous, risky population. A Canadian analysis of political, program and evaluation documents found that the political goals of MMT changed over a forty-year period (between the periods 1963–79 and 1980–2001) from an orientation towards meeting drug users' needs to one protecting the community from drug users. The author of that study concludes that

> changes in the way political agencies considered the harms associated with drug use confirm the importance of risk management in this field of regulation. These changes can then be summarised as a shift in the way drug use is now considered, passing from a manifestation of personal needs to the manifestation of a public nuisance.
>
> (Quirion, 2003: 253)

As we argued at the beginning of this chapter, Beck's 'risk society' is flawed in its individualising. It is also flawed in its failure to distinguish between the relationships that different kinds of people have with the state. Methadone clients are not just people at risk in the same way that Beck's individualised citizens are at risk of terrorism or nuclear war (Beck, 2004). They are also constructed as risky, imprudent and in need of management. The prescription of powerful drugs such as methadone is *always* risky, to some degree, and doctors bear the risk in cases of adverse incidents. But methadone clients are constituted as risky and almost axiomatically incapable of self-management; 'methadone dependence', as we will see in Chapter 5, constructed as a proxy for lack of agency. Liberal figurings of the subject, based on notions of autonomy and rationality, are denied methadone clients, whose agency is often reconfigured as pathology or recalcitrant non-compliance. Service providers working with methadone clients clearly feel that the responsibility for adverse events will be completely attributed to them, in a manner quite distinct from other patient groups. This is not because service providers are recognised as having expertise and power that clients do not: as is the case whenever drugs are misused accidentally or deliberately and service providers are held to account. It is because clients are constituted as risks to be managed, rather than people who are at risk with the capacity to share in the management of that risk. When MMT is discussed as risk management these distinctions are rarely made, and the operationalisation of risk as a technology of governance is rarely acknowledged.

Interpretation

So far we have considered one aspect of the rules governing treatment: the importance of risk and risk management in their operation. The second element of the regulations to be considered here falls under the broad rubric of interpretation, that is, how regulations are put into practice through being read, understood and implemented in various situations by different actors. As with the other aspects of regulation, these acts of interpretation constitute both clients and service providers. Neither clients, prescribing doctors, dispensing pharmacists nor dosing nurses are wholly constituted by the regulations governing treatment. Nor do the regulations act on wholly constituted pre-existing subjects. Instead, interpretive acts work to constitute the subjects of regulation, and regulation is enacted and brought into practice by these subjects. These acts of interpretation, and responses to those acts by clients, also demonstrate the agency of clients and service providers: subjects are produced through reading, intra-acting with the guidelines, with methadone and each other.

This is not to say, however, that the agency of clients and service providers democratises treatment. As in our previous discussion of risk, analysis of the interpretation of guidelines demonstrates the ways in which clients are figured as people to be managed (and in Chapter 5 we will discuss the ways in which this figuration is gendered). Interpretive power resides with policy workers and service providers, not with clients. Acts of interpretation have effects on service providers, but the biggest impact of differences in interpretation is on clients' experiences of treatment. Client interpretations of the guidelines, and responses to the failure of the guidelines to allow space for negotiation and consensus, are too readily figured as proof of their need to be managed. This does not mean that clients are inactive or passive, only that their activity and agency is constituted as illegitimate. As we will see in this section, and throughout this book, clients are active in interpreting the governance of MMT, and in many cases their interpretations are close to those made by service providers. The agency of clients is not in question here, only the recognition of that agency; and as much of our analysis is the regulatory production of clients, it is the regulatory work done by service providers that is central to the following discussion.

At the time our research was conducted, guidelines in NSW and Victoria stipulated that the maximum number of takeaways per week was four and one respectively. However, both clients and service providers report inconsistencies in access to takeaways, and variations in other rules such as frequency of urine testing.

> [W]e've still got people who have got five takeaways a week. We've got one guy who gets four takeaways in one hit and then often gets another four a day after.
>
> (William, Sydney, NSW, pharmacist, 43)

> Yeah, no, a mate of mine, he managed to scam five, five or six a week out of them, I don't know how he did it. It was, yeah, five a week [...] 'Cause [his dose] went up and down too. He was my flatmate, and, um, I don't know how he, he got, I think he could bloody sell snow to Eskimos, he's that kind of guy, you know.
>
> (Joel, Melbourne, Victoria, client, 33)

> [W]e have a very strange situation where we have someone who is, um, who picks up his methadone weekly [...] And it's been working fine for years. He doesn't sell, he doesn't, he just, you know, he just gets his seven bottles and takes, you know, picks them up every Tuesday and he's happy.
>
> (Teresa, regional Victoria, nurse/manager, 48)

It would be difficult to overstate the importance of access to takeaways and of consistent standards of treatment to many of our participants (Treloar, Fraser and valentine, 2007). Clients often know other clients, and differences in takeaway access are often communicated between them. Inconsistency in service provision is in part an effect of the guidelines, brought about by the practices of their being read, interpreted and acted on. The regulations governing treatment work to constitute clients through representation and practice, and this is evident in treatment in very practical ways. Interpretation of the guidelines is the means by which clients receive takeaways or do not, submit to urine tests regularly or do not, are treated with the same expectations as customers in a retail environment or are not. More broadly, acts of interpretation put guidelines and other rules into practice, and reveal the various modes of regulation of methadone subjects. The subjects of methadone are both service providers and clients but it is only clients who are governed according to the contradictory repressive/responsibilising logics of regulation.

Here, we will consider three modes of interpretation: the guidelines as law, as suggestion and as surveillance. There are a number of conclusions to draw from these, but excluding the possibility of interpretation is surely not one. Rather than calling for changes that stop service providers having any interpretive say at all, we argue that recognition of the inevitability of interpretation is a more productive step.

The lexical ambiguity of the word 'guide' (the *OED* has various meanings including 'leading the way' and 'directing the course') (*The Oxford English Dictionary*, 1989) readily enables an interpretation of guidelines as law, directing action. Some participants report being instructed in this way. Diane, a nurse in a public clinic, describes her reading of directives around takeaways, which, it will be recalled, specify the length of time on treatment before takeaways are to be prescribed:

> We had the little methadone book, and how you could have one after three months and then one again one month after. I used to live by it, you know, I'd read it and when the one year goes over you can give the third one and then the two years goes over and you get the fourth. They changed the guidelines and I gather the reason was there were some doctors who were prescribing five takeaways a week and they clamped down.
>
> (Diane, Sydney, NSW, nurse, 30s)

Dominic, a pharmacist, is explicit that the guidelines are in fact not guidelines, but law:

> [W]here they used to be, they're a guide, as it says, now they've got some legislative backup so those guidelines can be enforced, so in actual fact they're not guidelines, they're actually laws.
>
> (Dominic, Sydney, NSW, pharmacist, 44)

Interpretation of the guidelines as law brings with it the prospect of sanctions, of consequences for failing to comply. Diane and Dominic describe the legislative status of the guidelines as having impact on their own practice and perspective: if they are laws, then you learn them and live by them, conscious of the weight behind them. Sanction is possible, if only theoretically. Some criticisms of the guidelines deploy a similar logic, arguing that there should be consequences for failing to comply and that policing should be more vigorous. Cheryl, a NSW pharmacist, states that takeaways should be 'really tightly restricted and controlled'. Lawrence, who worked in NSW policy, argued the case for more 'policing'; Ryan, a client from NSW, used the same argument and the same term when discussing the 'few that do rort the system'. Alongside the argument that the guidelines are laws that should have penalties and policing more immediately linked to them, some participants argue that the guidelines themselves should be more restrictive. Bob, a pharmacist from regional NSW says that

> I think they need to be more heavily regulated. That's my opinion [...] for the reasons that I think they, too many are being diverted and sold. And, it's just too easy to get takeaways.
>
> (Bob, regional NSW, pharmacist, 52)

Bob's logic is that methadone is diverted to street sale, and access to takeaways is too easy. Client access to takeaways should therefore be restricted. Pamela, on the other hand, refers to the misbehaviour of doctors:

> I think there, and there are guidelines for those doctors to follow, but they're not always being followed. So who, who are they accountable to? You know, there should be strict guidelines and that, and that's it [...] I think there should be fairly strict guidelines about the take-aways. If they're going to continue to give them out, there should be, you know, I don't know, how do you police that?
>
> (Pamela, regional NSW, nurse, 46)

For Pamela, guidelines should be strict, and takeaways should be more restricted. However, a problem with the guidelines is that doctors fail to follow them, and are difficult to police. Here, the subject of regulation is not clients, at least not directly, but doctors. The question of adherence by doctors was also discussed in other ways, and they will be addressed shortly.

There are also arguments about the coverage of regulations. For example, Brendan, a client from Victoria, describes an insufficiently regulated system, in which one nurse's practice of measurement resulted in some people receiving a lesser dose than they had been prescribed:

> there should be a standard way to dispense methadone, because it's not something, we're talking about, um, you know, people's lives [...] she was doing it by syringe or something, or, I don't know, she had her way of doing it.
>
> (Brendan, Melbourne, Victoria, client, 37)

Each of the quotes above reveal a familiar interpretation of guidelines. The rules are restrictive, they suppress activity and dictate what happens and at what time. Or, conversely, the rules should be stricter, they should be more actively policed, and they should apply to more areas than they currently do. In either case, people who are supposed to be subject to the law are not submitting as they should. The guidelines are law and law acts, or should act, as a repressive mechanism. Failures of the regulations lie in their failure to monitor and punish. In this mode of using the guidelines in the practices of treatment, flexibility and judgement are much less important than adherence. This is an act of interpretation that is in fact a refusal to interpret, mobilised by an initial, founding interpretation that interpretation is proscribed.

In contrast, the second mode of interpretation is based on an assumption of active interpretation and selective use of the guidelines. In contrast to readings of them as prescribing action, this mode sees them as guidance, or even suggestion. Rosemary, a doctor from NSW, expresses some ambivalence about the content of the guidelines while acknowledging their assistance and denying any need for them to be given more weight, to become law:

> [T]he guidelines are difficult, they can be useful, and I guess that's what guidelines are about, it's about being useful. But I don't see that they need to be more harshly enforced.
>
> (Rosemary, Sydney, NSW, prescriber, 50s)

Colin, who works in policy in NSW, described them as exactly not law: 'they're only guidelines'. Clients, as we have already seen, are aware of the variations in the way doctors read and interpret, and argue that the discretion that service providers have when it comes to making decisions should be acknowledged and acted on. For example, Debbie describes a situation of recommencing methadone treatment and working in a new job:

> And [my employer] said to me 'ah, you're going to a conference in Sydney'. And what could I do? I couldn't say no, and I asked the doctor and he said, 'Nup, I can't do it'. And, which I thought was a little bit, I thought he could have done it. I think they're guidelines, I don't think they're set in concrete.
>
> (Debbie, Melbourne, Victoria, client, 34)

Danny, a client in Sydney (aged 46), says, 'I know there's set rules and criteria about methadone takeaways but I think the doctor, doctor can give it to you a bit quicker if he wants to.'

In Victoria, prior to June 2006, the system of permits for prescribing takeaways above the number specified in the guidelines seems to have served to cement the guidelines as law for some and render them suggestion for others. Some doctors reported that the permit system was more procedural than substantive. Kurt, for example, explains the system thus:

> **Kurt**: It's kind of, it's a pro forma where you, so you tick a box if they're stable and you've spoken to the chemist and, you know, you've told the person the the dangers of having someone else taking their methadone. Um, and we fax it to DPU, and they usually do their own check. They might ring the pharmacy, they might check how long they've been on methadone and what they're entitled to, and then they let us know if it's approved.
>
> *Interviewer: Does it happen often that it's knocked back?*
>
> **Kurt**: Ah, no, only occasionally.
>
> (Kurt, Melbourne, Victoria, prescriber, 36)

Others interpret permits and extra takeaways as available in exceptional circumstances only:

> **Howard**: Well I don't routinely apply for more than that which is approved, because they're not going to be approved, ah, unless there's a particular reason of quite, ah, some degree of substance.
>
> *Interviewer: Do you find that, um, people ask you to allow takeaways beyond the guidelines, or do people*
>
> **Howard**: No. Well if they do they very soon get put straight. They don't ask twice, if they do ask.
>
> (Howard, regional Victoria, prescriber, 54)

Besides the obvious point that these different interpretations of the guidelines make a significant difference to client experiences of treatment, it appears as though the permit system in Victoria added an extra dimension to the interpretation of the guidelines as law or suggestion. If the guidelines were thought to be suggestions or guiding best practice, then routine prescription beyond them through permits was practiced; if thought to be law, then permits would not be used. In the latter case, the interpretive act is again a refusal or proscribing of interpretation: the guidelines are to be read literally and as law.

In a number of our interviews with service providers, the question of takeaway prescription is one of the key areas on which the autonomy of doctors turns. This means that arguments for doctor autonomy are often linked to takeaways. This is particularly true in NSW where, prior to mid-2006, more takeaways were routinely allowed than in Victoria: although, as we have seen in the section on risk above, the permit system in Victoria also gave rise to the same questions. In our interviews, arguments for greater restrictions on takeaways were sometimes characterised as moves to restrict the activity of doctors, while the doctors' exercise of their judgement was classified as liberal or too-generous prescription of takeaways.

> I've worked on the committees that have come up with policy guidelines and too many cooks, too many cooks, too many bureaucrats, too many people with vested interests, just hasn't worked, I mean, you know, it should ultimately be at the doctor's discretion how things are done.
>
> (Otto, Sydney, NSW, prescriber, 50s)

> Guidelines shouldn't dictate just who gets it and what; the process by which the decision is made safeguards against people making hasty decisions that they then find very difficult to reverse [...] And we need to practice credibly and limit-setting is a critical skill in addiction medicine. It is the critical skill.
>
> (Phillip, Sydney, NSW, prescriber, 53)

Nothing inherently connects the extent to which doctors are regulated with the extent to which clients receive takeaways, but in NSW at least a strong current of policy formation and clinical practice links the two. This is almost certainly also influenced by the NSW Health audit of takeaways in 2000. As the arguments cited above show, access to takeaways is associated with doctor discretion, and restrictions on takeaways linked to regulation of doctors. Otto talks elsewhere in his interview about takeaways being an 'inalienable right of treatment'; Phillip talks here of limits and elsewhere in his interview of boundaries (and we return to the implications of his arguments in Chapter 5). It is perhaps unsurprising that such a connection should be made, given the contentious nature of methadone in general and takeaways in particular. But if arguments around regulations turn on the latitude granted to doctors in prescribing, then this is an unacknowledged element in the formation and enactment of treatment that could well not be in the best interests of clients. Our NSW interviews suggest that a predictor for clients receiving takeaways is having a doctor who chafes against restriction, and we consider again the implications of this construction of the doctor subject to regulation in chapter 4.

The interpretation of regulations as either law or suggestion reveals more than the idiosyncratic practices of individuals. Instead, these two modes of interpretation can also be seen as a contest over doctors' professional autonomy and the number and kinds of domains in which client activity should be regulated. Both modes of interpretation have significant effects on the treatment that clients receive. There is a third interpretation to consider, that of surveillance. Whereas the first two interpretive modes, law and suggestion, describe different understandings of the discretion with which doctors can act, the interpretation of regulations as surveillance is centred on an apparent desire to gain total knowledge of clients. This can be illustrated through calls for improved technologies of monitoring and regulation, of regimes of testing and scrutiny to extend the reach of written regulations. Again, in NSW the question of access to takeaways was one basis for these calls.

> Well, they would have to be stable clients, they would have to be people who are living in a drug-free existence now [to get takeaways], yeah, yeah. I believe that, and there are ways of testing that, it doesn't have to be with urine. They can do it with hair now, hair samples.
>
> (Pamela, regional NSW, nurse, 46)

> So if somebody's on methadone and they've still got dirty urines every time you check them, then you're not likely to be offering them takeaways.
>
> (Lawrence, Sydney, NSW, policy, 61)

> I think the, the regulation's currently okay. Um, as I said, the only thing that I would say is that a bit more random testing wouldn't go astray. Um, it'd be nice if the testing could show whether or not they've been taking their doses, too. I don't know whether that's, I don't know whether that's within the testing regime. You would think it would give a blood level of methadone, which would give them a rough idea.
>
> (Richard, regional NSW, pharmacist, 50)

There is something suggestive of Foucault's panopticon here, or, from *The Birth of the Clinic*, 'the great myth of a pure Gaze that would be pure

Language' (Foucault, 1973: 114). Physical testing of clients' bodies could, in a totalising regime of surveillance, be translated into the language of regulation. This is a dream of quantification, of obviating the need for communication or the testimony of clients, which in any case is often treated as suspect (Roberts, valentine and Fraser, forthcoming). Whether based on an imagined possibility of eliminating risk and judgement, or on the untrustworthiness of clients, the desire for more technologies of testing is the desire for materialising guidelines, putting them into different practice. These regulatory fantasies of pure surveillance are evident in the biopolitical operations of individual clinics and doctors (daily urine tests) and in the elaborated schema of risk assessments organised at state level.

So far we have discussed three ways of interpreting the guidelines, as law, suggestion and surveillance. There are two further functions of interpretation to be considered. The first operates in gaps and absences, in the spaces in which regulations are absent or ambiguous. The second addresses the question of compliance or its lack, a disobedient relationship to the regulations that is unsanctioned. During the time of our data collection, the NSW guidelines[4] had this to say about access: 'Ideally, all patients should have access to onsite dosing seven days a week, with no patient receiving takeaway doses simply because of lack of access to daily onsite dosing. An exception is in rural areas where access to methadone is difficult' (NSW Health, 1999: 24). Diane, a nurse in Sydney, explains her interpretation of this clause thus:

> As far as I'm concerned if they are working and they find it difficult to get anywhere to get it, then they have an access problem. So I see it loosely, some people see it very strict [...] Yeah I think that the wording of the takeaways now [...] is open to it being restrictive to clients.
>
> (Diane, Sydney, NSW, nurse, 30s)

In contrast, we heard many client reports of arbitrary decisions, inconsistency and illogical appeals to rules. Debbie, a Victorian client, acts according to contemporary norms of consumer sovereignty. She knows and asserts her rights and communicates clearly her needs, and here describes the not uncommon situation of planning travel and so needing to organise physeptone to take with her. Physeptone, methadone in tablet form, cannot be prescribed for use in maintenance programs in Australia. It is prescribed for overseas travel and offers the advantage in that situation of being more portable than methadone syrup (especially diluted syrup) and allowing privacy that syrup may not. Debbie asked her doctor to ring the Department of Human Services to organise the prescription, but

> he just doesn't get a lot of time to do that, so I thought 'I'll ring'. So I rang the general number for the Department of Human Services, like, their main switchboard, and, and said 'I need to speak to some-body about methadone'. And they put me through to this number, and I started talking, and I, I don't know if it was the language I was using, they kind of assumed I was a doctor. And then I said that it was for me, and they said 'oh, we can't talk to you, we're not allowed to talk to you'.
>
> (Debbie, Melbourne, Victoria, client, 34)

The request for physeptone was denied and Debbie says she was told by her doctor, '"You know, look, this guy from the department has said there's no way that you're getting physeptone". Like, it was like I was after it for some sinister kind of reason.' Whether or not she was punished for disconcerting the department, as she does not unreasonably implies here, there is much in this account that suggests opaque rules and unclear communication. Debbie's experience is not atypical.

Service providers may chafe against restrictions and attempt, more and less actively, to open up spaces for interpretation and autonomy. For clients, however, these modes of interpretation are much more restrictive and limiting. If their treating doctors or dispensing pharmacists interpret the rules 'strictly' and without scope for negotiation clients will experience a more restricted and repressive regime than otherwise. In other cases serv-ice providers see more autonomy to act than this: in the spaces where the rules do not strictly operate or ambiguity is perceived, or if they treat the guidelines as suggestion rather than direction. In these cases, though, clients are just as likely to view decisions made on the basis of whim rather than logic, or to experience one ruling at one time and a different ruling at another. Whether service providers are unreasonably (according to them) restricted or they act with autonomy, clients experience regulations as authoritarian and organised by fiat. This may not always be at the extremes of repression or infantilisation that characterise much of the treatment meted out to drug addicts, but nor is it much like the model clinical encounter of responsibilisation and choice (Helén, 2004).

There is a final function of interpretation to consider, that of compli-ance and adherence to the guidelines. Although familiar in literature on the clinical encounter as a term to describe patient conformity to pre-scribed treatment regimes (Gascon et al., 2004; Greene et al., 1982), 'compliance' here refers to policy compliance. We have already seen the function of risk management and auditing in the regulation of profes-sional practice. The regulatory power of policy *rules* is a different ques-tion, and is described as relatively weak. Colin characterises the regulatory power of the guidelines as minimal:

> Um, look, to me it's about adherence, not regulation, you know. I mean, regulation effectively doesn't work in the health system. You know, I can do almost anything I want [...] you're asking the key question in policy, which is how do you make policy real, the, the, the successful strategy is to make policy real enough to make every-one want to do it, at the end of the day.
>
> (Colin, Sydney, NSW, policy, 46)

Both clients and nurses used phrases such as 'doctors can do whatever they like' and William, a NSW pharmacist said a 'major source of problems' is that doctors are 'trusted, you know, they're basically trusted'. George, also a NSW pharmacist, said that he thinks that younger doctors 'are taking a little bit more care and they're doing it more correctly than the older ones', while Pauline, a client from Victoria reports a doctor who prescribed takeaways without applying for a permit.

> And apparently that's pretty standard for this particular doctor, he's very, um, I don't know, ah, yeah, slack, lazy (laughs). Yes, doesn't care much for the paperwork side of things anyway.
>
> (Pauline, Melbourne, Victoria, client, 33)

Aaron, a doctor from Melbourne, works with 'a bloke who never gets permission'. As we have seen, service providers report taking seriously the consequences of poor management and treatment decisions, and resent restrictions on their actions and surveillance of their practice. However, the consequences of prescribing outside the guidelines – as opposed to the consequences of diversion or overdose subsequent to prescribing outside the guidelines – appear to be uncertain. Certainly there was nothing like consensus reported among service providers about what could happen under these circumstances. Despite this, some doctors and pharmacists refer to the rules as reasons for their treatment decisions. The rules are attributed consequence; they are given a mandate to dictate action. This is reported by clients:

> I've tried to negotiate with my doctor each time I've gone in saying, 'you know I've got a full-time job and this is a hassle for me [...] Can you not, do you not have any leeway as my doctor to be able to negotiate with me the therapeutic way to treat me with this drug?' and he says 'no, I haven't and if I get audited, I'll get in trouble and blah blah blah'.
>
> (Sue, Sydney, NSW, client, 40)

> [M]y doctor, he said if he could have kept everyone on five takeaways he would have but, you know, he said legally he wasn't allowed to do it and [...] if he's going to be debarred or kicked off or whatever it is they do to doctors, you know, well it's not going to do much good for his patients is it?
>
> (Justine, Sydney, NSW, client, 41)

It is also reported by service providers:

> [Y]ou know for difficult patients you can say 'this is what it says, I cannot do this for you', um, so there's that benefit from it um you know, 'the guidelines say that I cannot give you a take away if you continue to use, blah blah blah', so there's that.
>
> (Rosemary, Sydney, NSW, prescriber, 50s)

Derek, a doctor who has worked in both NSW and Victoria, emphasises that prescribers have to bear responsibility for their actions, but also says:

> I think having fairly rigid takeaway provisions, which don't give a lot of flexibility helps, because you can sort of hide behind that a little bit. So you can, ah, 'look, you know, even if I wanted to give you takeaways I can't because, ah, you had a dirty urine and under New South Wales guidelines', ah, or Victorian guidelines, you know, 'your dirty urine means you can't have takeaways any more'. That sort of stuff is helpful [...] you can actually hide behind regulations, that's helpful.
>
> (Derek, regional Victoria, prescriber, 48)

Service providers appealed to a regulatory function of the guidelines that does not really exist, or is at least not practised, and which is known to not exist. These examples of doctors appealing to regulations to explain their decisions or to disavow responsibility for them may be instances of strategic interpretation of the guidelines (the doctors knew that the regulatory function of the guidelines is more minimal than they are claiming) or they may be instances where the ambiguity of the guidelines leads to uncertainty (the doctors did not know that the regulatory function of the guidelines is minimal and they are acting as they believe they must). In either case, these are instances of the guidelines being put into a particular kind of practice – lessening the autonomy of the doctors, and removing scope for negotiation from the client.

This, again, adds to the authoritarianism of rules governing clients' experience of treatment and contradicts contemporary models of open communication and choice-making in treatment. It also represents instances where the governance of service providers is deliberately brought into the therapeutic relationship. Phillip, a doctor who also worked in policy, called doctors' appeals to guidelines as the basis for decisions 'avoidant behaviour by puerile people', but this disregards three important elements in treatment. First, doctors inevitably act according to their dispositions or habitus in clinical encounters, as do clients (Bourdieu, 1995; Bourgois, 1995). As Derek points out, the resources of some methadone clients, developed in order to function in the world in which they live, amount to expertise in confrontation: 'I, like many people, don't enjoy confrontation. I particularly don't enjoy confrontation with people who are expert at it'. Second, while institutional means to guard the security for service providers often governs the spatio-temporal arrangements in large clinics (Chapter 3), individual doctors in private practice do not operate with the same measures. These doctors may, at times, be concerned for their safety and anxious to avoid conflict. They may well, in these circumstances, be without adequate resources to respond in ways other than by summoning an impersonal set of rules. Finally, the governance of doctors is, as we have already seen, mobilised by technologies of surveillance and audit. People who work in social work and psychiatry are identified by Castel as those who deal with risk factors rather than subjects.

> We have gone beyond the problematic of treatment (or, in critical nomenclature, that of repression and control). We are situated in a perspective of autonomised management of populations conducted on the basis of differential profiles of those populations established by means of medico-psychological diagnoses which function as pure expertises.
>
> (Castel, 1991: 291)

Methadone clients are not necessarily subject to the regimes of either social work or psychiatry but they share much in common with those who are, and, like Castel's dangerous populations, represent a 'dangerousness that it is more and more of a polyvalent entity credited with unfathomable causes and unpredictable ways of manifesting itself' (284). People who work with stigmatised populations, and people who themselves belong to those populations, have become habituated into these regimes of surveillance and technologies of regulation. Especially in Australia's changing organisation of welfare and health services, scrutiny and surveillance are increasingly a part of the every-day lives of many. Impoverished people are required to submit to rules and bureaucratic regimes that privileged people never experience (Peel, 2003). It reveals much about the social marginalisation of clients that they can be governed through these mechanical appeals to rules, audit and absent authority. Other people are subject to rules as well, of course, but MMT operates in ways unthinkable in other treatment formats. Clients recognise and protest this regulation, the means through which they are constituted and governed as an aggregation of risks – but they are familiar with it. It happens to them all the time.

The regulation of clients through the interpretation of guidelines, then, is about more than individual decisions. It is about a framework of authority in which the agents of governance are at least sometimes absent from the therapeutic relationship. In Castel's words, for those people who are constituted by 'factors' that render them dangerous:

> This is a form of surveillance, in the sense that the intended objective is that of anticipating and preventing the emergence of some undesirable event: illness, abnormality, deviant behaviour etc. But this surveillance dispenses with actual presence, contract, the reciprocal relationship of watcher and watched, guardian and ward, carer and cared.
>
> (Castel, 1991: 288)

As we have seen, this enacts MMT in irregular ways. At times the absent authority is used strategically by doctors; at times it frustrates them. For the methadone client, however, this surveillance and regulation results in a choice of submission or rebellion: compliance to rules, or disobedience. Negotiation and consensus are not possible. Far from being active consumers or patients sharing treatment decisions and responsibility with their doctors, methadone clients are positioned within an apparently out-moded, paternalistic relationship of compliance. Alternative choices and different courses of action, of which methadone clients are demonstrably capable, are not recognised as agency here, but can only be constituted as disobedience. Some of these choices and acts have been discussed here: arguments with doctors about the legislative power of guidelines, attempts to negotiate treatment decisions and use of methadone outside the rules (such as injecting). Contemporary accounts of patienthood and subjectivity emphasise the activity of patients. The self-constitution of patients as people with a particular relationship to their embodied vulnerabilities has been described as an important new mode of citizenship. Yet this kind of activity is authorised only for particular groups of people, while excluding others. As historians of medical compliance and adherence argue, socially marginalised populations have historically been given substandard treatment or even denied treatment, based on public health approaches to risk management. In the early days of highly active anti retroviral therapies (HAART) used to treat HIV, serious consideration was given to withholding medication from injecting drug users and other marginalised groups on the grounds that mutations of the virus could be generated through imperfect compliance with the treatment regimes. Non-compliance with anti-tuberculosis measures in the early twentieth century was defined as the action of 'derelicts' who were 'dangerous', 'ignorant' or 'recalcitrant' (Mykhalovskiy, McCoy and Bresalier, 2004). Management of risky populations sets up exceptionalist interpretations of agency and choice: models of contemporary patienthood based on negotiation and activity exclude particular kinds of patients, and treat particular kinds of activity *only* as non-compliance and risk. This is an adaptation of Castel's framework: as we have seen, treatment is enacted in various ways. Sometimes it conforms more closely to the contemporary biomedical mode of responsibilised consumers and Castel's 'top tier', sometimes more closely to Castel's 'dangerous' bottom tier.

Conclusion

Recognition of the regulatory functions of risk management and interpretation should of course coincide with recognition of the role played by individuals within regulatory frameworks. The interpretive acts of individual health care workers make an enormous difference to the experience of treatment. Doctors who regard takeaways as an inalienable right of treatment will make different decisions from those who regard takeaways as a privilege (assuming that the same doctors will not adopt both of these attitudes at different times and for different clients, which is by no means certain). Pharmacists who make continuation of treatment conditional on personal grooming will co-produce different environments from those who do not. Individual relationships are hugely important in MMT, and individual workers who are politicised, committed and experienced make an enormous difference to the treatment experience of individual clients. But reliance on generous and sophisticated interpretation of guidelines is hardly an adequate strategy in the management of medical treatment, and dependence on enlightened service providers starts to seem very much like paternalism, or benign authoritarianism.

Methadone clients are not the only people subject to rules and absent authority. Unlike other people, however, clients are constituted as risk populations. Service providers dealing with them always have the spectre of consequence, audit and accountability present. Clients cannot escape their risky status even with the most progressive and reflexive of service providers. The very best outcome for clients is that they be treated similarly to other patients prescribed dangerous medication, and be subject to the same risk management. Patients in severe chronic pain are prescribed strong opioid analgesics and may well find themselves considered at risk of depression and suicide. If this is the case, then it reveals the importance of risk and caution in the clinical encounter, and should be communicated to clients. In the best possible circumstances for clients, that is, the mechanisms for managing risk are identical to other kinds of patients. This is happening in some cases, but our interviews reveal that clients feel that they are singled out because they are drug users; they do not know that other people are subject to similar rules and regulations. Given the unique demonisation of drug users, knowledge of this kind could make a real difference. In many cases, of course, clients do not experience the best outcomes. Instead, risks are equivalised, or gossip and hearsay are treated with the same weight as other kinds of evidence, or moral judgements are used as proxies for clinical judgement. And this is *on top of* the range of criteria used by service providers to define if takeaways are reasonable: total abstinence from all drugs; a full-time job or some other activity that gives 'structure' to clients' lives; or, as cited above, a 'particular reason' of undefined 'substance'.

What would it take to change methadone regulation? How best to address arbitrary decisions, lack of communication, conflict, inconsistency and stonewalling? It is essential to recognise that these elements of treatment do not stand or fall on the interpretive capabilities of individuals. Instead, change can only be brought about by a thoroughgoing recognition of the constitution of methadone clients as a population, of the mechanisms of risk management and surveillance that organise treatment, and the capacities of both clients and service providers to negotiate risk and regulations. It would also take a thoroughgoing review of minimal acceptable standards of service provision and the responsibilities of the state in ensuring the conditions in which those minimal standards could be met. It would require a shift in understanding to recognise the dynamic, mutually constituting intra-activity of treatment and subjects. Perhaps most importantly, and most difficult in political and practical terms, it would take acknowledgement of the risks and uncertainties of treatment, and of the heterogeneity of treatment clients. Some clients have suffered trauma, have extremely limited access to material and other resources and have suffered and embodied the worst effects of poverty and deprivation. Some have not, and do not. Drug use is not the difference between these clients, although drug use may sometimes reflect or exemplify them.

The differences between clients, their differing needs and the injuries done by treating them as a single group are well known to service providers as well as clients; and practical strategies as alternatives to what is currently in place are similarly known. Indeed, some have already been tried. Penny, who works in NSW policy, said that MMT should be an integrated and holistic treatment, not just provision of a drug – for most clients. But, she says:

> There's another group of people for whom we might introduce methadone in what is exactly, what is essentially only a harm [minimisation] framework. And it isn't about people wanting treatment. Um, and Victoria did it with people, street kids and young people, and you didn't have to turn up every day for the program [...] You actually chose your dose to some extent [...] Um, and that to me would be better, than, um, forcing a system where people feel like they can sell it and get money. So all you're doing is encouraging, reinforcing that drug selling. Um, and if we don't provide enough spots on our methadone program, we don't think about why people are selling takeaways.
>
> (Penny, Sydney, NSW, policy, 44)

Penny describes individual behaviours (the selling of methadone); the resources and material conditions through which individual behaviours are constituted (available places on methadone programs) and the heterogeneity of clients ('street kids', those who need and want other services). Her account reveals the agency and capacity for choice clients deploy, sometimes through the frames of action set out by treatment and other regulations, sometimes outside them. Such action and choice confirm the repressive elements of regulation even as they work to challenge the pessimism of analyses that see only repression in the lives of those regulated. They confirm that MMT enacts both the repressiveness and responsibilisation of post-Fordist regulation, while demonstrating (and to a degree producing) the agency of those who are regulated. The next chapter will consider one critical enactment of this agency through the spatio-temporal arrangements of treatment.

3
The Chronotope of the Queue

> At all levels the drug trade operates without schedule. Nobody delivers on time except by accident. The addict runs on junk time. His body is his clock, and junk runs through it like an hour-glass. Time has meaning for him only with reference to his need. Then he makes his abrupt intrusion into the time of others, and, like all Outsiders, all Petitioners, he must wait, unless he happens to mesh with non-junk time.
>
> William Burroughs (1982)

Identifying queuing as one of the quintessentially mundane aspects of everyday life, Joe Moran (2005) notes that it tends to be associated with life at the low end of the socio-economic spectrum. This is especially the case for queuing/waiting associated with state institutions such as public transport. Indeed, and perhaps apocryphally, Margaret Thatcher is said to have declared, 'If a man finds himself a passenger on a bus having attained the age of twenty-six, he can account himself a failure in life' (quoted in Moran, 2005: 4). The link between queuing/waiting and disadvantage so superciliously captured in the above statement is perhaps no more directly demonstrated than in the case of MMT. As we noted in the Introduction, Australian MMT programs commit clients to regular contact with prescribing doctors and, in particular, with the agencies through which methadone doses are dispensed. In New South Wales, this means clients can expect to visit their dosing point between three and seven days per week, entailing a high degree of contact with service providers that, as we saw in the previous chapter, can have significant effects on both parties.[1] In this chapter we explore in detail the ways in which MMT clients describe their experiences of dosing, focusing on the issue of waiting and queuing, as this constitutes a central and abiding theme in client accounts of treatment. In part, our intention is to broaden the discussion of the co-constitution of methadone subjects provided in the previous chapter, in that this chapter will focus explicitly on the action of non-human actors as well as human ones. In doing so, we consider MMT as a temporal and spatial phenomenon, a set of practices and arrangements that operate intra-actively in response to, and in provocation of, certain kinds of subjects understood as 'methadone clients'. It draws on our interview data on everyday experiences of methadone dosing[2] to consider this aspect of treatment in terms of two sets of theoretical concepts: Mikhail Bakhtin's chronotope and Barad's formulation of the space-time manifold. The chapter explores the ways in which, in the context of the methadone dosing point, the specific actions of time and space co-produce each other as a chronotope of the queue, and it goes on to describe how this chronotope helps materialise particular methadone subjects – often the very kinds considered undesirable within modern liberal societies; that is, the 'unproductive', the 'disorderly', the 'illicit'. It also takes into account, to anticipate the argument made in Chapter 4 about the mutually constitutive actions of clients and treatment (both 'make up' each other), the ways in which the actions of clients fold back into the chronotope, sometimes creating change, sometimes reinforcing elements of the organisation and process of the dosing point. As we will see, this particular use of the chronotope (taking an intra-active approach to the relations between space and time) contrasts with approaches which tend to treat space and time simply as two *aspects* of the chronotope rather than as mutually constitutive of it in an active, contingent way.

What is a methadone dosing point?

This chapter focuses on interviews conducted in NSW. In this state, large-scale public and private treatment clinics form a significant part of treatment delivery. The chapter looks most closely at clinics and, in this respect, the argument we make has a great deal of relevance to the US context, in which clinics are also a significant part of treatment. We also note, however, that many of the issues identified here are relevant to pharmacy dosing, thus, consideration of their implications is also important in contexts where clinic dosing is minimal and pharmacy dosing the norm.

In NSW, approximately 40 per cent of clients are dosed at pharmacies, 22 per cent at public clinics and 19 per cent at private clinics.[3] Each of these types of dosing points is characterised by different arrangements, attributes, expectations and regulations, and within each category there is significant variation in operating practice. Public clinics have undergone change in the last few years, and now tend to treat only clients new to the program (under twelve months on treatment). These new clients access prescribing services via doctors attached to the clinic, and in some cases also access counselling and case work services.

Treatment is free in public clinics. This is a major incentive to attend these dosing points rather than private clinics or pharmacies, but unlike private clinics or pharmacies, public clinics do not generally provide takeaway doses. This means that clients attached to public clinics must attend each day to receive their supervised dose. This acts as a significant disincentive to remain on the public program, and over time clients usually shift from this setting (providing the prescriber agrees) to a pharmacy or private clinic in order to gain access to takeaways. The limited opening hours of public clinics also contribute to client interest in moving to pharmacy dosing (typical clinic hours might be 7 a.m. to 9:30 a.m., followed by 2:30 p.m. to 3:30 p.m.).

The interviews we conducted for our study include detailed descriptions of dosing points. It is worth beginning by quoting some of these in detail if we are to get a sense of the ways in which clients engage with the environment through which treatment is delivered. One interview participant, Lisa, described each of the dosing environments she had experienced during her time on MMT. Firstly, Lisa describes a public clinic environment:

> You walk in through the door and then you turn right, and there's a sitting room with some plastic chairs on the wall, and it's sort of all hospital-institutional looking. A big queue. The queue can extend right out the door of the waiting room. You have to queue up, and then there's a line that you don't go past, and then a thing 'dings' and the door unlocks, there's a 'bzzzz', and you can open the door and walk through. So it's all very highly secure. [...] If it's really busy then the queue might go out into the lobby of the whole building. [...] And, ah, then you go in around the corner, and there's, like, a glass window. I think there's more [queuing], like another line or something [...] And then you go in, and they look at your photo, and they dose you. And then [...] you walk back into this little corridor

thing and keep going forward out another door. You don't go back out the same door, you go out the other door. And then you, they have very specific instructions about which way to walk around and out the building. Like, I don't know why.

(Lisa, Sydney, NSW, client, 34)

Here, Lisa's account emphasises the institutional environment of the clinic, the regular queuing clients can expect, and the quite complex, highly regimented, mechanisms in place for managing the flow of clients within the clinic.

Private clinics operate in a similar way to public clinics in that they are purpose-run to provide opioid pharmacotherapy, and cater to a large number of clients. Like public clinics, prescribing doctors are available on site, and opening hours are often very limited, or, in some cases, very complex. For example, one clinic in inner Sydney lists the following opening hours:

Monday to Friday
6 a.m. to 8:25 a.m.
9:00 a.m. to 10:25 a.m.
11:00 a.m. to 1:25 p.m.
2:00 p.m. to 3.25 p.m.

Saturday, Sunday and public holidays
6:30 a.m. to 9:25 a.m.
10:00 a.m. to 12:25 p.m.

Unlike public clinics, private clinics charge a weekly fee of approximately thirty to forty dollars. As noted above, they also provide take-away doses. Lisa describes a private clinic setting as follows:

Okay, that one was really ugly. Um, there was a waiting room on one side, and there was the clinic on this side [...] A counter: not much security in terms of glass over it, I don't think. You queued up there for a while, and the waiting room was one of those ugly, dirty-carpet, mismatching broken chairs sort of environments. [...] There was usually a, a reasonable amount of queuing, yeah. Um, twenty minutes, up to half an hour, maybe.

(Lisa, Sydney, NSW, client, 34)

In this description, the clinic's presentation is described more negatively than in the previous extract, and queuing is again commented upon.

Like private clinics, pharmacies provide takeaway doses, and charge a fee (again, around thirty to forty dollars per week), but their opening hours are much wider. This does not mean clients are always free to pick up their dose at any time during opening hours, instead many pharmacies institute regulations around hours in which clients can pick up. By and large, however, these regulated hours are significantly broader than those offered by clinics. Clients who attend pharmacies for dosing must also attend a general practitioner (GP) for medical supervision and prescription of medication. Regularity of visits to GPs varies substantially, with some clients attending once a fortnight, and others attending monthly or less frequently. Frequency depends on both the overall management style of the GP, and on the perceived needs of (and risks associated with) each individual client. As Lisa's description of her pharmacy makes clear, other regulations are also often in place around pharmacy dosing:

> You sort of stand around a corner at a tiny part of the counter, which is out of the view of other people. So there is some sense of trying to keep it a bit private, I think. And I suppose keep it out of the way of the other customers, and to make it clear what you're there for, for any casual staff [...] But it's a chemist, so it's a reasonable environment to be in. They don't like you to bring other people in with you, that's I suppose the biggest problem. Because I took a friend in and her child once, and she's a perfectly sort of respectable person, and I was told not to bring her back. [...] That sort of stuff. I think maybe when you sign the thing [contract] at the beginning it says don't bring your friends in, you can only bring in immediate family with you, like your partner and your kids.
>
> (Lisa, Sydney, NSW, client, 34)

This description focuses on the restrictions clients face in attending the pharmacy in the company of friends, rather than on questions of waiting and queuing evident in the previous extracts. As we note later in the chapter, however, the queue is also a dominant feature for some clients dosing at pharmacies.

Lisa's descriptions of the three main styles of dosing points raise a range of issues relevant to the concerns of this chapter. Firstly, it is clear that methadone dosing points are highly regulated spaces in which movement is carefully managed. Also regulated is client social conduct, and in some cases, the conduct of individuals not enrolled in the program (for example, Lisa's associate, who is not free to enter the pharmacy while Lisa is present). Prominent in two of Lisa's three descriptions is the spatio-temporal practice of queuing, and in this respect, Lisa is not alone. This theme of queuing thoroughly suffuses the accounts of dosing collected for our study.

The temporality of drugs

In pursuing the issue of waiting and queuing that arises so powerfully in the interview material, it is useful to turn to the literature dealing with addiction and time.[4] Several authors have considered drug use and the experience of addiction in terms of temporality (Lenson, 1995; Reith, 1999; Keane, 2002; Klingemann, 2000). In his book entitled *On Drugs* (1995), David Lenson argues that becoming and being addicted to drugs involves a shift in consciousness in which time becomes 'atomised' (33), that is, broken up into separate moments given meaning by the search for and administration of drugs. As we noted in Chapter 1, Lenson argues that 'drug addicts' find it difficult to escape addiction precisely because they are faced with making the return to the monotony of 'horizontal' or 'pre-drug' (34) time, an unappealing prospect impossible to contemplate while the enticing memory of drug time lingers.

Lenson's account of addiction temporality is both thought-provoking and troubling, not least because, although he makes clear his view that drug use is a matter of degree not kind (31), his analysis implies a rather rigid distinction between addicts and others in its construction of addiction as temporal atomisation in contrast to the smooth waves of non-addicted temporality. Addicts, he suggests, remove themselves from 'conventionally measured time'. Thus, he states:

> What characterizes the condition of addiction is above all else ... the replacement of conventionally measured seconds, minutes, hours and days with a different chronometry based on the tempo of administration.
>
> (35)

It is not clear here what is meant by 'conventionally measured'. The term suggests something like Bergson's clock time, yet Bergson explicitly distinguishes clock time from lived time (Bergson, 1955). Who might it be that possesses a sufficiently generic relationship to time as to experience it as 'conventionally measured'?

Like Lenson, Gerda Reith (1999) also describes addiction as a kind of re-ordering of temporality, noting that in interviews conducted with 'ex-opiate addicts' (the totalising term 'addict' passes unqualified) the state of addiction was described as a period of 'lost time' characterised by an inability to envisage the future. Amnesiac episodes involving a kind of 'narcotic slumber' were described by participants, often seen as extending over the entire period of addiction. The recovery from addiction was expressed as a re-animation of the future and an 'awakening' from the previous state of present-oriented temporality. In that these accounts of addiction were provided by individuals identifying as 'ex-addicts', one might expect Reith's reading to be alert to the role of genre in their constitution, for example, in the use of familiar tropes of redemption and reclamation, loss and recovery, evident in the interviews. Interestingly, for a paper which expresses a strong interest in the significance of temporality in addiction, present accounts of past repudiated (addiction) states are treated as immediate access-points to addiction reality. In that most accounts follow a familiar disgrace/redemption pattern, the effect is to pathologise addiction and valorise departure from addiction. Indeed, Reith's view on the relative desirability of these two forms of temporality – that based in the future (non- or ex-addiction time) or that based in the present (addiction time) – is made clear in her choice of expressions. Living in the present involves a 'breakdown' of temporality, in which addicts are 'stranded' (105). Despite the varying evaluations of living in the present evident in the interview excerpts, Reith argues that this state of affairs produces a problematic 'addictive worldview' (105).

Both Lenson's and Reith's work raises an important question here – is it possible to draw a meaningful distinction between conventional ('normal', 'non-' or 'ex-addict') time and 'drug time'? This issue is canvassed briefly by Keane in her book *What's Wrong with Addiction?* (2002). She analyses the temporality of smoking, and the tendency to view smoking as a form of disordered temporality in which insufficient attention is paid to present activities and their likely impact on future health. In contrast to Lenson and Reith, she argues that

> The distinction between the disordered temporality of addiction and the natural, unthreatening passage of normal time is hard to maintain. It is not only the addicted who are unable to live in the present.
> (105)

Keane's observation is crucial: both Lenson and Reith rely on distinctions that assume and reproduce binary models of difference between drug users and non-drug users. As we have argued in earlier chapters, such models can become the basis for stigmatisation of and discrimination against drug users, and can shape treatment delivery.

It is worth staying with Lenson's argument a little longer at this point, so as to highlight some of the critical concerns we want to address in this chapter. In that temporality and subjectivity are closely aligned, it is perhaps understandable that Lenson does not confine himself to questions of temporality. Like the pre-drug and post-drug time described in his book and echoed slightly differently by Reith (as addiction and non- or ex-addiction time) he also writes of pre-drug and post-drug thought:

> Once time has been atomized according to a pattern of drug administration, the very existence of memory prevents an easy reversion to 'natural thinking'.
>
> (33)

Presumably in deference to critiques of the self-evidence of the natural (see Haraway, 1991a and 1992; Grosz, 1994), Lenson quarantines the last two words of this sentence in quote marks. Yet his investments are clear. He argues that once a drug has been consumed (or at least, consumed 'regularly'), consciousness is in some way permanently recalibrated. Implied in this assertion is the idea that there is indeed a distinct 'natural' ('pre-drug') consciousness in the first place. Both time and thought, in this account, are radically divided along before and after lines, constituting 'before' in naturalised terms.

This tendency to compartmentalise pre-drug and post-drug time and thought, to think in terms of one or the other, of an originary, naturalised 'before' and altered/enhanced 'after', is reflected in Lenson's metaphorical appropriation of quantum theory (he calls this non-Newtonian, or Einsteinian physics [37]). Lenson describes temporality and thought before drug use as wave-like, and after drug use as particulate. In the context of twentieth-century quantum mechanics, this is at best an idiosyncratic formulation. Famously, the distinction between wave and particle is problematised in quantum mechanics by reference to experiments into the nature of light. As Karen Barad notes (her use of quantum theory was discussed in the Introduction), early twentieth-century observations found that the attributes of light differed depending upon the apparatuses used to observe it (Barad, 1998: 96). Most notably, experimenters found that light possessed the attributes of both waves *and* particles, depending upon how it was measured. This is called the wave–particle duality paradox. From this point of view, Lenson's depiction of drugs in terms of wave *or* particle seems to neglect some of the most important insights of post-Newtonian physics. In this respect, as in others, Lenson tends to invoke compartmentalising conceptions of drugs, thought, temporality and knowledge.

In that Lenson tends to rely on commonplace divisions such as those operating in relation to notions of a priori naturalness or absence and post hoc alteredness or presence, it is perhaps unsurprising that conceptual categories such as time and space also remain divided in his analysis. In thinking about the issue of waiting in relation to the material collected for this chapter, however, it is clear that the queue cannot be seen purely as a temporal phenomenon. Consider the following extract from an interviewer's fieldnotes on her meeting with client 'Mary':

> As Mary left the clinic, she passed the queue of clients waiting to be dosed, and was suddenly punched in the eye by a waiting woman. [...] The sole entrance/exit to the public clinic is accessed via a ramp with a railing. The railing restricts movement along the ramp, that is, there is no way out except via the ramp and the queue running alongside it.

Despite the confusion that followed the attack on Mary, it is obvious to the interviewer[5] that the assault was the product of more than individual agency – that it would not have occurred (at least in the way it did) in the absence of a queue. Certainly, the issue of temporality is obvious here. Yet while the clinic's temporal mode (waiting) was clearly instrumental in the incident, the spatial arrangements in place also contributed to orchestrating the event. Without the peculiar set-up obliging clients to leave via a ramped exit directly in front of the waiting line (with the ramp and its containing rail actively funnelling exiting clients past those still waiting) the assault might not have been possible. In other words, both temporality and spatiality combined with individual agency to produce the event; indeed, they were always already inseparable in it. As will be argued below, time and space are indivisible: they produce each other in specific forms. It is true that Lenson grants a role for space in the texture and character of addictions. Along with time, and in keeping with his tendency towards the possibility of neutral forms evident in his reliance on notions of the natural, Lenson terms space a 'medium' for consciousness (37). His focus, however, rests almost exclusively on temporality.

The approach taken in this chapter bears some similarity to those taken by Lenson and Reith in that, prompted by the concerns expressed in the interview material, we too have turned to temporality in understanding drug use, and specifically, life on MMT. Shot through with intensely expressed concerns around time, most explicitly, waiting, many of the interviews place temporality at the very centre of experiences of treatment. Unlike Lenson and Reith, however, our analysis operates directly from an insistence upon the inseparability of temporality and spatiality, and specifically, on the temporality of waiting that is found in the interviews as also the product of spatial arrangements. In this respect, this chapter proceeds from three main insights.

The first insight is that the workings of time and space in MMT cannot be examined separately if an adequately complex picture is to be produced, and that quarantining the two from each other would likely provide cover for other questionable divisions.[6] Secondly, temporality and spatiality should not be treated as 'media' for consciousness and experience. Rather, following Barad's agential realist ontology, all manifestations of time and space must be treated as both contingent and specific; as active, in this contingency and specificity, in the production of consciousness, and, in turn, as themselves the product of consciousness. Thirdly, the temporality of MMT is not strictly distinguishable from the temporality of other parts or forms of life. That is, a 'normal' temporality against which 'methadone temporality' can be compared and identified as abnormal should not be assumed. Instead, the temporality of methadone should be understood as possessing characteristics found elsewhere in life. These characteristics, however, are invested with a specific intensity and significance in this context. With these insights in mind, we turn to the work of Mikhail Bakhtin and Karen Barad to elucidate elements of the relationship between time and space, and to begin to consider in more detail the ways in which this relationship might shape life on MMT.

The chronotope

Russian theorist Mikhail Bakhtin developed his theory of the chronotope (or 'timespace') as a means of analysing the historical development of the novel. Based on an analysis of literature, Bakhtin proposes several chronotopes including the chronotope of the road, and the chronotope of the castle. Inspired by Einstein's theory of relativity, he argued for the 'intrinsic connectedness' of space and time, and for the specificity of chronotopes in different genres and historical periods. According to Bakhtin, chronotopes are the

> organising centers for the fundamental narrative events of the novel.
> The chronotope is the place where the knots of narrative are tied and

untied. It can be said without qualification that to them belongs the meaning that shapes narrative.

(250)

This notion of the inseparability of space and time, and the constitutive role the chronotope plays in relation to narrative, can be adapted from literary criticism to social and cultural analyses. Bakhtin himself argues that '[o]ut of the actual chronotopes of our world (which serve as the source of representation) emerge the reflected and created chronotopes of the world represented in the work (in the text)' (253). Here, Bakhtin speaks of the material world in terms of the chronotope.[7] Vice (1997: 209) explains that Bakhtin's preoccupation with the social and political in relation to time indicate that the term can be extended beyond Bakhtin's original use in the context of fictional worlds to one encompassing other concerns.

Indeed, social and cultural analyses using the chronotope have already been undertaken (for example, Harden, 2000; Jones, 2003). Lainie Jones uses the chronotope to consider the events of September 11, 2001, asserting that September 11 can itself be seen as a chronotope. She argues that this chronotope can be read in texts both preceding and following the event, suggesting that common phrases such as 'in the wake of September 11' have specific effects. In her view, they 'communicate a shared understanding not only of a time but also of a place and an event' (2). Jones goes on to refer to the 'interrelationship of time space and history' (2), and to the value of Bakhtin's theory in elucidating this interrelationship. Jones's approach presents events as having many aspects, among them, a location in time and a location in space. This insight is a valuable one, although in its implicit adherence to the idea of 'aspects' it tends to reify temporality and spatiality by attributing to them a priori attributes. Thus, she describes an event in Afghanistan as a 'chronotopic *intersection* of time, place and history' (3) (my emphasis).

This treatment of time and space as *aspects* of events or situations leaves the potential of the chronotope for analysing social and cultural phenomena at least partly unrealised. It is our intention to mobilise the notion of the chronotope in such a way as to exploit its ability to treat time and space as always already co-constitutive. We argue that time and space always shape each other (that is, that each is a necessary constituent of the other), and, in relation to the focus of this chapter, that it is the contingent intra-action of time and space under specific circumstances that produces the particular chronotope of the methadone dosing point, simultaneously producing particular methadone subjects. Likewise, the dosing point and its clients also produce the forms of time and space at work. In order to explain and draw out some of the implications of this notion of time and space as always already co-constitutive, we now turn to Barad's work, which, like that of Bakhtin (and, for that matter, Lenson), takes inspiration from quantum physics.

The intra-activity of space and time

Karen Barad's agential realist account of materiality was described in the Introduction. We build this chapter on this, focusing on her theorisation of space and time. Barad's theory challenges conventional assumptions about the ontological and epistemological autonomy of three elements: the knowing subject, discourse and matter. In doing so, it opens up ways of understanding the co-construction – the intermingling and fluid intra-action – of all kinds of phenomena, such as methadone itself, the program's clients and the chronotope of the dosing point. Indeed, Barad has much to say of relevance to the chronotope, focusing in one paper on the iterative intra-activity of what she calls, after post-Newtonian physics, the 'space-time manifold' (2001: 93). In keeping with her formulation of the phenomenon and intra-action, Barad conceptualises space and time as mutually constitutive, and as productive of material realities:

> Intra-actions are causally constrained but nondeterministic irreversible enactments through which matter-in-the-process-of-becoming is sedimented out and becomes an enfolded ingredient in the further materialisation of human, nonhuman and cyborgian bodies; such a dynamics is not marked by an exterior parameter called time, nor does it take place in a container called space, but rather iterative intra-actions are the dynamics through which temporality and spatiality are produced and reconfigured in the (re)making of material-discursive boundaries and their constitutive exclusions.
>
> (90)

Here, Barad recognises that time and space are more than pre-existing agents that act on pre-existing subjects and objects to produce stable outcomes. Rather, they are always already the product of each other and of specific intra-actions with other always already intra-actively produced phenomena. This insight can be applied to the chronotope, providing a productive starting point from which to consider the action of space and time in the case of the methadone dosing point. Having questioned Lenson's tendency to reify and compartmentalise drug time and thought, and Jones's reading of Bakhtin's time and space as 'inter-related' (read pre-constituted) aspects, our intention in the remainder of this chapter is to consider the action of space-time in the materialisation of the methadone dosing point in a manner that eschews assumptions about points of origin and about causality, and which asks the following questions: what emerges when Bakhtin's chronotope is overtly formulated as a product of the iterative intra-action of space and time, and of discourse and material objects? How does space-time help produce the character of the methadone dosing point, and how does the dosing point (its location, layout, staff and clients) produce particular forms of space-time (particular chrono-topes)? Similarly, how is the client (assumed to be merely observed and 'treated' by the program) intra-actively constituted by the dosing point and its chronotope? Most importantly, what implications do these multiple iterative intra-actions have for methadone clients and their relationships to the program?

A chronotope of waiting: The queue

As Bakhtin has noted, a chronotope structures every story (1981: 250). The chronotope that structures the stories in many of our interviews with MMT clients, especially those picking up their dose from a clinic, is that of the queue. Alison (who has experienced both clinic and phar-macy dosing) describes the public clinic queue she waited in as a per-manent feature of treatment: 'Each morning people would arrive long before opening hours, sometimes as early as four a.m., to place them-selves near the front of the queue, some because they needed to get to work, and the clinic's opening time of eight am allowed for little scope if they were expected at work at eight thirty or nine'. According to Alison, this long, slow queue generated all kinds of 'ruckus' as individ-uals negotiated and jostled for a prime position. In winter, it was not uncommon for some in the queue to build small fires to keep them-selves warm:

> You know, they'll, they might make a fire or something because they're cold, like in winter. You know like, not big bonfire, but I mean just a little fire or something, and, I mean, it gives everyone a bad name.
>
> (Alison, Sydney, NSW, client, 44)

In Alison's account, images of clients queuing for hours in the pre-dawn morning, building fires to keep themselves warm, evoke not so much an Australian medical treatment program as a wartime breadline.[8] Other participants also emphasise harsh conditions faced in the queue. Chris recalls a period in which his job as a carpet-layer demanded he reach his clinic at 5 a.m. to be first in line when it opened at 6 a.m. Likewise, Danny travels a long distance to attend a clinic that opens earlier than his local one (6:15 a.m.) in order to find a favourable place in the queue and be dosed before work.

Moving to a pharmacy dosing arrangement reduced some of Alison's queuing time in that management aimed to keep the clients spaced apart rather than encouraging them to arrive for dosing together. For Alison this was a vast improvement, although other temporal issues, such as negotiating last minute dosing, figured more prominently after the move:

> They have their, I suppose, little pets, so to speak [...] if their clock says six o'clock, and it's only three minutes to six, you know, they'll close the doors, I mean they'll close the door in your face [...] and then someone will come in a car, even a taxi cab, you know [...] and they let this person in. And like why?
>
> (Alison, Sydney, NSW, client, 44)

Under these circumstances, closing times could lead to a particularly agonising form of waiting, that is, for the following day's dose.

Lisa's descriptions of clinic dosing (given above) also highlight conditions in some respects incongruent with Western conventions around provision of medical treatment. In Lisa's account of a public clinic, queuing is extensive, and clients spend a significant amount of time in each others' company.

Interviewer: What, what happens in the queue?

Lisa: Um, people talk and, talk about jail and stuff (laughs) [...] a lot of them are just out of jail, and they go straight on to the program there, and they all seem to be comparing war stories about jail and their crimes and stuff [...] I remember a guy saying, making small talk by asking if I was just out of jail, and ...

Interviewer: And what did you say?

Lisa: 'No, what are you talking about', you know. Like, I was surprised, I mean, I didn't know how many people were out of jail, and why you should assume that I was just out of jail, you know. And I didn't really want to talk to him anyway. Um, the people there, I suppose [...] seemed to be kind of dangerous type people, a lot of them. I suppose the jail connection, the sort of people who might openly sort of talk about, do those kind of violent crimes, and might – you wouldn't want to meet them in a dark alley kind of thing. You wouldn't want to run into them outside the clinic, unless there were a lot of other people around, you know [both laugh]. Especially if you had something that you knew they wanted.

Interviewer: Yeah, right.

Lisa: Like takeaways or something.

(Lisa, Sydney, NSW, client, 34).

Here, the organisation of dosing guarantees (indeed requires) that clients engage with each other for a substantial amount of time each day. As in Alison's account, Lisa provides insights into the ways in which life in the queue comes to be managed, necessary social relationships are negotiated, and new social relationships are forged. Yet this process is clearly fraught for some. Overheard conversations about criminal activity and violence render Lisa wary of others in the queue. The possibility that some clients may present a threat to security is acknowledged in the design of the clinic's floor plan, which rigidly controls traffic with automatic doors. However, the benefits of this arrangement accrue only to the staff. It is an arrangement in which all parties acknowledge that some individuals in the queue may constitute a danger to others, yet the queue remains a compulsory element in dosing, and efforts to secure safety (or at least, to control exposure to individuals in the queue) are made only on behalf of the staff.[9] This is one of many ways in which the queue is a site of anxiety as well as of boredom and frustration for clients. Others include waiting causing lateness for work, and waiting while experiencing withdrawal symptoms.

Although community pharmacies generally offer far wider dosing hours than clinics, many are also subject to queuing. In these cases, queuing may occur for reasons similar to those producing clinic queues: bottlenecks around popular hours and limited numbers of staff. Other reasons, however, include regulations around the number of clients who can enter the premises at any time. In these circumstances, clients arriving to be dosed at similar times are obliged to form ad hoc queues in the street outside the pharmacy or often, a nominal distance away from the pharmacy as 'congregating' outside pharmacies is also discouraged.

Under these circumstances, queuing becomes especially arduous as position in the queue is not as easily maintained, and issues of confidentiality around being on the program emerge. As Renée explains:

> You are a methadone client so you're treated differently [...] you're only allowed to have two methadone clients in the shop at one time so and you're not allowed to wait outside the store either so you've got to go to somewhere else, which I think like, where do you go when you've got kids and things? [...] I've got to stand out the front, like most people actually stand out the front and down two stores, and there's a group of them. And nobody will leave because their place will be lost [...] and it's obvious who they are, and I was standing there one day and three of the mothers from the school walked past, looked and then did a double take [...] now I stand up the other end.
>
> (Renée, Sydney, NSW, client, 37)

Ivan is also required to queue for pharmacy dosing on occasion, and like Renée, in his dissatisfaction, finds ways of queuing without queuing: 'I don't, I sort of sit down in the road [on the kerb] until it opens. I won't be seen queuing there like that – like cattle' (Ivan, Sydney, NSW, client, 34).

Dosing is not the only stage at which clients must wait, however. Some prescribing doctors also create queues by operating on a first come, first served basis. As Danny explains:

> There are no appointments made; they just say a doctor is in [...] first in best dressed [...] I can understand why people don't get a job. I don't know why they don't open clinics up earlier.
>
> (Danny, Sydney, NSW, client, 46)

Here, Danny points to an issue many clients consider a central irony of the program. MMT aims to restore a lifestyle that is broadly in keeping with contemporary neo-liberal values in that clients' daily activities are expected to become regular and predictable, and they are expected to find paid work and free up cash to make improvements to their standard of living. However, the demands of regular queuing make securing and keeping paid work difficult, especially for those in trades and other positions expected to begin work early in the morning.

These stories provide an indication of the extent to which queuing and waiting form the central chronotope of MMT for many. As explained earlier, the chronotope literally means timespace. In elaborating this notion, we also noted three points in relation to the chronotope:

(1) the workings of time and space should not be examined separately
(2) temporality and spatiality should not be seen as 'media' for consciousness but as active, in their specificity, in the production of consciousness, and, in turn, as themselves the product of consciousness
(3) the temporality of MMT should not be seen as strictly distinguishable from the temporality of other aspects of life (that is, there is no 'normal' temporality against which 'methadone temporality' can be compared and identified as abnormal).

How do these insights relate to the phenomenon of the queue in MMT? Perhaps most obviously, the queue is itself an inherently spatio-temporal phenomenon in that it is the product of the intra-action of specific temporal conditions with specific spatial arrangements, at the centre of which is dosing. In other words, the queue would not exist if either the relevant spatial or temporal conditions did not occur: each is a necessary but insufficient element in the materialisation of the queue, and the nature of each is intra-actively produced by the other. These spatio-temporal intra-actions differ for clinics and pharmacies. In what follows, the discussion will focus on clinics.

In Chapter 2 we demonstrated the importance of regulations to the surveillance and management of clients. Such regulations have profound effects on the way dosing occurs. At clinics, dosing involves observation and occasional urine testing for illicit drug use. All onsite dosing involves close observation which itself takes time. The relatively few number of dosing staff usually on duty means that the number of clients who can be dosed at any one time is strictly limited (usually at most two). Narrow dosing hours then concentrate client visits, creating more pressure on time. In addition, urine testing can slow progress further, both because clients cannot always produce a sample on demand, and also because collection and processing of samples takes time, particularly where urination is observed by staff. These temporal issues are also necessarily spatial issues. The number of clients observed during dosing is constrained by the available counter space and concerns around security and public order. The latter organises space around the preference for one or, at most, two clients occupying counter space at any given time. Some clinics' preference for dosing clients at an external window (an even more pronounced desire to control space and circumscribe responsibility for the contents of space) heightens the queuing/waiting experience by reducing dosing area to a single hatch and by providing few or no comforts for those waiting. Indeed, one interview participant describes dosing arrangements in which clients queue outside the premises, dosing takes place via a hatch, and clients are expected to access their dose by passing a straw through the bars covering the hatch:

> Renée: [I]t was a real shock to the system to go down and to see how people were treated. It was a real meat market sort of, yeah [...] when I first came [into treatment], the clinic that I was at had, the toilet had a shower screen on it so [...] as people walked past, the shower curtain would fly up, and they took blood in full view of all the other clients and that [...] and they had a big grille on the, um, the dosing window and the nurse used to hold the cup and you had to put a straw through the grille. (laughter)

> *Interviewer: You're kidding?*

> Renée: No. The straw [goes] through the grille and [you] drink it and then open your mouth to show her that you'd swallowed it. And it, I felt like I was in a gaol or something like that, it was a really awful experience.

> (Renée, Sydney, NSW, client, 37)

In these cases, in which waiting is largely conducted out of doors, dosing involves explicitly distancing arrangements such as barred hatches and straws, and procedures such as urine and blood testing are undertaken without attention to privacy, waiting comes to present as a kind of exile, carrying with it an implicit judgement. These are cases in which the stigma and disadvantage associated with methadone treatment are rendered highly visible. As we argued in the Introduction, methadone treatment does not simply reflect the social marginalisation of clients: it also enacts it. Perhaps unsurprisingly, self-sufficient practices such as the building of fires emerge, as does the practice among clients and non-clients of taking advantage both of the temporal dimension of the queue (waiting) and its spatial dimension (no supervision, distribution of clients in a convenient array) to approach individuals to buy or sell takeaway doses. Indeed, queuing both indoors and out can co-construct illicit sale of methadone. As Lisa spells out in relation to her dislike of extensive clinic queuing:

> You know, sometimes you don't necessarily want to be hanging around all those other people [because] you're more likely to have,

there are people there who want to do things like, sell methadone, buy methadone or um sell drugs, buy drugs, whatever.

(Lisa, Sydney, NSW, client, 34)

All of these arrangements are the product of the intra-action of particular forms of time and space – that is, they would be qualitatively different if either time or space performed differently in this context.

As point two above notes, space and time should not be considered 'media' of consciousness. This is no more clearly highlighted than in the queuing described here. Although clinics tend to operate as if they are observing and treating clients who have pre-existing attributes (in Barad's terms, relata), they can also be viewed as co-constituting clients through a process of intra-action. In other words, the client and the queue co-construct each other. The program does not take pre-formed 'addicts', observe their behaviour and then treat them to produce a reliable outcome that can be understood as the reproducible effect of the program. Rather, clients, themselves already multiply co-constituted phenomena, intra-act with the chronotope of MMT (that is, the queue – itself also always already multiply co-constituted). In the process, both the client and the queue impact on each other, reproducing each other differently. Thus, the specific forms of time and space at work at the clinic help shape the client and his or her experiences, rather than simply acting as a conduit for these experiences. This can be seen in those acts such as the lighting of fires (a product of queuing outdoors, yet likely to be understood by many as a public order problem – as indeed, does Alison), and the buying and selling of methadone, which is to some extent cultivated by the queuing process. Indeed, violent acts such as the assault on Mary, described earlier, can be seen as the product not simply of individual agency, although this is an important element, but of the 'phenomenon' (in Barad's terms) of MMT. The assault is in part the product of the particular spatio-temporal phenomenon of the queue in place at the clinic Mary was attending: individual clients intra-act with a temporality of waiting, a spatiality of outdoor queuing (configured to run alongside the railed exit ramp), and, possibly, a corporeality of withdrawal, to produce an act of violence. Our intention here is not to argue that the assault should not be treated as a serious act perpetrated by the woman in question – overlooked or excused, as it were – but to point out that the chronotope of the clinic acts as much to produce particular kinds of clients as it does to treat them.[10] As Barad explains, the human is also phenomenon, that is, the human is the product of other intra-actively produced phenomena (such as methadone policy, clinic infrastructure, and temporal and spatial arrangements), its attributes stable only in the moment of intra-action. In short, in rendering the maintenance of paid work difficult, in providing few protections and comforts, and in making clients available to black market purchasers and sellers in a public space for long periods of time, the chronotope of the clinic (more specifically, the queue) regularly runs the risk of intra-actively producing the very clients it seeks to 'cure', the very clients MMT has been introduced to manage within liberal societies: unproductive, disorderly clients involved in illicit drug markets. Equally, acts such as assaults, the building of fires, the buying and selling of medication and so on also act to materialise the design of the clinic in certain ways (attention to security and public order infrastructure, surveillance of dosing leading to increased waiting) via a process in which causation, rather than being readily traceable from one pre-constituted actor to another, emerges, as Barad argues, from multiple past and present intra-actions.

In making this argument, it is also important to recall, as noted in point three above, that the temporality and consciousness of 'drugs' is not separate from or unique in comparison with 'normal' or non-drug time and consciousness. Indeed, methadone is another interruption of Lenson's comfortable distinctions in that it is both drug and drug treatment, both drug time/consciousness and 'non-drug' or 'pre-drug' time/consciousness. In highlighting the similarity between the methadone queue and other kinds of queues, our earlier likening of the clinic queue to a wartime breadline begins to make our argument. There are many reasons for rejecting the kind of distinction Lenson makes here (some of which have already been explored) – for example, it sets up the possibility that 'non-drug' time or consciousness can be read as a kind of authenticity or purity against which drug use and drug users are likely to be defined as diminishing or diminished, sullying or sullied (even if defined as enhancing or enhanced, the effect is to produce an 'other' to the normal). More practically, in insisting on their absolute difference, it opens up the possibility of problematising drug use and drug users, allowing for diagnoses of social problems in which drug use is assumed to be the operative factor. Thus, behaviour in queues tends to be attributed to inherent characteristics of methadone clients and of the specific state of methadone dependence, while parallels and similarities with social behaviour in other kinds of queues (particularly those involving comparable levels of duress, as noted, for example, by Moran [2005] in his discussion of violence in British bus queues) go unrecognised. A sense of this can be identified in the use of security doors and bars at clinics. Here, a blunt distinction is made between dangerous clients and vulnerable staff, while questions of client security, and of the role of the queue itself in fostering violence, and thus, in performing the violent subject (for instance, via the generation of frustration, or merely in providing the material conditions for violence) is neglected.

Conclusion

There is no doubt that many of the circumstances and processes described here present MMT in a poor light. Our intention in making this argument is not, however, to deny the value of the program. On the contrary, the view we have taken throughout this book is that, notwithstanding its flaws, MMT represents a critical practical, and in some respects compassionate, response to some of the severe problems that can arise in the context of opioid dependence under contemporary social and political conditions, including those in Western liberal societies. Our intention, instead, has been to encourage new ways of thinking about the processes of treatment, the ontology of the client and the organisation of the clinic so as to provide insights into how clinics operate in relation to their perceived aims. From this point of view, the queue offers a significant challenge to these aims in that, rather than simply containing or organising pre-existing clients, it intra-actively performs particular kinds of clients. At times, these clients can be seen to:

- trouble public order;
- fail to approximate the liberal goal of independence through paid employment; and
- use the time and opportunity afforded by the queue to buy or sell methadone.

Perhaps most challenging of all, it is possible to argue that the demands of the clinic and its queuing reproduce rather than depart from the model of waiting and dependence widely seen as characteristic of lifestyles associated with regular heroin use. Not only is waiting and a sense of uncertainty around when and whether access to the drug will be achieved characteristic of heroin use, for many it is also a central experience of MMT. From this point of view, it is perhaps only a small stretch to argue that rather than gaining access to a new and liberating lifestyle, treatment can, under certain conditions, merely shift the waiting, the service, the attentiveness, from the illicit drug market to the licit drug market. If waiting and uncertainty are the essence of 'junk time', as many, including William Burroughs and Lou Reed (quoted at the very beginning of this chapter) have said, MMT can be seen as a refinement of and expansion on this relation, rather than a departure from it. Indeed, Burroughs's own confusion around the normativity or novelty of waiting in 'drug time' ('the drug trade operates without schedule' versus 'he must wait, unless he happens to mesh with non-junk time') echoes this unacknowledged dynamic in treatment. Here, we do not, of course, mean to invoke Lenson's concept of 'drug time', which neatly distinguishes the temporality of regular drug use from that of non-drug use. As the critique provided at the start of this chapter makes clear, such distinctions are essentially untenable. Rather, we argue that these assumptions inform critiques of regular drug use, including within methadone treatment. It is more than ironic, then, that treatment tends to produce the very conditions subjected to criticism, indeed, those considered to be *overcome* by treatment.

These observations suggest the need to alter policy so as to allow for changes in treatment delivery and the constitution of different treatment subjects. Put simply, the chronotope of the queue should be avoided. To achieve this, a range of issues need to be considered (some of these are broad, regulatory matters, as outlined in Chapter 2, and others are local matters). Is the program adequately funded? The number of staff on duty during opening hours intra-acts directly with other factors such as client numbers to establish the prevailing chronotope. Is the program infrastructure (building location and layout) suited to the numbers of clients being served? Location and layout often produce levels of intra-action between clients considered by some to be counter-productive and unsafe. Should the question of client safety at the dosing point be considered when takeaway policy is developed? More takeaways mean less time spent in the queue and less exposure to other clients, so it is worth asking how consideration of space-time in the clinic might reshape safety. Is the current system of urine testing conducive to timely and respectful treatment? How does the phenomenon of testing intra-act with other phenomena such as staffing levels to help produce the chronotope of the queue? Are clinic opening hours sufficiently broad to support clients in leading satisfying lives? How do opening hours intra-act with other client responsibilities and opportunities to create specific ways of life? Are opening hours straightforward enough to contribute to easy access to treatment and a minimum of confusion?

In sum, there is no decisive way in which to separate the attributes that 'belong' to clients and those that 'belong' to the process of program delivery. On the contrary, it is necessary to acknowledge that the program helps constitute those very behaviours and attitudes understood to be a priori attributes of clients. For this reason, careful consideration should be given to the specific chronotope of treatment likely to be co-produced by any particular policy.

4
Treatment Identities

This chapter is concerned with the everyday operations of power and agency in MMT. Like Chapters 1 and 2, it is concerned with sanctioned, 'official' material-discursive practices, such as clinical guidelines. Like Chapter 3, it is also concerned with the details of clients' day-to-day experiences of treatment, and the ways in which the mechanisms of treatment materialise subjects. Here, our focus is on the identities and roles of the human actors who enact the worlds of MMT. Its purpose is to describe the identities that are produced, altered and contested, and discuss the implications that these treatment identities may have for social agency and biological citizenship (Rose and Novas, 2005). Building on Chapter 1 in its use of the agential realism of Karen Barad, it is also indebted to sociological and philosophical approaches to identity that are not concerned with materiality in the same way.

What are the advantages of adopting both these approaches? As emerges in this and other chapters, a consideration of methadone as materially co-constitutive of subjects allows a broadening of the analytic lens from that commonly used in drugs research. Considering methadone to be neither determining of what happens to people who consume it due to its physical properties, nor wholly available to the imposition of preferred meanings, entails thinking the worlds of treatment differently. Barad, following Bohr, argues that the scientific experiment introduces a constructed 'cut' between the 'object' and the 'agencies of observation' (Barad, 1998), and does not establish any ontological separation between what is observed and what is used to observe it. Rather than claiming that MMT is an object or referent that exists independently of its observers, and rather than doing the opposite and claiming that MMT is only intelligible in terms of (non-material) discourses or 'social construction', Barad's agential realism offers a means for studying the dynamic co-constitution of methadone subjects and non-human bodies.

Barad has not specifically engaged with the question of identity, but her work contributes to Foucault's conceptualisations of power, bodies, and technologies of surveillance and discipline. The question of identity and classification is important to a study of illicit drugs and treatment, however, and addresses these questions of power and surveillance directly. This chapter begins, then, with two very influential examples of Foucauldian scholarship in the field of identity and social change: Ian Hacking's historical ontology and Nikolas Rose's biological citizenship. Hacking's work illuminates the profound changes wrought by the interplay between classification and classified. Rose's account of biological citizenship emphasises that the agency of medical patients brings about changes not only to medical classification but also to social identities and networks, and to the ways in which claims are made on the state. The chapter then goes on to describe five instances of the creation of new identities through MMT. The first of these speaks to the role of expectation and repetition in the experience of treatment. Conventional understandings of what methadone is, and what treatment involves, have powerful effects on the production of treatment (we return to this point in Chapter 5). The other examples are all new, which is to say they are all produced through treatment: the dissatisfied customer, the 'stable' user, the person in need of guidance and the lay carer. Although not exhaustive, these examples of new identities instantiate key questions of power, knowledge and ethics at work in treatment. Each of these identities complicate what is known about drug users and the biomedical domain of treatment, suggesting new 'boundary articulations' for the 'object of investigation' that is the methadone subject (Barad, 1998). While these identities may turn out to be neither as robust nor historically enduring as other, culturally dominant figurings of the 'drug addict' (Derrida, 1993; Room, 2003; Sedgwick, 1992), they do suggest alternative ways of recognising both the constraints imposed by treatment and liberal models of subjectivity, and the capacity of drug users to negotiate them.

Making up people

Barad cites Ian Hacking's *Representing and Intervening* as an inaugurating text for critiques of representationalism in science studies (Barad, 2003; Hacking, 1983). The phrase for which Hacking is best known, however, is 'making up people', and the project of historical ontology is one of his elaborations of that phrase (Hacking, 2002). Historical ontology describes 'ways in which the possibilities for choice, and for being, arise in history. It is not to be practiced in terms of grand abstractions, but in terms of the explicit formations in which we can constitute ourselves' (Hacking, 2002: 23). Making up people is a process where new kinds of being are created, both through the actions of people 'from below' and the effects of expert discourses 'from above'. The identity categories of homosexuality and heterosexuality are very well-known examples of this process: before the nineteenth century, people did not identify and were not identified as heterosexual or homosexual, because those categories were not available. There were of course practices and desires that can be retrospectively identified as homosexual, but to map a gay or lesbian identity onto them is anachronistic. Identity is not formed only through practices and desires; it does not exist until it is an object of study and a means by which the self can constitute itself as that identity. Equally, to retrospectively diagnose a Crimean War soldier as suffering from post-traumatic stress disorder is to misrecognise the power of identity categories, expert knowledge and biomedical technologies in forming individual experience. Along with others influenced by Foucault, a number of Hacking's projects examine what creates the conditions of possibility for individual subjectivities and experiences. Hacking's examples include child development (we understand children as developing entities) and trauma (we understand that abuse of children occurs and has severe and longstanding effects). A very important element of this is a feedback effect, or

> the looping effect of human kinds. People classified in a certain way tend to grow into the ways that they are described; but they also evolve in their own ways, so that the classifications and descriptions have to be constantly revised.
>
> (Hacking, 1995: 21)

There are a couple of points to emphasise from this. First, the processes in question may circulate around the discourses of experts or other forms of authority, they may emerge from science or from self-help, they may happen during transient historical moments and pass away or emerge and remain in place. However, they all – if only eventually – act upon the conditions of possibility for individual subjectivity, and are not experienced as impositions on fully constituted persons. They refer to the historical conditions not of particular representations of people but of particular ontologies. Second, saying that it is possible to historicise the emergence of conditions of possibility for individual experience is not the same thing as saying those experiences are inauthentic or fabricated. That is, arguing that the identity category of child abuse survivor did not exist until quite recently is not arguing that such an identity is contrived or that its impact on individual experience is somehow artificial. The truth claims of these arguments, in fact, work in the opposite direction: these conditions of possibility are empirically verifiable and entirely real, and it is important to understand their historical formation precisely because they have such an impact on people's lives and selves.

Does MMT count as an instance of 'making up people', in the sense used by Hacking? Insofar as it is a particular drug treatment for opiate addiction, probably not. This is a difficulty with Hacking in that his exclusion criteria are a bit opaque. Insofar as it is concerned with the category of 'drug addicts', almost certainly. Drug addiction, a historically specific, and historically locatable, condition that is an established part of medical taxonomies and a recognisable cultural stereotype could surely be a part of any project of historical ontology. The domain of drug treatment is a specific, contemporary enactment of this. As a treatment program that operates on addiction and is often undergone for a considerable length of time, it enacts in particular ways those relationships between clients/consumers and coercion/consent that feature in many analyses of contemporary biomedicine. On the one hand, most contemporary drug treatments situate addiction in the domain of illness rather than criminality; on the other, medicine itself is constituted through technologies of regulation, surveillance and 'responsibilisation' (Bourgois, 2000; Fraser, 2004; Moore, 2004). An effect of this, as we will argue shortly, is the constitution of clients as unreliable and immature, in need of moral guidance and social structure. In this respect, MMT operates as an instantiation of the broader phenomenon of 'biopower' as well as a specific technology of managing addiction.

Biological citizenship

It is here that the work of Nikolas Rose (1996; Rose, 2001b; Rose and Novas, 2005) becomes particularly useful, in its analysis of the ways in which contemporary negotiations of medicine co-produce new forms of responsibility and obligation, as well as new kinds of social action and claim-making. Rose and Carlos Novas (2005) refer to 'biological citizenship' to describe specific instances of this. Making up biological citizens refers both to changes in the means by which medical, legal and other authorities understand people and those in which people have come to understand and produce narratives of themselves. Identity categories such as 'the chronically sick, the disabled, the blind, the deaf, the child abuser, the psychopath' now organise the ways in which groups of people are regulated by experts. Equally, biological citizenship describes the creation of persons with a certain kind of relation to themselves. These citizens use biologically inflected language in narrating their own experience and subjectivities:

> For example, they describe themselves as having high levels of blood cholesterol, as vulnerable to stress, as being immuno-compromised, or as having an hereditary disposition to breast cancer or schizophrenia.
>
> (Rose and Novas, 2005: 12)

They may also organise collectively to advocate for change based on these relations to themselves and domains of medical diagnosis and treatment.

Hacking and Rose have made significant contributions to an extensive body of work on medicine as an important force in the production and regulation of contemporary subjects in liberal societies (Hacking, 1995; Rose, 1996, 2001b). Hacking's work illuminates the profound changes wrought by the interplay between classification and classified. Rose's account of biological citizenship emphasises that the agency of medical patients brings about changes not only to medical classification but also to social identities and networks, and to the ways in which claims are made on the state. MMT, a medical response to addiction freighted with many of the criminal and political meanings attached to drugs and addicts, is productively studied using both.

There are two ready examples of methadone's productivity in forming treatment identities. The first is liquid handcuffs. As we saw in Chapter 1, this is a dominant metaphor for methadone, and is used internationally by clients and service providers. Given the emphasis in contemporary critical understandings of power on its internalisation and productivity, it is important to note that methadone also invokes responses to power in a much more externalised sense of the term. When clients use a term like 'liquid handcuffs' they also describe themselves as prisoners, constrained by methadone and by the treatment regimes: a point to which we return in Chapter 5. The second example comes from the precriptiveness around socialisation and re-education in our interviews and in policy documents. Indeed, the openness with which moral prescriptions around behaviour and discipline are delivered is a striking feature of medico-legal drugs rhetoric (Stengers, 1997). In some ways it is not the subtext that clients are infantilised, deviant and in need of moral education, but the text. This is illustrated by Barry, who works in policy and is a doctor.

> I suppose that there's a certain paradox that they [clients] feel that they are being treated like children and criminals, and yet the medical profession is saying one of the wonderful things about medicalising drug and alcohol is of course that we take away from the model of the judgmental and the criminal. But actually in practice, we actually do treat them as untrustworthy children.
>
> (Barry, Sydney, NSW, policy/prescriber, 40)

This paternalism can also be read as explicit, visible power that makes use of metaphor and analogy. Alongside our investigations of how MMT works to change the terms by which people understand themselves and the empirical categories through which the world is ordered, we also need to consider the effect and uses of *existing* categories. Liquid handcuffs and errant children: these are examples of the circulation and re-animation of existing repertoires and of the circuitous, recursive effects of language on experience and experience on language. A phrase by which methadone has long been known to clients and service providers represents a shared language to describe a shared experience, and its repeated use informs and shapes experience. Similarly, the infantilisation of drug users is reproduced and embedded in treatment, at once shaping the expectations of experts and deployed as a tool to confirm those expectations. Both obtain through their availability as repertoires and their experiential 'fit'. Expectations are formed by available repertoires and inform the experience that clients and experts have of treatment, which then is recirculated through these repertoires. As we saw in Chapter 3, expectations around the malign agency of clients materialise the layout of clinics, and Chapter 5 shows that expectations around gender inform treatment decisions.

In some ways, this is quite a mundane point: people constitute their experiences of drug treatment (of addiction, of clinical practice, of anything) through the language that is available. However, there are a couple of stronger claims to make from it. The first is a reiteration of the argument made in Chapter 1 that language does not only describe experience, but also shapes it. The metaphors and analogies that circulate through the world of MMT have more than descriptive power. The second is that these available categories confirm and embed some of the more pernicious effects of treatment. As we argue throughout this book, many clients do experience methadone as repressive and are constrained by restrictions on their movement, time and privacy. Many service providers do view clients as asocial and deviant, in need of surveillance and discipline. These repertoires work towards reproducing the effects of treatment that other repertoires, such as value-neutral policy language, can mask.

As we argue throughout this book, existing identity categories are very important to the production of treatment. The focus of this chapter, however, is the effects of MMT in producing new kinds of identities. In making a claim for new identities, we are not arguing that we have discovered hitherto unknown experiences and practices: on the contrary, clients and service providers will be very familiar with them. Rather, we are arguing that MMT is materialising new ways of being that inflect the notion of biological citizenship in particular ways, especially in their dimensions of ethics and power. While liquid handcuffs, 'chaotic' users (Fraser and Moore, in press) and errant children are familiar enough figures to most people associated with treatment, the identities described below are also very common in treatment worlds, and reveal as much about what and how methadone materialises as do other, more stale and constrained subjects.

Throughout this chapter we will argue that there are at least four important elements to be added to the usual accounts of the ways in which new identities are materialised through MMT. First, new selves are produced that occupy oblique positions relative to the positively and negatively remade selves described in many methadone texts. Second, these new selves may crop up in counterpoint or opposition to 'official' categories, become accommodated into the official accounts but also work to change them. This is Hacking's looping feedback effect. Third, and similarly, the work of MMT in creating new identities is not, or at least not always, a one-way process. New selves and identities also work to change the elements of MMT, including its practical objects: service counters, waiting rooms and the drug methadone. Finally, when we are talking about the new identities materialised through MMT and the ways in which they act to change the identity categories they occupy, we are not only talking about clients. The service providers who work in the field are also 'made up' and remade in this way.

This chapter is indebted to Foucault, Rose and Hacking, but we are not arguing that this single treatment is analogous to homosexuality, childhood, madness or the technologies that produced them. MMT, as already noted, does not qualify as an instance of historical ontology; although it does enact important developments in biomedicine, governance and the constitution of the self under the conditions of neoliberalism. We do not (yet) see much to be gained in pursuing an argument that the 'methadone client' is a historical development analogous to the 'gay man' or the 'child abuse survivor'. But the identity of methadone client is important because it both relies on and disrupts the identity of the 'drug addict'; and because it proposes important nuances to biological personhood and contemporary discourses around addiction, consumption, patienthood and care.

Dissatisfied customers

Some of the rhetorics of drug treatment offer only two subject-positions that clients can occupy: the chaotic addict or the compliant/subdued 'stable' consumer. However, much of our interview data show resistance to these narrow categories and activity in a mode familiar from other contexts, notably consumer complaints. Here, is a description of the day-to-day frustration of being made to wait for no apparent good reason from Steve, a Sydney client. A description of the experience of attending a methadone clinic for dosing, it would not be out of place in a register of complaints of poor service anywhere:

> And, it's like they get their kicks out of you sitting there and making you wait. You go in there and they'll be having conversations, drinking coffee, and then like, and you'll stand there, and they'll finish the conversation before they dose you.
>
> (Steve, Sydney, NSW, client, 29)

Similarly, Lisa, also a client from Sydney, complains of distracted and ineffectual treatment from her doctor:

> I mean I tend to get on okay with my doctor although at times I think she is inconsistent and she, she works very long hours and often seems tired and only seems to be half listening to what I'm saying. She'll get interrupted with phone calls and she's sometimes written the wrong thing down on my prescription.
>
> (Lisa, Sydney, NSW, client, 34)

Being made to wait, and being treated indifferently, has happened to most of us at some time, for example in the queue at the bank or the airport. In this sense the experience of treatment is described as comparable to other experiences of customer service. However, as Rowan indicates, there is an inflection to poor service provision in the retail environment of the pharmacy that is peculiar to MMT:

> Like [in a rural pharmacy] they used to, they used to make me wait a bit, and maybe that's just paranoia, I'm not sure, but, you know, I got the feeling that 'oh, yeah, he's just a junkie, we'll, you know, just let him wait there and serve him when, when we're ready' sort of thing.
>
> (Rowan, Melbourne, Victoria, client, 41)

Drug users often are not seen, and often do not see themselves, as the same as customers who are not drug users. Their drug use separates them from others. In some cases clients are constituted as quite radically different from customers. For example, Sam, a client from regional Victoria, describes the hostility between staff and clients in one setting as an effect, rather than a cause, of deliberately impersonal and distant service:

> They, they were behind a sheet of glass so you couldn't even talk, have any contact with them. They just passed your methadone under a little window. Because, and that fostered an atmosphere of tension and animosity between the staff and patients. To the point where people would throw furniture and yell and scream at them, because they couldn't, they didn't feel they were having contact with their provider. And, you know, they felt like they weren't listening because they were behind the sheet of glass, you know, someone is pressing a button to talk to them.
>
> (Sam, regional Victoria, client, 31)

As we have seen in other chapters, everyday conflicts, frustrations and degradations can play important roles in the experience of treatment. What is perhaps less obvious is the uncertain boundary between patient and customer at work here. Ivan, a Sydney client, describes getting his methadone from a pharmacy as 'just like shopping' and in some ways treatment is enacted through procedures that resemble buying a newspaper or catching the bus: turning up to the same place every day, paying, collecting the same thing. In other ways, however, it is performed through biomedical repertoires and constitutes clients as patients. It requires intimate information, such as that gained through urine and blood testing, and these requirements can enact conflict or humiliation. For example, Faith, a client from Sydney, says that 'it just seems like even if we just need to use the toilet to [pass] urine you have to go through this big spiel with them'.

Disrespect, poor communication and lack of flexibility appear to characterise relationships in some cases. Faith and Kimberley describe attitudes of hostility and the threat of withdrawal of service that would not be countenanced in most shops, or indeed in most health services:

> I walked in there one day and they were running late with their dosing and I said to them 'running late?' next thing they're saying, she turned around and says 'oh well we've got things to do, we've got to set up this machine, we've got to do this, we've got to do that', you know all these excuses and then it ended with 'if you don't like it go somewhere else'.
>
> (Faith, Sydney, NSW, client, 50s)

> That's what I notice with, um, my new pharmacy, is that it's got like a stand over tactic. You've got your hostage here, if you don't like it, go somewhere else. And going somewhere else out there is like, going three suburbs away.
>
> (Kimberley, Melbourne, Victoria, client, 27)

When daily dosing is required, proximity to home or work and to transport is critical; refusal of service at one place can mean massive disruptions. Moreover, discipline to the extent of removal from treatment altogether is a possibility for all clients at any time. Ned, a pharmacist from Melbourne, reveals the contradictions in treating clients as both retail customers and unreliable drug users:

> [W]hen I have an interview with them I ask them to treat us like a normal retailer, and we'll treat you as a normal customer. Now, if, if they understand that, I mean I ask them not to come in with anyone else. Um, I mean, we've got a few with kids but, so that's fine, but the kids have got to be kept under control.
>
> (Ned, Melbourne, Victoria, pharmacist, 48)

To risk labouring the point, 'normal customers' are not routinely told that they have to come into shops without their family, nor warned as a matter of course that they have to keep their children under control.

Other logics are also at work here. Conflicts are not rare, and, as Chapter 3 showed, the operations of treatment are often conducive to conflict. Yet the identity categories circulating around drugs place these conflicts in a particular frame, such that complaints about treatment dovetail readily into interpretations of 'chaotic use' or 'drug-seeking behaviour'. This underlines both the limits of clients' capacity to legitimately complain and the consequences when complaints are judged as unreasonable. Some clients reported that staff expect or assume dishonesty from clients. This means that changes to client routines or occasional requests for treatment variation, which in most circumstances would be regarded as normal practice, are treated as suspicious.

> I get, sometimes like even last week I had to ring up my doctor and he, I can hear it in his voice, he gets a bit annoyed and, and probably suspicious. I can hear that as well like because, I mean I know people that will ring up and chuck on that many excuses. I feel sorry for the doctors because some people genuinely do it just to rort the system.
>
> (Ivan, Sydney, NSW, client, 34)

This constitution of clients as unreliable and dishonest is also enacted through practical measures. For example, in some locations intrusive and humiliating procedures have been implemented as a blanket response to methadone diversion, implemented universally. Isaac, for example, describes the response of a hospital (where many rural clients have to receive some of their doses) in regional Victoria to diversion of buprenorphine:

> [T]here'd be a couple of nurses just watching you have it, and they'd both just sit there and stare at you the whole time, then you had to come up and lift your tongue up and all this shit. It was just embarrassing. Because sometimes, you know, someone would come in the door, you might know them, and you're standing there with your hands in your mouth with these two nurses looking down your throat, you know. And that was because of what, what somebody else did.
>
> (Isaac, regional Victoria, client, 38)

Our interviews with service providers also illustrate assumptions of client dishonesty. Bob, a pharmacist from regional NSW, reports implementing systems to keep track of what clients tell him because they cannot be trusted:

> I'm a bit smarter now. I record the date their grandmother died in my files. And I record, you know, the date their grandfather died and all of that sort of stuff, and the date that their children died.

So they can't go and tell me [...] it's the anniversary of their grand-mother's death, or whatever, because I've already got it recorded.

(Bob, regional NSW, pharmacist, 52)

Scott, who works in policy in Victoria, makes a more general point about the trustworthiness of clients reporting drug use when they receive takeaways:

There's a lot of trust involved in it. And there's a lot of self reporting. I'm not saying that urine testing or whatever is a, is a good idea, but, um, yeah, it's trust and self report, and, ah, I mean these, these are people who have drug issues otherwise they wouldn't be turning up to the service. It's a big point.

(Scott, Melbourne, Victoria, policy, 47)

William, a pharmacist from Sydney, reported dishonesty or unusual behaviour as an indicator that clients are using illicit drugs or misusing prescribed drugs:

[T]he urgency and the height that the arguments reach just suggests something else is going on. Uhm, the lack of rationality, or the lack of response to rational argument, but you know the construction of these incredibly elaborate reasons.

(William, Sydney, NSW, pharmacist, 43)

The pharmacy or clinic shares elements with retail settings, and complaints about poor service follow the logic of the dissatisfied customer, at least in some respects. However, there are very important limitations to this. Beyond a certain point – and the location of this point resides mostly in the judgment of workers – complaints reveal more than their content, become suspect, and shift or entrench the complainer not into the category of difficult *customer* but unreconstructed, chaotic *user*.

At work here, then, is the deployment of some existing categories and the creation of new meanings for them. Dissatisfied customers complaining about indifferent or inefficient service are hardly unfamiliar types, and neither are disaffected service workers talking about having to tolerate unreasonable things from customers. However, there are also some new things going on in this context that are not often recognised. The first is the very presence of the register of customer complaints at all. When methadone clients are constructed as intelligible only as either out of control drug addicts or functional and stable clients, there is little space for recognition of the grinding, quotidian harms and insults that enact the client as dissatisfied customer. Binaries like this also foreclose the possibilities of recognising clients as people with expectations of service that are sometimes met and sometimes not. Such recognition brings to light the particular frustrations of occupying the position of 'dissatisfied customer' simultaneously with the position of 'drug addict', when the latter places significant limits on complaints being heard or respected at all, much less acted on.

There is a further point to make from this, to do with the ways in which the quality of treatment and service has been recognised. Research on respect and courtesy in services indicates that the manner in which services are delivered is important (Ashton and Witton, 2004). Yet a focus on treatment retention tends to present clients as either in treatment, an indicator of treatment success, or absent, an indicator of treatment failure. The effect of treatment on participants is oversimplified in these kinds of binaries, as is the understanding of what and whom treatment produces. Further, these binaries assume a one-way process of treatments acting on clients, pre-existing subjects who remain constant in every respect except for the fact of receiving treatment, being acted on. While this can be a valid approach to improving treatment services, it is of limited use in improving understanding of how treatment acts on people and changes them. The relationship between clients and treatment is not a one-way process and, as we argued in Chapter 3, treatment both makes changes to people and is changed by the people on whom it acts. A more nuanced approach is needed to think through some clients' readings of surveillance and care, as suggested by this comment by Rowan:

> Well I don't think she cares that much really. Um, and I just get the feeling that she just wants to get people through and, as quick as she can. Whereas I used to go to another, another doctor for a while in Melbourne, and, um, he was really good, and I got a urine test every time I went there. And, I'm happy to do that.
>
> (Rowan, Melbourne, Victoria, client, 41)

Rowan suggests that the time and labour of urine testing equates to care, whereas for other clients the procedure is humiliating and an indication that their word is not trusted. Clients and service providers also discussed the gratitude with which basic courtesies are sometimes received by clients, which supports other research into the reduced expectations of disadvantaged groups, including drug users (Bath, 2006;

Sitzia and Wood, 1997). However, the comment below from Jack indicates that more is going on in treatment than this:

> I see all of them every day or every second day. You know I've been out with them to music, music's one of my things, and often they're musicians and things. And, I've been out to a couple of things, I've been to a couple of their funerals. I, they would say, and I would say, I treat them with respect. Um, they often say, 'this is the first place that I have not been treated with suspicion and as a lower form of life'.
>
> (Jack, Melbourne, Victoria, pharmacist, 62)

Participation in the program changes service providers, and positioning health care workers as static subjects misrepresents the impact of worker–client relationships on workers as well as clients. Some pharmacists reported very close connections with clients, some clients very close connections with pharmacists. In-kind arrangements for payment were sometimes in place, for example, whereby a methadone debt was paid by fixing the pharmacist's computer, or doing some gardening. Pharmacists and clients see each other between two and seven times a week, often for periods of months or years, and this can lead to tension, open hostility or, sometimes, friendship and closeness. Alongside the dissatisfied customer and instances of startlingly insulting treatment, then, are instances of relationships and support that cannot be captured under the rubric of either customer or patient.

What is revealed by a consideration of the case of the methadone client as dissatisfied customer? In the first place, we can see that complaints and criticisms made by clients and workers are part of the activity of the drug and program, working to change the program and also working to change people such that they inhabit particular spaces relating to consumption, service and obligation. Examples of these are the changes in service brought about through such things as conciliation meetings between clients and workers, through the rapport between service providers and clients just described, and through clients positioning themselves successfully as entitled to higher standards of treatment. Second, we can see that the consequences of this can also be invidious in that situating the client as a customer can occlude the real dilemmas and restrictions placed on clients, and distort the power relations at work. In producing an identity position of dissatisfied customer, MMT puts the lie to any idea that clients are zombies or too passive to talk back to power. However, the transformative possibilities of customer dissatisfaction are pretty evident in any context, let alone a drug treatment one. Moreover, the positioning of clients as customers distorts their obligations and the consequences of failing to meet them.

Third, the identity of clients is not an unhappy combination of the identities of 'patient' and 'customer' but, in the context of MMT, has very particular meanings and effects. Some of these are transplanted from customer service, some are from patient–doctor relationships and some produce clients as analogous to client states, bound by contracts and agreements that belie inequalities (Newbury, 2000). All of these work together to produce an identity of methadone client that cannot be reduced to either patient or customer. The identity of drug treatment service *consumer*, however, is one instance where this irreducibility is giving rise to new categories. Rose and Novas (2005) argue that biosocial groupings include new forms of activism ('rights biocitizenship'), new forms of knowledge, especially about health and medical status ('informational bio-citizenship') and new forms of collectivity and organising, mediated by information technologies such as websites and email lists ('digital bio-citizenship'). Each of these is evident in the work of user groups such as the Australian Injecting & Illicit Drug Users League (AIVL). Using mental health and disability services as analogues, these groups act in a number of ways for the inclusion of user views and experience: developing policy position statements, conducting peer research, publishing policy and user magazines and representation on government committees (Australian Injecting & Illicit Drug Users League, 2006; Bryant et al., forthcoming[b]). This model of advocacy shares similarities with other patient support groups and social movements, and also departs from them in important ways. It argues that consumers of services have specific expertise as well as experiential perspectives, and that specific resources should be dedicated to ensuring their active involvement in policies and program. In particular, it argues, the discrimination and stigma imposed on drug users lends particular urgency to the need for consumer representation. This relatively new identity construction of the drug user as treatment service consumer suggests possibilities for the biological citizenship of clients.

Finally, while any treatment or service relationship is bound by explicit and implicit rules of conduct, the client's position in treatment is especially precarious, and felt to be so. Dishonesty and violence are not tolerated anywhere, and anyone who threatens the person behind the counter can expect to be told to leave at the very least. However, the expectation of dishonesty or antagonism, combined with the lack of real choice of doctor or dosing point in many cases, effects limitations on client complaints and dissent that are probably unique within medical treatment. Access to methadone has an enormous impact on clients' lives, and the fragility of that access, its felt instability and the constant danger of its being lost, is unlike either customer service or other kinds of treatment.

The enactment of the client as dissatisfied customer reveals much then about treatment relationships, power and what is known about drugs and users. The next identity to be considered also illuminates new categories and new possibilities for understanding what and who MMT produces.

The stable user

When drug treatment is discussed as transformative, familiar typologies of drug use such as addicted and 'clean' are used. Our interview data revealed less use of terms such as recovered or recovering addict than of other terms, particularly 'stable' and 'chaotic'. This may be because, as Chapter 1 suggested, MMT functions in public discourse as an extension of addiction, or, as Chapter 5 will argue, a repetition rather than escape from addiction. Both 'stable' and 'chaotic' recur in service provider and client interviews, and the terms recur partly because their meanings are flexible and can be vague, as the following examples show. Barry, who worked in NSW policy and is also a doctor, uses 'stable' to refer to compliance with treatment agreements, arguing that takeaways should be seen as an indicator of stability.

> [A client's reaction to receiving takeaways should be] 'shit, I'm being quite stable, I'm attending and getting my dose, I'm not being refused my dose, I'm not using drugs in a dangerous way, this is, this is a good thing'.
>
> (Barry, Sydney, NSW, policy/prescriber, 40)

Beverley, a nurse in Melbourne, uses the term to describe both drug use and social circumstances:

> She's twenty-three, and she is what we would call stable. She is on a massive dose, I think a hundred and fifteen, well that's not massive, that's what she needs. She, um, other indicators are there. She's got a relationship, an intimate relationship that's really going well for her, she's got stable affordable safe housing,

she has reconnected back with her family [...] she's swallowing her methadone every day.

(Beverley, Melbourne, Victoria, nurse/case worker, 50s)

Danny, a client, uses the same term to describe approval in the eyes of his doctor, while Jenny, also a client, has a more specific use of the term: she was judged to be stable because she behaved appropriately, but in reality she was not.

I like [the] respect of the doctor giving it to me quicker, it means that he thinks that I'm stable, sure but the bottom line is I actually have got the takeaway.

(Danny, Sydney, NSW, client, 46)

I was deemed to be, you know, like a stable client, for want of a better word, which I wasn't but, I mean I did pay and I didn't cause a fuss.

(Jenny, Sydney, NSW, client, 46)

Graham uses the term to describe the absence of diversion or unwarranted drug use, Kara in terms of managing withdrawal:

I'd say definitely the first six months you should be going five days a week to the chemist and you should have to go weekends if they're open. I honestly believe that, when you start. 'Cause you are most likely to do the wrong thing, and you need to get that stability. Once you've got the stability [...] then we should progress, we really should.

(Graham, regional Victoria, client, 39)

It actually stabilises me so I don't actually want to go out and get a hit. Um, it makes me feel normal, so I don't feel like I'm hanging out, or I'm sick, or wanting to have a taste really. [...] Because once I've got that I've got that stability and then I can start working on getting back to work.

(Kate, Melbourne, Victoria, client, 27)

'Stable' can refer to the client in a holistic sense, or to levels of drug use, or to demeanour in clinics, or to employment. It can have more or less precise meanings; have a narrower or a broader sense. In contrast, while 'chaotic' describes what stability is not, it also commonly evokes more dimensions than drug use or behaviour in drug treatment. This is revealed in comments from clients:

[M]y own chaotic drug use um that meant that yeah I didn't really know what was going on.

(Sue, Sydney, NSW, client, 40)

[W]hen we go onto methadone, our life is just chaotic, you know. It's not like 'hey, oh, I'll go on methadone, you know, it's trendy'. It's not trendy at all, it's just, you know, your, your life becomes unmanageable.

(Brendan, Melbourne, Victoria, client, 37)

Descriptions of chaos are more commonly evoked from health care workers than clients, however. The uses of the term are illustrated by the following quotes from Rosemary, Beverley and Tom.

I think the level of chaos is the [issue] [...] they're getting people from gaol, they're getting people who are homeless who are living on the streets.

(Rosemary, Sydney, NSW, prescriber, 50s)

You've got access, transport wise, you've got poverty, you've got homelessness, transience, in and out of jail, domestic violence. You know, there's just so many factors that contribute to this person's chaos.

(Beverley, Melbourne, Victoria, nurse/case worker, 50s)

So if they stay in the treatment, they settle down, they stop using, they stop doing crime, their kids start getting looked after, they pay their bills, and they change pretty drastically within, you know, weeks, months, days sometimes. Um, you know, so people go from being very messed up and distressed and chaotic, to being pretty, pretty reasonable sort of folks.

(Tom, Melbourne, Victoria, pharmacist, 56)

Whereas 'stability' can be used to refer specifically to drug use, 'chaotic' is almost always about things other than drugs, such as housing, employment, family, crime and poverty. In the context of this 'chaos' that describes drug use but is always about more than drugs, methadone is often discussed as a means of addressing these non-drug problems. 'Chaotic' and 'stable', then, are not simply synonyms for addicted and not-addicted, and use of these terms highlights two connected points. First, drug addiction can be about more than drugs and, second, methadone addresses things other than other drugs. This recognition of the not-drugs dimensions of drug addiction has, in turn, another implication, which is that methadone use can coincide with illicit drug use and, further, that illicit drug use does not erase the effects of methadone in addressing addiction.

'Chaotic' and 'stable' are among a range of binary oppositions common in discussions of drug use. Probably the most simplistic is that between drug use (bad) and abstinence (good). Others distinguish between different kinds of use and different kinds of users (Boeri, 2004; Rødner, 2005; Southgate and Hopwood, 1999). In these typologies the key question is often that of addiction, or dependent use. The distinction between chaos and stability is different. In many respects, this distinction is problematic (as indeed are distinctions between use and addiction). It can conceal assumptions and disguise moral values as clinical. However, the vagueness and flexibility of the terms 'stable' and 'chaotic' also give rise to the possibility of a new identity: the methadone client who is a stable user.

> [E]ven if they're still casual users they still, they still become a lot more stable, you know they're not out running around stealing and ripping people off and things like that, you know it does stabilise people up even though they might still be using. It's not a bad thing like that.
>
> (Darren, Sydney, NSW, client, 47)

> [T]he general attitude is that if people are using they're not stable. But the truth is that some people can be stable and still using. They may be, they just may happen to be using at the time that they had the urine done, and that may be once a month. We do have recreational heroin users who, who were using a lot and now just use as a treat every fortnight when they get paid.
>
> (Diane, Sydney, NSW, nurse, 30s)

Any opposition between illicit drug use and abstinence due to treatment is undermined by an identity particular to MMT: the stable client-user. For this identity, whatever methadone is doing it is *not* substituting (completely) for heroin and it is not blockading heroin. In other words it is not acting in either of the two roles prescribed for methadone. Yet this is not to say it is doing nothing. If methadone – as our data and other research indicate (Koester et al., 1999) – effects change to 'chaotic' drug use and can be used alongside illicit drugs, then this has the potential to unpack some complacent assumptions. For example, when methadone is used alongside illicit drugs in a strategy to correct or change behaviours defined as chaotic, one-dimensional arguments about drugs causing chaos do not make sense.

Equally, the category of 'stable use' may unpack distinctions between use and addiction, in that use of heroin, usually understood as inherently unmanageable, addicted and chaotic, can coincide with stability and broad compliance with the rules of treatment. Moira, a client from Melbourne, is explicit in her refusal of both the notion that her use of heroin was chaotic and the idea that methadone caused huge changes to her, or her use:

> I suppose I would be on methadone if I wasn't working, but if I had the access to the money that I do from working, then I would prefer just to use rather than be on methadone. But because I do have to work to get that money, and because, to get that money I have to turn up to work and be functional and do a job, I can't really rely on an illicit supply. Um, it's sort of putting the responsibility for my capacity to work on an illicit black market [...] I sort of need to be on methadone, you know, in case there is a drought, or in case, um, you know, my dealer does stop or run out, or get busted or, you know, whatever.
>
> (Moira, Melbourne, Victoria, client, 38)

Moira uses MMT to ensure that the relationship between her heroin use and her capacity to work is predictable and continuous. Rather than methadone effecting changes to her level of 'stability', it effected other changes to her heroin use, namely that heroin is not the only drug available to her. Émilie Gomart's (2002) analysis of the two clinical trials of methadone reveals that the question of whether heroin is the same as methadone or different is not resolved through reference to an inert, pre-given substance. Instead, 'methadone' is constituted through the event of the trial and the drug is one actor in a network that produces it. Similarly, the stable user reveals that methadone is not a given, pre-existing substance with universal effects. Methadone is different from one context to another, and changes according to circumstance. It replaces heroin, complements it, provides backup in its absence. It differs between individuals, and may change over time for particular individuals.

The stable user, then, illustrates the importance of agency, negotiation and resistance to rules in MMT. Clients who continue to use heroin figure in treatment guidelines and other texts, but usually, as Chapter 2 showed, in terms of risk. The stable user cannot be accommodated into narratives of risk or chaos and shows alternatives to both pessimistic accounts of liquid handcuffs and redemption narratives of socialisation and abstinence. Importantly, the substance of methadone does not have pre-determined effects, nor is it simply the product of social construction. As Chapter 1 argued, the particularities of methadone lie in it being *like* heroin but also *not* heroin. Methadone is not the same as heroin; the client who is a stable user is different from both the client who only consumes methadone and the drug user who only consumes heroin. The drug methadone is co-constituted through regimes of governance and regulation, government subsidies, medical training, transnational pharmaceutical companies, randomised control trials, political arguments and the substance 'itself'. Its agential capacities are neither determined independently of its consumption, nor determining of its effects.

The stable user exemplifies making up people from 'below'. Our next example considers an instance of people being made up from 'above'.

In need of guidance

In the language of drug treatment, judgements about the reliability and stability of clients often give rise to assessments of the guidance they need. In our interviews service providers reported that treatment brings benefit to clients through the provision of 'structure'. Their point and the language they used to make it echoes the NSW Clinical Practice Guidelines' description of treatment as providing

> stability and structure, and within methadone programs the therapeutic relationship established with each patient can facilitate social reintegration and access to other services.
>
> (NSW Health, 1999)

Assessments of drug users as requiring introduction or restitution to legitimate, routinised ways of life are not unfamiliar, and have been subject to analysis for some time. Getting up in the morning, conforming to normal standards of grooming, keeping appointments, having self-discipline, accepting life's disappointments and inconveniences: all of these are assumed to be lacking in the drug addict and present in everybody else. Recall Jacques Derrida's argument that drug addiction is vilified because it is read as an escape from reality:

> What do we hold against the drug addict? Something we never, at least never to the same degree, hold against the alcoholic or the smoker: that he cuts himself off from the world, in exile from reality ... that he escapes into a world of simulacrum and fiction.
>
> (Derrida, 1993)

Restitution to society includes incorporation of norms and the adoption of prescribed class and gender roles. Drug treatment is designed to facilitate these changes, although, as we saw in Chapter 3, its specific operations often work against them. NSW's treatment guidelines describe an instrumental socialisation process, access to services and so on. The 'structure' of treatment described by health care workers suggests something slightly different, which is that without the discipline of daily attendance clients may just hang around all day, in thrall to the pleasure principle:

> [T]his chaotic group that I'm talking of are generally not employed, they're generally not doing a lot. There doesn't seem to be a lot of structure in their lives, so almost coming to the pharmacy every day is a point of structure.
>
> (William, Sydney, NSW, pharmacist, 43)

> You know, the client is working every day of the week, he needs takeaways. He can't, you know, the pharmacy doesn't open till nine, he's got to be at work at seven. Um, things like that. So, I mean, that's totally reasonable that the person has some, but, but then the guy who is just, you know, doing the me-too thing, it's like 'I want takeaways 'cause he's got them, but I'm just basically in bed all day'.
>
> (Tom, Melbourne, Victoria, pharmacist, 56)

Perhaps less evidently, methadone treatment also produced another figure who cannot be trusted, who requires regulation and structure: the unreliable health care worker. This figure is sometimes incompetent.

> I think that private doctors need to be regulated [...] I do tend to think that there are some doctors out there who don't necessarily have an idea of what they're doing, which is very unfortunate. Um and

they can be seeing clients for many, many years um without really knowing what's going on.

> (Diane, Sydney, NSW, nurse, 30s)

Sometimes they are insufficiently scrutinised.

> [T]here are guidelines for those doctors to follow, but they're not always being followed. So who, who are they accountable to? [...] When I work in the wards, and I still do, and when we give out, you know, schedule eight drugs, we have very strict guidelines that we have to abide by. But, ah, doctors, you know, can do what they like (both laugh). And they do, you know, they do.

> (Pamela, regional NSW, nurse, 46)

Sometimes they are dishonest and exploitative.

> Some doctors you can see are just there for the money and they'll exploit the people and they couldn't care less about them.

> (Dominic, Sydney, NSW, pharmacist, 44)

And sometimes they have failed to do what was expected of them.

> [W]hy would I want to jeopardise my program because a doctor either doesn't know the guidelines or is too lazy to follow them? So [arguments with doctors] can often cause some angst, but only with guys that, as I say, are either lazy or, um, you know, just obnoxious, or, you know, sticks in the mud.

> (Mario, Melbourne, Victoria, pharmacist, 40)

Health care workers, then, were seen as oddly similar to clients, as not only imperfect but imperfect in the same ways clients are. And just as clients were active in protesting their construction as childish, dishonest and irresponsible, so too service providers protested what they see as attacks on their autonomy. Otto, a doctor, describes treatment guidelines as not simply trying but punishing:

> [I]t should ultimately be at the doctor's discretion how things are done and the doctor should have guidelines, but I think they need to be, they need to be clear, unambiguous and uhm, and with less, with less of the kind of punitive aspect that's been going around lately.

> (Otto, Sydney, NSW, prescriber, 50s)

Again, MMT enacts both clients and service providers, and in their resistance and reaction to these actions, both clients and service providers work to change both the treatment regime and themselves. This is another example of a new identity produced through treatment. In this case, it is the imperfect agent in need of guidance and structure which, in a neat circularity, treatment itself is said to provide.

The lay carer

Diversion of methadone to street sale is one of the two major problems associated with methadone, the other being overdose (of the client, or of someone else). As a category, 'diversion' sits readily alongside 'drug dealing'. The latter term is so freighted with meaning that diversion can then be seen as a pathological activity by a client who, as an unreconstructed chaotic user, uses methadone only as a means for getting more drugs. The drug dealer is a demonised figure and mythic predatory characteristics are ascribed to them. For example, a few health care workers in our interviews reported their horror that methadone is sold to young children, a practice for which no evidence exists.[1] Diversion recurs in our interview data as problematic for both clients and service providers, but in ways that complicate these stereotypical ideas of the methadone client as a compulsive, black market seller. For example, clients may be victims of diversion: some report being threatened and otherwise intimidated outside clinics to sell their methadone. This pathologising is also troubled by recognition of the fact that many clients are impoverished, that most have to pay for their methadone, and that diversion of a partial dose or one day's dose happens in some cases so people can remain on the program.

Another disruption to conventional understandings of diversion as pathological commerce is the program's informal networks of sharing and exchange. Clients and service providers report that diversion takes the form not only of selling but *sharing* methadone with friends and partners who are withdrawing from methadone or from other drugs. Sharing is identified in the Victorian guidelines as a type of diversion:

> One characteristic of substance misuse is the phenomenon of sharing with other drug users. Pharmacotherapies are no exception, and patients may share their prescribed drugs with non-tolerant associates, with serious adverse consequences. Deaths have occurred as a result of patients sharing their takeaway doses of pharmacotherapies with friends or partners.
>
> (Drugs and Poisons Regulations Group, 2006: 22)

This appearance of sharing in the Victorian guidelines seems to be a recognition of the unremunerated circulation of drugs through social networks and suggests the range of practices that are normally grouped into categories like 'misuse'. Our reports from interviews, however, emphasise that sharing most often occurs between opioid users, to assist during periods of withdrawal (often described as sickness), not between users and 'non-tolerant associates':

> Yes, I was just helping out friends that aren't on programs, that use. And, before I went on the program, I had a friend that would help me, you know, like, I had to go to hospital, and um, she was a legend, she brought me methadone down and, and stuff. And I was in there five days before the drug and alcohol worker came to see me.
>
> (Alina, Melbourne, Victoria, client, 39)

> I've given [my partner] some of mine to get him through and things like that. And we've had friends that have been um ahh have been really sick and um we've given them some to get them through. I don't mean physically sick, I wouldn't give someone, I mean sick hanging out sick.
>
> (Renée, Sydney, NSW, client, 37)

> But I, I've seen, like people before, like, you know their mate's hanging out, and they'll go 'oh, here, have a sip of this', you know, 'and it'll help you out a bit'. That sort of thing, where there's not money exchanged, but 'just have a sip of my methadone, and you know, you'll feel a bit better'.
>
> (Kate, Melbourne, Victoria, client, 27)

Sharing with non-tolerant friends, and taking methadone without permission, the examples described in the new Victorian guidelines, were not discussed by clients or service providers in this way. (Theft of takeaways in share houses and other communal spaces was discussed, but as theft, not as sharing.) In some cases people describe sharing between treatment clients, in some cases between a treatment client and an opioid user who is not a treatment client.

> Like, it's a bit hard if, you know, your boyfriend or partner is, like, hanging out in withdrawal, and obviously if you're on methadone you know what that's like [...] Depending on the relationship of course, but, like, you know, 'glug glug glug, oh, I'm fine, oh well,

we've got no money, bad luck, you hang'. It's, you know, it's like, if you love someone, you're going to, and even, um, you know, if someone turns up on your doorstep and they're just desperate and sick and fucked, you're going to give them some of your take-away.

(Moira, Melbourne, Victoria, client, 38)

As these examples show, and service providers and policy workers acknowledge, sharing is a form of sociality and care. Rose and Novas (2005: 18) describe biological citizenship as involving 'a set of techniques for managing everyday life in relation to a condition, and in relation to expert knowledge', and while sharing of methadone is utterly at odds with most orthodox notions of normative citizenship, sharing of methadone can involve, to cite Rose and Novas again, 'ethical seriousness'.

It's a generous thing to do, ah, a generous thing for an opioid dependent to give an opiate away. You know, there are, these things are valued.

(Colin, Sydney, NSW, policy, 46)

This then is our final example of new identities created by MMT: the lay methadone carer. Concerns about methadone diversion circulate around the program's sustainability in general and access to takeaways in particular, so it is important to clarify the range of activities that are grouped under the rubric of diversion (Fiellin and Lintzeris, 2003). From another perspective, criticisms of drug treatment on ethical and political principles could also benefit from this knowledge. These activities and the new categories of client to which they give rise operate in the dimensions of care and self-care. Drug treatment has been criticised as regulation and surveillance masked as care. Drug treatment itself is linked to the control of deviance, the making docile of unruly bodies. Helen Keane points out the pessimism, if not quietism, that can result from this:

[A]n overarching suspicion of regulation can lead to a situation where all health programs and medical care are diagnosed as inherently oppressive. This stance can bring about a conceptual and practical impasse in which attempts to care for others and oneself can only be diagnosed as paternalism, surveillance or co-option into a disciplinary regime.

(Keane, 2003: 232)

She writes that there are 'other ways to envisage the demands of care' (232). The production of the new identity of methadone carer is an example of alternative means of understanding caring than capitulation into an oppressive social order. It suggests negotiations of the field of medical regulation and care that are largely unrecognised. Moreover, it also suggests a means of addressing the gloomy assessments of treatment that circulate. Recognition of the nuances of diversion has the potential to add a new dimension to knowledge of treatment. Of course, sharing of drugs is not peculiar to treatment; people who are not opioid dependent also share illicit and prescription drugs. However, the sharing of methadone is distinct from this and adds weight to arguments that diversion of methadone has more dimensions than reckless incompetence or greed. Diversion of methadone is often considered in a calculus of risks and advantages in methadone programs: on the one hand, access to takeaways makes programs much easier for clients to handle and so is associated with retention; on the other, takeaways allow criminal behaviours such as diversion. Equally, a great deal of policy anxiety is generated, as it should be, around rare and catastrophic incidents of diversion that result in the death of a child, or an opioid naïve adult. Recognition of the nuances of diversion is therefore essential for effective policy responses; grouping all irregular use of doses under the rubric of reckless and dangerous diversion misreads those instances of diversion as informal care. The sharing of methadone, as with selling and buying among small social networks, also raises different policy questions from zero-sum arguments about diversion. Methadone gets sold among peers because of difficulties in getting access to treatment, because the operations of treatment regimes are such that clients cannot stay on them, and because agreements on appropriate dose can't be reached between clients and health care workers. The lay carer is produced not only by the practices of illicit drug users around care and sociality, but also by the resource deficits and rules of the program.

Sharing also undermines critiques of drug treatments as necessarily paternalistic and debilitating. The sharing of methadone demonstrates that people do things in response to the drug and treatment rules that they would not otherwise do, that the program provokes new forms of activity. It is not necessary to celebrate methadone lay caring in order to recognise that clients can behave outside prescribed rules while being scrupulously careful about following different, informal codes of responsible treatment: looking after others and themselves, keeping doses safe. These behaviours can only occur within treatment and construct an identity peculiar to it. Analysis of methadone programs outside Australia emphasise client passivity and capitulation to dehumanising rules (Friedman and Alicea, 2001). The possibility of occupying a space of care may be a point of differentiation between Australian and other programs. This could have implications not only for policy and assessments of treatment retention, but also for other, political considerations of drug treatment as suppressing deviance and producing docile, obedient bodies. Once again, easy distinctions between addicted and not, stable and chaotic, compliant and disobedient are troubled by this new identity. Conforming to neither stereotypes of degraded, reckless criminality nor functional subjects perfectly reinstated to work and consumption, the lay methadone carer suggests new ways to understand the program's imperfections and possibilities.

Conclusion

This chapter has been concerned with two new products of MMT. The first relates to identities, and the second to the agents that bring them about. First, new identities and new possibilities for personhood are co-produced by treatment: the dissatisfied client/customer, the stable user, the professional and client in need of guidance, and the lay carer. As with other examples of making up people, it has been our purpose to argue here that new identities are created from both 'above' and 'below'. As with other examples of biological citizenship, the shared experience of methadone consumption and 'patienthood' is creating new forms of identity and advocacy, especially through user organisations such as the AIVL. Broad cultural narratives, social expectations and clinical judgments effect changes to clients and service providers, and so too do the activities of clients. The identities produced are also important to recognise in both empirical and conceptual terms. Some of these identities are only rarely recognised; others, such as lay carers, are familiar to both clients and service providers working in the field but scarcely known outside it.

Second, concepts, practices and objects are behind these new identities and we have attempted to foreground here those concepts, practices and objects. Complaints and arguments between clients and workers, clinic practices, waiting room counters, social networks, methadone 'itself', heroin 'itself' are all productive. As Chapter 1 argued, analysis of methadone often examines treatment as a nether world in which clients are no longer addicts but not straight either, in which they struggle with uncertain identities of patient or client, 'not quite junkie, not quite conventional' (Murphy and Irwin, 1992: 258). The analysis undertaken here supports much of this, but emphasises what is produced in and through MMT rather than the inexactness of existing categories. Defences of pharmacotherapy treatments argue that addicts can be transformed into the non-addicted citizens from whom they are supposed to be distant; criticisms of treatment point to its oppressive, normalising effects or argue that in fact very little change happens at all. That treatment has benefits and shortfalls is not in dispute here. Our purpose has been to examine what and who is produced through treatment, and to argue that these new identities and ways of being cannot be comprehended in simplistic terms such as good/bad, successful/failed and stable/chaotic. From this argument, the next chapter takes up the crucial identity category of gender, and other binaries that are both reproduced and troubled through the intra-action of the 'subjects' of MMT.

5
Repetition and Rupture: The Gender of Agency

Addiction is commonly understood to be a problem of compulsion: the compulsion to repeat an activity that brings harm to the self, to others and to society as a whole. MMT is concerned with satisfying this compulsion, again through repetition – the repetition of dosing. Indeed, the interviews we conducted with MMT clients and service providers emphasise heavily the theme of repetition in treatment. There are several respects in which addiction is associated with femininity within Western society (Keire, 1998), and the compulsion positioned at the heart of addiction and treatment, along with the repetition that signifies and materialises it, are prime sites of this gendering (other sites were also described earlier). As we argued in Chapter 1, this association with the feminine is partly responsible for the stigmatisation of addiction, indeed, for the construction of addiction as a meaningful problem in the first place. Conversely, however, the specifics of addiction and of treatment for addiction also construct gender in particular ways. In this chapter we build on the observations we have already made about gender and addiction to explore some of the ways in which MMT materialises differently for men and women, how the values and practices enacted with it rely upon and co-produce certain forms of femininity and masculinity, and equally, how notions of femininity and masculinity shape how treatment is understood. To do this we focus on a prominent issue in accounts of treatment, one directly related to the question of compulsion and repetition, and which has been alluded to in previous chapters: that of agency. We begin with a brief discussion of the literature on gender and MMT, highlighting some of the concrete ways in which the two phenomena intra-act in the research findings reported, and follow this with discussion of an aspect of the work of Simone de Beauvoir, which we then use to think through the gender of repetition. Having established the ways in which repetition is gendered in the feminine in Western liberal discourse, we go on to examine in detail the interview participants' constructions of gender in their statements on the clinical encounter, and on two factors that influence treatment practice: heterosexual relationships and gender violence. In the final section, we consider repetition from the point of view of Judith Butler's work on the performativity of gender, posing questions as to how repetition might be thought differently in relation to MMT. Thus, our argument attends to the gendering of MMT in a double sense: first in terms of the everyday conditions of treatment that affect men and women differently, and second in terms of some of the gender implications of the very notion of the 'everyday' itself – that is *routine* and *repetition*.

Little formally reported national data exist on methadone use in Australia, but it is thought that overall around twice as many men as women are enrolled in methadone programs.[1] Thus, while numbers of men and women in treatment are not equal, significant numbers of both sexes participate in the program each year, experiencing the program in different ways. The contemporary sociological, ethnographic and cultural studies literature on gender and pharmacotherapy is not extensive, but nevertheless elucidates some of these differences. As is the case in other areas of research, a focus on gender tends to mean a focus on women, as the implicit focus of most 'general' research is the circumstances and experiences of men. This is reflected in the scope of the work described below.

Perhaps most relevant to the issues under consideration here is the book *Surviving Heroin: Interviews with women in methadone clinics* by Friedman and Alicea (2001). As we noted in the Introduction, this book examines the social and political context of women's stories about drug use and treatment programs, deliberately avoiding an individualistic interpretation of addiction and recovery. The book is based on interviews conducted with 37 women in three treatment clinics in the southeast and midwest of the United States, providing a detailed source of data on the ways in which MMT encounters femininity to produce treatment experiences specific to female clients. The authors emphasise women's struggle to negotiate contemporary notions of the 'good' woman and 'good' mother in participating in treatment, and focus on resistance in women's interpretations of their own journeys through the 'heroin social world', hitting 'rock bottom', and the governing environment of the methadone clinic. For example, they argue that their participants 'rejected the status quo through their pursuit of pleasure' (204) via illicit drug-taking, but that at length this approach proved exhausting, leading them to choose a relatively routine and conventional life on treatment and the compromises this entails.

Like Friedman and Alicea, Banwell (2003) explores the agency of women in juggling MMT and motherhood. She describes the ways in which the drug-using Australian women she studied worked to maximise their efficacy as mothers and minimise any negative effects of drug use on their children. Although many described MMT as a means of achieving a more 'normal' life, they also noted that in re-enacting the drug-taking previously associated with heroin, they remained excluded from designations as normal women or mothers: 'Within the abstinence discourse they are still failures ... Thus their aspirations to the identity of a normal mother are accessible but not truly achievable through the medium of methadone. Instead they become a methadone mother, an identity that is not easily relinquished, nor as socially or morally valued as they would wish.' (2003: 31)

Catherine Waldby's 1986 report on pregnant women and women with children in NSW MMT programs describe many of the same issues noted above, and, despite the gap of 20 years since its publication, remains strikingly relevant. Waldby argues that a reliance upon the medical model of treatment and care tends to negatively impact on pregnant female clients, and by implication their children, by conceptualising the foetus as the primary medical client and the drug-using mother as, at best, an incubator, and, at worst, an obstacle to the health and well-being of the foetus. This can have far-reaching negative effects:

> Wherever the mother's interests and needs are regarded as antithetical to those of her child and relegated to second place, her incentive to cooperate with services in the care of her child is diminished.
>
> (1986: 83)

Waldby argues that treatment services need better training and resourcing for pregnant clients and women with children.

All these studies point to important ways in which MMT and the clinic are implicitly designed around male clients, rarely offering services such as childcare, or demonstrating awareness of issues such as the risk of gender-based violence among clients (see also Broom and Stevens, 1990; J. Fraser, 1997). As we will see later, many of these concerns are echoed in the interviews with participants in our study. Other gender issues related to treatment and the treatment environment are also highlighted. As in the literature above, agency and repetition emerges as an abiding theme in these interviews, and we focus on this to draw out our argument. In the process, we build on the existing approaches to women's agency in pharmacotherapy described above to consider the ways in which methadone treatment itself constructs particular gendered understandings of agency, and how these act in turn to materialise treatment in concrete ways.

Defining addiction

A key element in definitions of addiction is the notion of repetition. Consider, for example, the *Oxford English Dictionary*'s (1989) entry on addiction:

a. The, or a, state of being addicted to a drug (see ADDICTED *ppl. a.* 3b); a compulsion and need to continue taking a drug as a result of taking it in the past. Cf. *drug-addiction* s.v. DRUG *n.*[1] 1b.

Likewise, its definition of 'addicted' is as follows:

b. Dependent on the continued taking of a drug as a result of taking it in the past; having a compulsion to take a drug, the stopping of which produces withdrawal symptoms.

In both these entries the emphasis is on compulsion, and the continuation of past practice. The second contains a related element, that of the inability to 'stop'. Other sources also refer to compulsion and repetition. Savage et al.'s (2003) exploration of definitions of addiction demonstrates the ubiquity of notions of compulsion and repetition. Thus, for example, the current *International Classification of Diseases* terminology defines 'dependence syndrome' as involving withdrawal symptoms and tolerance, but specifies that these must be accompanied by 'compulsive use' to qualify as 'addiction' (Savage et al. 2003: 660). The *Diagnostic and Statistical Manual (Edition IV)* eschews the term 'addiction' in favour of 'dependence', yet its definition suggests close alignment to conventional understandings of addiction. Criterion three of 'substance dependence', for example, includes the twinned ideas of compulsion and repetition: 'substance often taken ... over a longer period than intended' (quoted in Savage et al. 2003: 660). Likewise, US federal and state policies use terms such as 'habitual' use of drugs and use of drugs on a 'continuous basis' (660).

This focus on repetition and compulsion as the essence of addiction finds expression also in critical scholarship. For example, as we explained in Chapter 3, David Lenson characterises addiction in terms of an altered relationship to time, that is, drug users experience time as 'atomised' instead of as wave-like. This atomisation emerges out of drug users' focus on administration of the drug, and the sense in which the time between these repeated moments of administration is somehow meaningless or dead time. Accordingly, and here we revisit an extract given in Chapter 3, Lenson argues that

> When the next dose comes is as important as what the drug actually does. This is partly because of the diminution of novelty: what began as a *kairos* – a special occasion or privileged moment – through repetition assumes the role of *chronos* or horizontal time. What characterises the condition of addiction is above all else the atomisation of time, the replacement of conventionally measured seconds, minutes, hours, and days with a different chronometry based on the tempo of administration. As a result, the drug's reordering of consciousness loses, over time, the elements of play and pleasure. It becomes as compulsory as a clock.
>
> (1995: 35)

Here, the emphasis is also on repetition and compulsion, and the sense that repetition precludes agency, creativity and enjoyment.

What does this emphasis on repetition in definitions of addiction mean for an analysis of gender and agency in MMT? To think this through, our first question might be, what is the status of 'repetition' within Western discourse? Middleton (1996: n.p.) provides a survey of this issue in a paper on repetition within music. He points out that repetition has long been associated with the absence of originality, with mass culture, with the status quo:

> From Baudelaire through Nietzsche, Freud and Adorno to Barthes, Derrida and Deleuze: the sign of critique, the moment of jouissance, is rupture, a break with the code, a transgression. The terms of debate are set, it would seem, with repetition at one side, shock at the other.

This organisation of repetition as located in a binary relation to the new, to progress or innovation, is reflected and produced in the ways repetition has been used to co-produce the categories of 'folk' and 'black' (especially African) art and culture. Likewise, it has been associated with the feminine, both through attention to women's consumption of popular culture (such as through the reading of romance novels in the

nineteenth century, and more recently in the consumption of magazines and daytime television) and through longstanding associations
between women and 'natural cycles' such as menstruation and reproduction (see Middleton, 1996; Huyssen, 1986). As Middleton (n.p.)
explains, cultural products associated with any of these categories –
blacks, the folk, women and the masses – have been denigrated as
'objects of reproduction, devoid of historical grandeur'.

There are many ways in which repetition figures as feminine in
Western thought, and simultaneously judged inferior. Indeed, the reference to 'reproduction' above is a clue to this. Simone de Beauvoir's
canonical work, *The Second Sex*, is a particularly vivid example of the
denigration of repetition, although her intention diverges, of course,
from most instantiations of this figuration in that she aims to benefit
the status and circumstances of women. In elaborating her gendered
approach to the existentialist themes of immanence and transcendence,
and the ways in which these illuminate the standing of women in the
middle of the twentieth century, de Beauvoir argues that repetition
figures especially strongly in relation to femininity (via, for example,
reproduction and housework). In doing so, she both highlights and sub-
scribes to (though in no simple way) the alignment of repetition, femininity, and impaired or absent agency described above. Thus, for
example, she depicts the 'housewife' as follows: 'Few tasks are more like
the torture of Sisyphus than housework with its endless repetition ...
The housewife wears herself out marking time: she makes nothing,
simply perpetuates the present.' (1984: 470) On reproduction she is
equally insistent that women are trapped in repetition: 'Her misfortune
is to have been biologically destined for the repetition of Life'. Earlier
she makes clear what kind of process reproduction is: 'this creation
results only in repeating the same Life in more individuals' (1984: 96).

These extracts are also quoted in Penelope Deutscher's (2006) paper on
de Beauvoir and repetition. Deutscher challenges the accepted view that
de Beauvoir simply dismisses reproduction and housework as inherently
valueless, as mere repetition, that she is simply echoing masculine values.
In Deutscher's view, de Beauvoir's objection is more that women reproduce activities and roles (themselves at least understood culturally to
constitute nothing more than mere repetition) out of habit – repetition –
itself (2006: 331). It is this repetition, that of habit and stereotype, that
de Beauvoir sees as the main problem with becoming a mother and
housewife (although it does seem she argues that the 'repetitious' acts
women undertake in these 'habitual' roles mean they participate in a
double whammy of repetition). Whether or not de Beauvoir's objection

to reproduction and housework, and her view of women's activities, are as Deutscher argues, there is no doubt that repetition per se figures in her thesis in thoroughly negative terms. As Deutscher notes, 'So, repetition is depicted as animal, dehumanising, a-temporal, death-like, unrewarding, unstimulating, boring, uncreative' (2006: 335). In this, femininity is portrayed in *The Second Sex* as possessing an especially potent (if not essential) relationship to the denigrated notion of repetition.

Across these literatures, then, we can link a series of intra-active ideas: addiction, repetition and femininity, all mutually constitutive, all associated with an absence or impairment of agency, and all judged inferior to the masculine values of autonomy, creativity and activity. In this sense, it would appear that MMT, itself associated with addiction, is likely to figure in culture, and thus to materialise, in terms of repetition, passivity and femininity. Indeed, as we explained in Chapter 4, Lenson himself points out that the origin of the word 'addiction' relates to the Latin *addicere*, meaning to say or pronounce, to decree or bind. This etymology references loss of control over language and of consciousness. That is, and again it is worth revisiting an extract given earlier, it asserts that drug users are 'already "spoken for", bound and decreed. Instead of *saying*, one is *said*' (1995: 35). Given the centrality of language to Western liberal formulations of the subject, this has significant implications for understandings of addiction in liberal societies. Where regular drug use is designated by a term that implies the inability to generate or enact speech; where, indeed, the drug user is designated by the ontological state of being defined rather than by the ontological act of defining (that is, of passivity rather than activity) addiction comes to be aligned with an ontological deficit in agency. As Lenson notes, through the representation of regular drug use as a kind of surrender to (and of) the powers of speech, 'the addict is changed from a subject to an object' (35).[2] How does this figuration of addiction as repetition and absence of agency help shape the phenomenon of treatment? What implications for women in treatment might it have? These questions will be explored via an analysis of the treatment of men's and women's agency in interview material on methadone programs.

Constructing Sisyphus

We have already argued that addiction, repetition, femininity and lack of agency are connected in Western discourse. This alignment of concepts is directly relevant to MMT in that, as we argued in Chapter 1, opioid pharmacotherapy is understood to be a form of addiction as much as a treatment for it. Chapters 2 and 3 built on this observation to argue that methadone treatment clients are understood to possess compromised, or pathological agency due to their status as addicts. Here, we want to expand on this analysis by drawing explicit links between these understandings of agency and understandings of pharmacotherapy as intensely repetitive. As we will see, the conceptualisation of treatment as mere repetition has significant implications for the perception of clients, both male and female, as lacking agency.

Central to the experience of treatment for clients, it seems, is the sense that onsite dosing constitutes a repetitive daily burden, emblematic of the low status drug users hold in society. Sydney treatment client Alison, for instance, has spent several years on the program and currently accesses four takeaways per week. When asked what the removal of takeaways would mean to her, she replies:

> Well, [you'd have] no choice. Either [daily dosing] or be sick. It would be just like having to go and get a shot every day, basically. That's exactly what it would mean to me, just like back to square one.
> (Alison, Sydney, NSW, client, 44)

Alison's remarks indicate the role of repetition in her understanding of heroin addiction, as well as her sense that MMT has the capacity to repeat the repetition of heroin addiction. Also clear, in her use of expressions such as 'no choice' and 'having to', is the sense in which addiction and treatment both involve passivity, forms of compulsion and a lack of opportunity for self-determination.

Melbourne client Cameron, too, sees MMT in terms of repetition: 'It's like you don't achieve nothing, you just go up and down without achieving anything. It's like a roller coaster ride. And that's the hard part' (Cameron, Melbourne, Victoria, client, 42). Like Alison, Cameron presents takeaways as able to introduce an element of flexibility disruptive of the otherwise pure repetition of treatment. Danny (Sydney, NSW, client, 46) appears to feel the same way. Without takeaways, he says, 'I just don't think there's any light at the end of the tunnel, going every day and weekends too. Oh no, no, I just wouldn't do it.' Darren (Sydney, NSW, client, 47) makes a similar point. As he succinctly puts it, 'All of a sudden you've got this appointment you've got to make every day and it drives a lot of people nuts.'

Daily dosing is mandatory in Victoria in the first two months in treatment, and in NSW in the first three months in treatment, and remains common among clients in their first year in both jurisdictions (NSW Health, 2006; Drugs and Poisons Regulations Group, 2006). After this time, clients are closely assessed for suitability for access to takeaways, and many receive only one per week, at least in their first year. The remarks made above reflect clients' experiences of this practice of daily, or near daily, dosing. Ryan, who at the time of interview was still required to attend every day for dosing, clarifies further the impact of this dailiness of treatment for many:

> Um, it's the liquid handcuffs routine. It's like being on parole or on bail where you have to report every day. You have to, you know, you're locked into going to a chemist every day and it does play tricks on you. It does make you think that you've lost some sort of freedom and you have got a prison sentence.
>
> (Ryan, Sydney, NSW, client, 39)

In referring to liquid handcuffs, Ryan makes use of a common analogy for MMT, one we have explored elsewhere in this book, arguing that it operates as a powerful metaphor that intra-acts with other factors in treatment to co-produce clients and their daily experiences in terms of entrapment and surveillance. His other comments likening daily dosing to other aspects of the criminal justice system reveal the extent to which the repetition involved in treatment constitutes a form of constraint on agency ('freedom') for many, and both assume and require passivity.

In these extracts there is a strong sense in which MMT's mandating of a period of daily dosing helps shape perceptions of treatment as a whole. While takeaways alleviate this dailiness to some degree, clients regard their continuing provision as fragile – easily lost – either at the hands of individual service providers or shifts in policy. This fragility tends to constitute treatment as always either actually or potentially highly repetitive and constraining. Service providers are not unaware of this, as the following remarks indicate:

> But you can imagine, two or three years in a program, you'd be getting mighty sick of fronting up every day.
>
> (Beverley, Melbourne, nurse/case worker, 50s)

> In time, they all get fed up with the routine as much as we try to make it quick and not unpleasant for them.
>
> (George, Sydney, NSW, pharmacist, 55)

Some clients explain that the repetition associated with daily dosing is all the more arduous when it is associated with the repetition involved in long-term treatment. In a few cases, these issues were framed within yet another context of repetition, that of intergenerational methadone attendance:

> You know, there's guys in their forties and fifties who have been on the methadone merry-go-round for, you know, twenty-five years. My uncle has been on it for nearly thirty years, and it's just never ending, yeah. Just awful.
>
> (Sam, regional Victoria, client, 31)

This last quote also indicates the extent to which, leaving aside the practical sense in which MMT constitutes a form of repetition through daily dosing, it also functions symbolically for some as mere repetition of heroin addiction itself. Sam laments the fact that some clients do not move on from treatment. This objection to repetition or continuation per se can be read as a criticism of MMT as too much like the repetitiveness or continuation of drug use itself. In this respect, MMT is reminiscent of de Beauvoir's critique of housework and reproduction: it not only adds up to repetition through individual daily acts, but always already comprises repetition through its perceived recapitulation of the status quo: women reproducing femininity out of habit; clients reproducing addiction out of habit.

Gender and agency

Clearly, MMT figures as mere repetition for many of those involved in the program, both service providers and clients. Also evident in many accounts is a sense of the obstacle to agency that this repetition represents. Inasmuch as repetition is aligned here with femininity, passivity and addiction, MMT must be aligned with these. How are these alignments co-produced? How do they signify and play out materially? As we will see, the alignment of femininity with repetition and its companion concept, passivity or absence of agency, helps shape relationships, processes and treatment decisions. Yet these do not operate in the same ways for male and female clients. Perhaps most useful for the argument we are making here is the room the alignment of addiction, repetition, agency and femininity discussed above leaves for acknowledging the differences between representations of male and female clients. After all, it is more than likely that the intra-actions between notions of femininity and women in treatment will produce different effects from those between femininity and men in treatment. Following Barad's formulation of agential reality, each materialises in specific ways in its encounter with the other. Importantly, our approach to gender matches that taken to other phenomena discussed in the book in that we see gender as made in intra-action. Gender is co-produced via treatment and treatment is co-produced via gender. Indeed all the concepts discussed above: gender, agency, repetition and passivity gather meaning only in their intra-action with each other and with other concepts and material objects. In this sense they do not pre-exist the encounter: the nature of their intra-action and effects cannot be taken for granted, as we will see. De Beauvoir notes, for example, that there are some men, such as working-class male factory workers, for whom repetition (or for our purposes, 'repetition' and all that certain understandings of it entail) is also constraining of agency. This does not mean, however, this process is identical in effects to those experienced by women.

Many of the ways in which gender figures in treatment are implicit in the design and processes of treatment. In Chapter 3 we described the lack of attention paid to client security at dosing points, and this too affects men and women differently, operating under a look-after-yourself ethos common to mainstream constructions of masculinity, but serving neither male nor female clients well. Some constructions of gender, however, are more explicit, emerging, as they do, in the comments healthcare professionals make about their work with clients. Aaron, for example, talks about the clinical encounter, describing some of his female clients as follows:

Aaron: I'm terrible with manipulative young females. In that I, you know, I tend to sort of think, you know, I'm not good for them. If I get someone who is real, you know, borderline personality disorder female, I just sort of see red immediately. I think, 'I'm not, I won't be good for you'. So, you know, I'm better off to say to them, 'look, this is not going to work with us'.

Interviewer: Yeah. And would you forward them on to someone else?

Aaron: Yeah sometimes I will, or [...] I'll tell them what my problem is, you know. I'll say, 'Look, sometimes people who carry on the way you've just carried on annoy the crap out of me, and I can't deal with that, so, you know, if you're going to carry on like this when you see me, I'm going to say to you "move on"'. And they go, 'Oh'. Sometimes it's actually worked, you know, they've pulled their fingers out [...] and then we're okay. But I know that about me, that I'm not therapeutic necessarily for some of them. And I don't think it's in their interest for me to carry on like that either, so I've got to sort of say 'well I'm not good for them, so get out of it'.

Interviewer: [...] Yeah, so [can] I get a bit of an idea of what sort of situa-tions you're talking about?

Aaron: Just where, you know, some of them have got all the jargon of everything and then you sort of get ... the story just comes out all down pat. They constantly dig at you. Um, you can't sort of get a word in edgeways. They'll be smiling at you while they're saying things like, you know, what their mother has done and hasn't done to them, and everybody else has done, and I'm thinking this is inappropriate rubbish. And I find that it just, you know, it starts to annoy me, and I'm thinking 'you're the problem, not everybody else'.

(Aaron, Melbourne, Victoria, prescriber, 59)

There is much that could be said about Aaron's remarks. They follow statements about the importance of being 'realistic' about what clients can achieve, and the likelihood that clients will create problems for themselves and others. Of particular relevance to our argument is the way in which gender is explicitly addressed, and expectations of femi-ninity, in particular around agency, are elaborated. In, for example, speaking so much that Aaron cannot 'get a word in edgeways', and in commandeering the very psy 'jargon' that Aaron employs himself ('borderline personality disorder'), the 'manipulative young female' client transgresses traditional ideals of femininity as quiet, retiring and subject to, rather than sovereign of, expert discourse. At the same time, in voicing difficult histories, in requiring of Aaron that he engage emo-tionally with them, these clients also enact familiar notions of feminine excess. As such, it seems they are both too feminine, and not feminine enough, and this ambiguous feminine agency is enacted through vari-ous forms of repetition, from the re-telling of the 'down pat' story and the constant 'digging' to the recycling of 'jargon'.

These understandings of feminine agency on Aaron's part are partic-ularly important in that they have practical implications. Aaron makes clear that where young women in this way are present, they are some-times declined treatment and referred on to another prescriber. The implications of this last sequence of events for clients – that is, of iden-tifying a prescriber, meeting with the prescriber, providing the prescriber with details about past history, then being referred on in the terms described above – are not explored in the interview, but it is clear they would be significant and very likely negative. We have already noted (see the Introduction and Chapter 2) that inadequate treatment places mean there is a high unmet demand for treatment in Australia. In describing these circumstances Aaron acknowledges his professional and personal limits. It would, therefore, be inaccurate to suggest that he locates the 'problem' solely in the clients. Yet, given that methadone prescribers are not always easy to find, ethical questions persist about Aaron's willingness to wash his hands of clients he finds too challenging.

These issues are especially important in that Aaron appears to relish his work with other (male) clients whose behaviour might be considered equally or more challenging, if rather different. Below he describes his experiences with these clients and with another (male) prescriber. In the process he references traditional constructions of masculine agency as both informed – and properly controlled – by the threat of violence:

> **Aaron:** But, you know [...] I think there are some doctors who practice in a way that they would be totally done over. I mean, I had one bloke come to me for a bit of mentoring one morning, and because I knew he'd been being stood over in his practice. [...] I'd arranged to get my worst clients there that day, told them what it was about, and [...] the first one comes and says, 'Oh, Jesus doc, I couldn't get a fucking park'. And this guy has gone red already. I thought, 'We're in for a good day here' [...] And I then gave him to my colleague for the second half of the day, and I said, 'What do you think?' And [colleague] just shook his head and said, 'Shouldn't be doing it'.
>
> *Interviewer: And what is it that you think is a required attribute to do –*
>
> **Aaron:** Do it?
>
> *Interviewer: Yeah, successfully.*
>
> **Aaron:** Oh, I think you've got to be a low class prick like me (both laugh). I think you've got to be able to function on all levels. I've never had a problem, I'm not intimidated by it, um, I'm fifty-nine years old now, and most people sort of deal with me as a nearly sixty-year-old. You know, I [give as] good as I get, pretty much. I think you've got to be able to do that. You don't get right down in the gutter with them, but you can go down there if you need to. [...] I tell them that, basically, in the words of the vernacular. I mean, I will say to some of them that I think might be a problem [...] 'Don't muck me around', I say, 'because I can fuck you over a lot harder than you can do it to me, so just remember that'. And they sort of go, 'Ooh, gee' [...] And after that they're right. Most of my clients I get on really well with, and they'd do anything for me.

Interviewer: Yeah, yep.

Aaron: Um, the odd one will give you trouble, and occasionally you have to remind them [...] 'I'm the one who calls the shots here, not you, and remember that because you start carrying on, you're going to be out of here so quick you won't even know how you got out'. [...] I remember there was a bit of a carry-on outside my door a month ago, and I sort of flew out to see what it was, and [client] was swearing at [colleague] and carrying on, and [colleague] was saying, 'Just get the fuck out of here', you know. This is in the middle of the waiting room. And the bloke is going, 'You bastard, you', you know, and I just looked at him and I said, 'Hey [...] this is our place not yours. You do what you're told here, so get outside. Cool down, when you're ready I'll come and get you.' You know, he looked at me as though he wasn't going to do it, and I said, 'I mean it', and grabbed him by the scruff of the neck and started dragging him out the door, you see. And they just do it. I think if I was twenty years, thirty years younger they might fight back. But they don't, now, particularly if they see that I really mean what I'm saying.

(Aaron, Melbourne, Victoria, prescriber, 59)

This account is rich in detail. Most relevant here is the masculine economy of implied and explicit violence mobilised in Aaron's management strategy. The contrast between the circumstances under which female clients are judged too difficult and referred on, and male clients are confronted but ultimately retained in treatment, is striking. What might account for this contrast? It is as though Aaron materialises as two different practitioners in his encounters with these different clients. Or, more specifically, he *dematerialises* as a practitioner altogether in his encounter with the 'manipulative' female clients he describes. It could be argued that, unlike the behaviour of these female clients, that of the male client described is essentially in keeping with gender norms in its conventionally masculine resort to aggression and the threat of violence. This might partially explain Aaron's relative comfort with the client. Equally, however, it might be argued that the male client is feminised in the account in that he is reminded who 'calls the shots', and depicted as having to submit to Aaron. This is a complex issue. In keeping with the alignment of addiction, repetition, passivity and the feminine described earlier, the data leave no doubt that contemporary notions of addiction, and the arrangements in place around MMT, often intra-act to co-produce both women and men as passive. Yet this particular case is ambiguous. After all, Aaron accounts for the client's submission largely by assuming that the client exercised ethical restraint in declining to respond to Aaron violently (the ethical consideration being Aaron's age). In other words, Aaron suggests that the client could well have dominated him physically, but chose not to. In this sense, his access to agency is not entirely denied by Aaron. The comments presented here begin to suggest some of the ways in which gender norms and stereotypes around agency shape treatment. Women are accorded agency here, but it is represented as pathological, particularly in relation to certain forms of repetition. Men are also accorded agency, but Aaron makes clear he is far more at home with the tenor and implications of this agency.

A rather different example of the ways in which the gendering of agency affects treatment relates to understandings of heterosexual drug-using couples. Sydney pharmacist George, for instance, talks about his observation that some female clients return to illicit drug use after establishing or re-establishing a sexual relationship with a man. In doing so, he assumes a dynamic of 'influence' between men and women clients:

> Then there were the other ones where girls would be stable [...] they'd meet an old boyfriend, they'd have a one-night stand sort of thing, and bang, before you knew it – these guys must have massive powers of persuasion or they're sexually so empowered, you know – they've got this hold over their women and they seem to make them do what they want. Then, whether it's a self-esteem thing with the women that these guys came around and tell them they love them or whatever, the women just seem to fall for it and bang, you can see them go downhill and then they have to come back up again [methadone dose must be increased].
>
> (George, Sydney, NSW, pharmacist, 55)

In one sense this account treats female clients rather favourably in that their return to (repetition of?) illicit drug use is attributed to the bad influence of male partners rather than to their own malign agency. Of course, in doing so it reflects faithfully gender stereotypes of masculine activity and feminine passivity and impressionability. It is equally possible that the male partners described here had also been abstaining from illicit drug use prior to their contact with the female partners, and that both partners returned to illicit drug use simultaneously. Alternatively, it might be that contact with the male partners offered the female partners easier access to cash or illicit drugs, and that they acted upon this opportunity to resume illicit drug use. There are many alternative interpretations of the pattern described by George, some of which can be found in our interviews with clients. Melissa, for example, describes her own experience of renewing contact with a past sexual partner in rather different terms, suggesting as she does so some of the complexities of the relationship, and its impact:

> *Interviewer: And so, and so you were injecting the bupe [buprenorphine] for a while?*
>
> **Melissa**: Yes.
>
> *Interviewer: Yep.*
>
> **Melissa**: I was doing that, and then, um, and then I jumped off, and then started dabbling, I was starting to use again. My boyfriend got out of jail, and we both started using again together. Well, then I ended up falling pregnant with [child]. So then I changed back to the methadone program because I didn't know the effects of the bupe for my baby, because they didn't know what the effects were yet.
>
> (Melissa, Melbourne, Victoria, client, 35)

In this account Melissa reports involvement in illicit activity (the injection of buprenorphine, the occasional use of heroin) prior to renewing contact with her partner. It is not clear whether she had 'jumped off' methadone (abandoned the program) before resuming contact with him or whether she decided to do so as a sresult of the resumption of their relationship. In any case, following the resumption of contact they both began consuming heroin regularly until Melissa discovered her pregnancy. At this point she re-evaluated her heroin use, electing to return to pharmacotherapy treatment, this time to methadone treatment as, unlike buprenorphine, it is widely recognised as safe for pregnant women and their foetuses.

Melissa's account describes circumstances that, from a pharmacist's viewpoint such as that of George, might well look like the effects of the undue influence of a male partner. Yet, as we have seen, Melissa was involved in illicit activity prior to her partner's return (something a pharmacist would not necessarily know). She resumed regular heroin use in tandem with her partner, but there is no reason to assume her partner instigated or drove this. When her pregnancy was discovered, Melissa made a decision to return to treatment, actively choosing between methadone and buprenorphine. In sum, Melissa's account indicates both how a gendered 'bad influence' theory of agency might seem to make sense to those witnessing client relationships, and how such a theory, and its implication that women are able only to repeat their past or the wishes of men, may oversimplify (or even misconstrue) events as understood by clients. As will be demonstrated later, the tendency to accord agency to male drug users and the passivity or compliance of repetition to female drug users impacts materially on some aspects of treatment, for example, in access to takeaway doses where women are known to have a partner who is taking illicit drugs.

Beverley's approach to the question of the effects of sexual relationships on resumption of drug use among female clients is different again:

> **Beverley**: You can enable them and empower them, and I think that's a role I've enjoyed a lot, and I've seen it work, and I think it's good fun, that part of it. But, of course it's disappointing when you see them slide backwards. Usually associated with a partner coming out of jail, but ...
>
> *Interviewer: Right, right.*
>
> **Beverley**: Who is the last person they should be hanging around with.
>
> *Interviewer: Yeah, right. That must be hard to advise people on.*
>
> **Beverley**: Well a lot of, ah, women relapse into heroin use for that reason, to survive those sort of relationships. I mean, there's no rocket science in that.
>
> (Beverley, Melbourne, Victoria, nurse/case worker, 50s)

In this formulation of the relationship between renewed contact with past male partners and resumption of illicit drug use, Beverley both downplays women agency and assumes it. On the one hand, women are described as passively repeating the past in 'sliding' back into abusive relationships, and 'relapsing' into drug use, while on the other they are depicted as actively self-medicating to 'survive' these relationships. Like George, and notably unlike client Melissa, Beverley presents the male partner as the source of corruption. As will be discussed later, the threat and fact of gender-based violence is referred to by many study participants. Our intention in analysing the depiction of agency in these accounts is not to deny the challenges women face in their relationships with men, or the structural problem of male violence in drug-using social worlds as in others. Rather, our point is that in this material, repetition and agency, innocence and culpability, are often ascribed rather uncritically along gender lines. This ascription tends to exonerate women, at the cost of full acknowledgement of their agential subjecthood.

The approach to agency indicated here is similar to Aaron's in that both suggest some discomfort with women's agency, in particular with women's agential undertaking of challenging or criminal behaviour. Thus, Aaron avoids this agency by refusing to treat 'manipulative' women, and George and Beverley deny it by accounting for women's conduct via the agency of male partners. All three produce agency as gendered along traditional lines (although in ascribing women some legitimate agency as 'survivors', Beverley's account is rather more complex than that of Aaron or George). These co-productions of gendered agency in the views and assumptions of service providers is significant both because of the specific events and practices they institute and reflect (such as Aaron's referral of some female clients) *and* because they contribute to the gender dynamics of MMT more broadly.

Indeed, the issue of repetition, agency and gender in treatment is not confined to the relationship between heterosexual partnerships and illicit drug-taking. It also bears on one of the most commonly evoked gender themes in the interviews: that of domestic violence. The following comments, made by prescriber and policymaker Barry in describing his experiences of treating clients, indicate some of this crossover:

I don't like the fact that some of my clients do really shonky things. Male clients of mine who beat their wives up, I think are scum of the earth and should be battered around the head. Regardless of what experience they've had [...] If I see women who are abused I will very strongly [tell them] 'There are services here that you can go to, you do not have to go back to this, blah blah blah.' And when the psychopathic men talk to me like this, you know, I will feed back and say, 'This is not an acceptable right of behaviour, I don't care what your wife has said. There is nothing you can possibly tell me that says she deserved to be smacked.' You know, and it's not colluding with crap like that [...] I remember being in an A&E [Accident and Emergency] department once, four o'clock in the morning, some eighteen-year-old girl came in, black and blue, bruised ribs, and she was saying, 'There's my Johnny, he really loves me, he's really sorry for what he did.' And Johnny turned up at about half-past-four, and wants his girlfriend, and I just had to go and get the nurse to go and see him, because I wanted to smack him.

(Barry, Sydney, NSW, policy/prescriber, 40)

As with some of the extracts reproduced above, this response is dense and extremely vivid. Barry indicates a high degree of clarity on the ethical status of male violence against women, that is, that it is never justified. This is laudable and, in that he reports making concerted efforts to inform women of their options where domestic violence is involved, he might be effective in dealing with these issues. In the context of this chapter, however, it is also important to consider the ways in which agency is constructed in his description. Perhaps most striking about the account, beyond its generally heightened language (perhaps appropriate for the topic), is the use of figures of speech that themselves reference violence. In this respect, Barry compares rather closely with Aaron, in that both take for granted an economy (however symbolic) of violence between men. His account also tends to emphasise his own agency in dealing with domestic violence rather than that of the women he encounters, in that the women are depicted (namelessly) only in terms of being informed and enjoined by *him* to act to change their circumstances. Similarly, his portrait of the teenage girl focuses on her acceptance of her partner's violence – her willingness to 'go back to', to return to, to *repeat*, the relationship as is. As above, Barry's remarks tend to reproduce gender along traditional lines, with female clients seen as passively willing to repeat the circumstances of their abuse, even as the remarks also indicate a valuable awareness of gender-based violence.

Beverley, too, makes graphic reference to domestic violence experienced by the female clients she works with:

> I think people who are significantly unwell with addiction almost always have a co-existing mental health problem [...] And the other thing of course that's overlooked time and time again [...] is the significance of any acquired brain injury that these people have, due to this chronic relapsing remitting condition of addiction. Most of my work has been with women [who] have significant histories of domestic violence where their heads have been pounded up against walls, on floors, kicked. They've overdosed several times, they've been exposed to doing some pretty horrendous things to get their needs met and their partners' needs met, in terms of supplying the goods. So they've got a lot of trauma. That's not even going anywhere near any childhood sexual abuse, physical abuse and neglect, abandonment, blah, blah, blah. Giving up their children, all that stuff, which is significant for women, as you would appreciate. And [...] I get a bit passionate about that. And I really do see way past the addiction stuff to all the other stuff. I work with the people I work with in a very holistic way.
>
> (Beverley, Melbourne, Victoria, nurse/case worker, 50s)

This discussion also positions women in at best an oblique relation to agency, drawing together a range of factors in which lines of causation are ultimately ambiguous. Beverley begins by stating her conviction that many of the women clients she deals with suffer from acquired brain injury caused by 'chronic relapsing remitting' heroin addiction. Yet her following comments suggest that it is domestic violence that is the cause. She then lists a number of other life events and circumstances associated with addiction, again leaving causal lines unclarified. It seems that Beverley's focus is on the female client as a whole, and the constellation of issues she might face. Yet it is the repetition of drug use – women's repetitious return to drug use – that is at the heart of their problems. In this framework, female clients are presented largely as the target of abuse and disadvantage, rather than as agents. For example, Beverly says of the women: 'They've been exposed to doing some pretty horrendous things to get their needs met and their partners' needs met'. Here, the agency of female clients is muffled by the initial passive construction, 'been exposed to'. The use of the term 'needs' further mitigates agency by suggesting compulsion or necessity. Located between these semantic bookends, of course, is the observation that women actively carry out difficult tasks for their own reasons and to support their partners. There is no doubt that women face significant structural disadvantage in Western culture and elsewhere, and that sexual assault and domestic violence enact and reinforce women's disadvantage. Yet recognition of the structural should not necessarily preclude recognition of agency. Indeed, as many feminists have argued (see Fraser, 2003: 76–7), without a theory of women's agency, change in women's status is literally inconceivable.

Simon, too, refers to the threat and fact of domestic violence faced by some women in methadone treatment:

> I think [...] people are often stood over for their dose, and sometimes that can be from partners and I think probably more often than not it's from people they know or from partners. And I'm sure it's generally males standing over women. I'm sure it could happen [that] women stand over women and other things, but generally I think it's usually the blokes standing over the women. Sometimes, you know, they've both tried to get on a program and maybe only one person's been able to get on or the other person's just reluctant to get on the program for whatever reason, maybe because they've got a partner they can stand over to get methadone from.
>
> (Simon, Sydney, NSW, case worker, 32)

The construction of agency in this extract bears some similarity to those in the extracts above in that the malign agency of (some) men is fore-grounded, and that of women is backgrounded. In broad terms, masculine agency is formulated as relatively unimpeded, while feminine agency is accorded limits or constraints. Thus, while male drug users are thought to menace various acquaintances and partners for methadone, female drug users are thought to do so only with other women. Even where Simon implies that it is female drug users who act to enrol themselves in methadone programs, this activity is framed by an emphasis on the impli-cations of this access to methadone for male drug users, and the sugges-tion that such acts primarily operate in the service of the male drug users. In this respect Simon's comments correspond with Beverley's and Barry's: women's agency is minimised by a greater focus on men's agency.

In all of these examples, women's experiences of domestic violence are understood in a framework that emphasises male agency (the instigation of independent, if malign, acts) and female passivity (the relapse into repeated acts). This tendency to view women as objects of male agency rather than agents in their own right, and as destined either to repeat the past or reproduce the desires and needs of men, is significant because it co-constructs women's experiences of treatment materially. Notably, it can affect their access to highly valued takeaway doses. Where, for example, female clients are known to be associating with male illicit drug users, service providers sometimes withhold takeaways on the basis that they might be passed on. As we noted in Chapter 2, service providers interpret the treatment guidelines differently, and these inter-pretations (as well as the scope available for interpretation) also help materialise treatment in particular ways. As Anya explains:

> Yes, I'm usually probably a bit more – stricter for women who have got a partner who's an active heroin user, and I would just say 'no', even if she'd been compliant with the program and she'd been good, she'd been all right.
>
> (Anya, Melbourne, Victoria, prescriber, 45)

Elliot presents a similar approach to evaluating the appropriateness of takeaway access:

> We often meet the mothers during pregnancy, and are involved even before, sometimes, the child is born, so we know that there are high-risk circumstances in the home environment. Um, we might have knowledge that, that the father or the spouse [...] is abusive and also

may steal methadone, and she might divulge that in a confidential meeting, but she doesn't want to take action. All those sorts of things.

(Elliot, Melbourne, Victoria, policy, 51)

Elliot makes clear that the presence of a drug-using male partner, especially one who might illicitly access methadone supplied in takeaway doses, can lead to female clients being denied access to takeaways themselves. It is notable that none of the participants we interviewed refers to reciprocal circumstances in which a male client's domestic arrangements with a female drug user were inquired into, or used to evaluate his access to takeaways.

Clients too make reference to domestic violence in the interviews. As with Melissa's account of the dynamics between heterosexual couples, the understandings of power and agency at work in them do not always correspond with those of the service providers. For example, Linda (mother of a child who was a very young baby at the time of interview) describes her past involvement in a violent relationship and the impact of this on her dose levels:

Interviewer: So you're still on the same dose as what you started on?

Linda: Yeah, yeah. I've like, they say to me, 'we better put you up, we better put you up.' I don't want to go up.

Interviewer: Why do they want to put you up?

Linda: Ahh, because I've had a lot of stress. I was in a relationship for thirteen years and he bashed me, you know, and I was pissed all the time and I [...] went to see my doctor last week, the week before, and I said 'you know, I'd like to come down a bit.' He said, 'not with the baby, because you're stressing at the moment, you're only going to stress even more if we start bringing you down', and they said 'how about we wait till the baby's four or five years old before we start to bring you down.' And I said, 'Well, meanwhile, what happens?'

(Linda, Sydney, NSW, client, 38)

In this extract Linda makes reference to her involvement in an abusive relationship and to a co-existing drinking problem without directly according causal agency for the drinking to the abuse or the abuser. Agency is most clearly evoked in the suggestion she makes to her doctor that her dose be reduced. Linda's account suggests that the doctor responds to her agency by resisting it: not only should Linda's dose remain the same while she is experiencing the stress of new motherhood and of the conclusion of her abusive relationship (or of the residue of this relationship), she should abandon her intention of reducing for at least four more years. Linda's frustrated agency is revealed in her final question, 'Meanwhile, what happens?'

There are many other instances of the gendering of agency as outlined above, which, for want of space, we cannot elaborate on here. Most importantly, Linda's anecdote, along with those analysed above, bears directly on the chapter's central set of questions: how does the gendering of agency and repetition in methadone treatment materialise treatment in particular ways? Likewise, how does treatment materialise gender in particular ways? So far we have seen that this gendering can potentially affect which clients are seen by which service providers, and how readily some clients are retained in a program while others are referred elsewhere. We have also seen that particular formulations of gender issues such as pregnancy and domestic violence can sometimes dominate service providers' responses to women's agency.

In all these respects, then, gendered notions of agency and repetition form treatment. We can see, for example, how female clients are presumed to be dominated by their partners at the same time they are understood to be properly subject to the power of service providers themselves. Indeed, in some cases, there is the sense of a power struggle taking place between service providers and male partners through the bodies and subjectivities of female clients. The same cannot be said of male clients. There is no doubt that, as suggested in the alignments described earlier, male clients too are in some ways 'feminised' in MMT (that is, co-produced as possessing stereotypically feminine attributes such as passivity). Thus, as we saw in Aaron's account, male clients are frequently reminded that the clinic is not their domain, that 'rules' have been established by others and that they must simply follow them. Yet, as also noted above, male clients are not described as subject to surveillance around their partners as are female clients. In short, they appear to be conceptualised less relationally, more autonomously, and as less subject to or responsible for, their partners, than are women. In this respect, female and male clients are positioned differently in terms of power. Both are understood to be subject to the power of service providers and the treatment system as a whole. This power relation is often presented by service providers as benign, indeed it is understood by some to be part of the therapeutic action of MMT. As Phillip argues:

> You know, it's like a parenting role and if you don't set limits you can cause disasters for your kids. But if you have no limits, they grow up uncontained and chaotic.
>
> (Phillip, Sydney, NSW, prescriber, 53)

This is not to say Philip is unaware of the problems associated with the repetition involved in mandatory daily dosing. Indeed, he argues that the centrality of repetition to treatment requires a handing over of agency for clients:

> It's the biggest obstacle to entering treatment – people are surrendering their autonomy by entering methadone treatment [...] The stigma of coming in each day and taking a supervised dose is awful. It creates an atmosphere in methadone clinics which is essentially adversarial. We could work against this, you can try, but that's the definition. You're here to be contained and controlled. I think there are few greater problems. It's a necessary safeguard and many people will always need to have daily supervised attention. But it's precisely because you're tarring everyone with the same brush that you create problems and therefore there is a real issue about judiciously deciding who should or should not be eligible for takeaways.
>
> (Phillip, Sydney, NSW, prescriber, 53)

Phillip recognises the problems associated with requiring all clients to attend daily without distinguishing between them (of, it might be said, blindly repeating one approach to dosing), but his formulation concludes by reinforcing the power of the service providers he problematises in the first place: it is they who must 'decide' client access to takeaways. Not surprisingly, given his earlier construction of clients as children in need of firm parenting, they are not represented here as party to decisions around their own treatment. In these respects, both men and women are conceptualised in terms of a deficit of agency and as subject to the power of service providers. For women, however, this subjection is understood more broadly in that they are also conceptualised as subject to the power of male partners. In this, female clients can be said to be doubly subjected through treatment, both to partners and to service providers, and this impacts on treatment delivery.

Repetition as change

Our aim in this chapter has been to demonstrate the ways in which a group of related concepts – addiction, repetition, femininity and passivity or lack of agency – operate intra-actively to materialise treatment in different ways for male and female clients. We have looked at the tendency within Western thought to accrue to repetition negative associations, and for this negative judgement to both reflect and enact other judgements, such as those around perceived feminine attributes, and the question of addiction itself. As Deutscher (2006) notes in relation to de Beauvoir's unstintingly negative take on repetition, however, there are ways in which repetition can be reconceptualised along more positive lines. She turns to the work of Judith Butler, itself inspired partly by de Beauvoir's assertion that one is not born a woman, but rather 'becomes' one. Butler famously conceives gender as performative, as materialised through the repetition of particular gendered acts. As she explains: 'all signification takes place within the orbit of the compulsion to repeat; "agency," then, is to be located within the possibility of a variation on that repetition' (Butler, 1999 [1990]: 185). Indeed, one of the strengths of her approach is the way in which its focus on repetition and citation allows for both the reproduction of norms of gender and for the introduction of change and resistance. As Deutscher (2006: 336) puts it, 'Beauvoir sees sameness as sameness and repetition as repetition rather than [like Butler] difference in sameness and repetition'. She notes that it is the centrality of repetition to the maintenance of social norms that renders them vulnerable. In each re-enactment lies the possibility of change or difference. In Deutscher's view, Butler's work raises a central question, one which Karen Barad, in her emphasis on the phenomenon and on the contingency of realities, might well also ask: 'Is repetition ever just repetition?'

Given that negative valuations of repetition as emblematic of passivity and a lack of progress strongly inform broader social estimations of MMT and of those who undertake it, there is some merit in extending this question to the repetition perceived to be at the heart of treatment. Indeed, there are many instances in the interviews we conducted of repetition in treatment as generating change as much as sameness. Some clients, for example, recounted the ways in which daily dosing can produce a departure from routine. Darren, for example, explains:

> It's like I've got a special little place I put the bottles down there when I take them home, you know, so they're safe and everything

[...] And after you've been, like a couple of months I've been on it, the weekends now, sometimes, um, was it last Sunday or the Sunday before? I woke up at 11 o'clock Sunday night and realised I had just forgotten to take my dose for the day.

(Darren, Sydney, NSW, client, 47)

Graham tells a similar story:

I'll sometimes wake up the next morning all sore and that, and I can't get out of bed. And [partner] will say, 'Well, did you have your 'done last night?' I say, 'I don't know, did I? Is the bottle empty? I mean, go and have a look'. She'll go, 'No, there's still two full bottles', so I didn't take it yesterday. Completely forgot, gone to sleep, you know what I mean (laughs) and then woke up sore the next morning.

(Graham, regional Victoria, client, 39)

Here, change enters subtly, unbidden and only belatedly noted. Where once Darren and Graham had anticipated their doses with some intensity of feeling, the processes of treatment (in this case incorporating take-aways as well as onsite dosing) now mean they are liable to forget to take their methadone at all, until, that is, physical symptoms remind them. With repetition comes rupture: this is the nature of the phenomenon of treatment. Indeed, the contingency acknowledged in the concept of the phenomenon finds no more productive expression than in this subtle yet highly significant process.

In the context of this book, we can, of course, think of repetition as an alternative, or complementary, chronotope to that of the queue described in Chapter 3. Repetition and waiting are heavily implicated in each other, both symbolically and practically. Waiting, too, is constructed as passive, and as such, feminises both men and women, albeit differently. And certainly, it is the repetition of queuing that makes waiting so unbearable for many clients.

Beyond the accounts given by Darren and Graham above, there are other ways in which change is introduced through repetition in treatment, and these can be conceived as far more intentional than those described above. Diversion, the off-label use of methadone such as in selling it to others, sharing it, injecting it, or splitting the dose into two, does happen in MMT (Ward, Mattick and Hall, 1998: 82–3). As we argued in Chapters 2 and 3, by deliberately resisting the rules and regulations of treatment, such acts introduce significant change into the routines of dosing. Not all agency, not all refusal of repetition as sameness, is valued, of course. The agency associated with these (in some cases illegal) acts is generally cast in the negative, or even as another form of compulsion in some instances. Thus, Phillip is able to frame client agency as that of children: in need of containment.

While the material presented earlier indicates the possible role of takeaways in disrupting routine and in allowing agency and change rather than mere repetition, it would be a mistake to think takeaways alone can significantly alleviate concerns about repetition or have the power to change public perceptions of treatment as repetition. After all, takeaways form part of the dailiness or routine of treatment in many clients' estimation. The problematisation of treatment as repetition is based much more strongly on the intra-action of two elements: (1) the broader implications of the status of methadone as 'just like heroin' (see Chapter 1) and (2) the open-ended nature of treatment – its status as chronic – and the reliance of dosing on routine, whether onsite or at home. Both of these aspects exclude clients from qualifying as proper liberal subjects in that they disrupt the fantasy of autonomy and self-determination central to liberal norms.

Conclusion

In concluding this consideration of gender in MMT, two questions remain. Firstly, given the material presented above, is there a sense in which MMT can, or should, be reconceived along lines that emphasise the role of repetition in change, and in so doing potentially raise the status of treatment from that of mere passive maintenance? In Chapter 1 we argued that public understandings of methadone might be improved if it were identified less with ideas of replacement and inauthenticity. Similar shifts around treatment as repetition might be beneficial. As indicated earlier, however, the negative associations operating around methadone are tightly interconnected. As such they might be difficult to change. By the same token, Barad's agential realism reminds us that phenomena perform differently in different encounters. In other words, the very contingency of negative valuations of repetition – their reliance on a series of other negative valuations – can be said to point to their instability. In any case, questions remain here around the denigration of sameness in the first place. Is denying the sameness of treatment, insisting that change too is possible, nothing more than an acceptance of the terms of the debate, of the liberal values of progress and activity that inform MMT's marginalisation? There is no doubt that the conditions of treatment need to improve before clients are likely to find treatment more bearable, but this is a practical issue rather than a matter of the inherent value of change.

Given this chapter's focus on gender, our second remaining question follows from this last dilemma: are current estimations of repetition especially damaging to perceptions of women's agency in treatment, and if so, can this be confronted? The interview material presented above demonstrates clearly the ways in which women's agency is constituted differently in treatment from that of men. Women are understood as doubly subjected, both to service providers and to male clients, and the latter subjection is taken as grounds for treating women differently, indeed, often disadvantageously. While all clients are to some extent 'feminised' by treatment, it seems that women can be doubly so. Again, notions of repetition and passivity are central here, and again, it might be that shifts in the meaning of repetition are called for, both in terms of how repetition is conceived, and also in terms of the need to question the alignment between MMT and repetition in the first place. From this point of view, the repetition of methadone treatment relates to all those involved in it as clients, service providers, researchers, and policymakers. How is treatment – both our understanding of it, and its materialisation in practice – repeated by those involved? This question applies equally to treatment in its immediate contexts, such as in clinics and pharmacies, and its broader contexts, such as in policy, medical literature and research analysing drug use. As we have suggested, it is repetition that opens up the possibility of change. In other words, these many instances of repetition are also potential sites of rupture.

Conclusion: Dependence, Contingency and the Productivity of Problems

As Deleuze has reminded us, intellectual freedom lies not so much in devising answers or solutions but in formulating problems. As he puts it,

> A solution always has the truth it deserves according to the problem to which it is a response, and a problem always has the solution it deserves in proportion to its own truth or falsity ...

> (1994: 159)

The processes by which problems come to be formulated, and the shapes they are given, powerfully influence the kinds of answers and solutions thinkable and enactable. This insight into problems and solutions is precisely what *Substance and Substitution* has been about. There is no doubt that MMT is a curious phenomenon. It is a means of converting an illicit practice into a licit one, largely through two strategies. The first strategy is the replacement of one substance with another only marginally different in molecular makeup. Indeed, as Émilie Gomart (2002) so crucially says, despite our deepest convictions, the properties of substances such as methadone and heroin are performed in practice: they are not ontologically anterior to it. The second strategy is to change, again only marginally or in some respects (as we have seen, the changes are not as radical as they seem), the conditions under which this substance is consumed. What are the implications of these relatively small, but uncannily profound, changes for drug-using individuals and for liberal society as a whole? How does MMT intra-act with(in) liberal values? *What kind of problem throws up methadone maintenance treatment as its solution?* These are the questions we have sought to answer (at least partially) in this book.

In order to approach these questions, we have been obliged to theorise our project and our method along new lines. In the Introduction we brought together the work of Karen Barad and John Law, both of whom start from two ideas. The first is explicitly stated: things (such as method, such as facts, such as realities) could be otherwise. The second is implicit in the ethico-political project of Law and Barad, and of other scholars to whom we are indebted (Foucault, Hacking, Nancy Fraser and de Beauvoir): some phenomena must become otherwise. MMT is one such phenomenon that both could, and must, become otherwise, as much as it is valued and valuable even as it stands. However, as this book has shown, this becoming otherwise is deeply implicated in, indeed it necessitates, the becoming otherwise of many other phenomena. As Barad's concept of intra-action reminds us, all phenomena are contingent upon each other, thus change can never be isolated. Indeed, and this is one of the major methodological insights taken up in this book, phenomena are so ontologically contingent that delineating the boundaries of the object of study is not in itself a straightforwardly methodological, or indeed a logical, procedure. Rather it is one of politics. Delineating the object of study is one part of the process of formulating the 'problem'. Our aim has been to delineate our object's boundaries broadly: to begin from our own initial theoretical and political reflex, that is, from a critical relation to the received wisdom of liberal modernity, and to proceed from a point beyond the standard notion of the individual that so deeply informs understandings of drug use, its problematisation, the solutions offered, and even much of the research conducted around it. Yet, to proceed from a point beyond the individual is not as simple as it seems. If the individual is not the central category – the basic building block – upon which accounts of agency, efficacy, change and politics should be based, what is? Of course, Barad has helped us here: her work has shaped many of the directions our research has taken. Using her notion of the phenomenon, and her focus on materiality and the agency of objects, it is possible to construct accounts of reality that move beyond the obsession with individual human agency. The phenomenon reminds us that all objects rely upon other objects to take shape, and that the shapes objects take vary in relation to their specific encounters over time. This contingency belies the logic of the individual. Related to this, the *agency* of objects, of matter, also disrupts the centrality of the individual. Beyond humans and their supposed autonomous activity, there are material objects which also act (though not, Barad insists, in predictable or essential ways). In this, our work resembles that of Gomart (2004), whose attempt to find instances in which 'the drug user would not be the toy of the drug' (85), leads her to observe that '[t]he drug performs the user as active and, in turn, is performed through the activity of the user' (105).

Already it will have become clear that we are talking here of two nested, or related, issues: MMT as phenomenon, as solution, as object, and our own research project (and this book) as phenomenon, as 'solution' (or response), as object. As Law would put it, we are talking about two method assemblages. MMT is one. This book is another. To reiterate, all method assemblages are responsible for producing realities, and this includes both these assemblages. If, as Barad (among others) argues, representation and reality cannot be separated, it would not be appropriate to instate a formal distinction between our object of study and the research that has emerged from our intra-action with this object. To research and write on a 'problem' is to become a part of that problem – to co-produce it, to become responsible for it. As Barad (1998: 7) says:

> [R]eality is sedimented out of the process of making the world intelligible through certain practices and not others. Therefore, we are not only responsible for the knowledge that we seek but, in part, for what exists.

But perhaps we are getting a little ahead of ourselves here. It is necessary to speak both of the reality 'out-there' of which this book speaks, and also to speak of *how* this book speaks, what it 'gathers', what it makes present. We will begin concluding by addressing the first of these tasks.

Gathering methadone maintenance treatment

Our aim has been to explore the tensions and contradictions entailed in MMT's role within Western liberal societies, to consider the ways in which it attempts to produce the proper, law-abiding, autonomous, responsibilised subject ubiquitous to liberal discourse. As the preceding chapters attest, these tensions and contradictions exist in abundance. Indeed, perhaps the most significant of the book's overall themes is the way in which MMT takes up and then confounds almost every familiar dualism in Western liberal discourse's exquisitely interlinked series of binary oppositions. As we have argued throughout, addiction or dependence is one of liberalism's most despised, and most necessary, creatures. After all, dependence is the concept against which the individual is produced. The elaboration of the binary relation between autonomy and dependence is one of the many operations of the concept of addiction, one partially undertaken by MMT, although, as we have seen, holding this binary stable is no easy feat for this profoundly riven phenomenon. MMT, then, can be seen as a point of condensation through which a whole range of interrelated dualisms flow, ostensibly led, or perhaps compelled, by the intensely political dualism, dependence/autonomy. In the process, these dualisms and their demands shape this site of condensation itself.

Of course, in exploring this central question – precisely how, and to what effect, MMT and liberal discourse/society co-exist – we have also examined a multitude of circumstances, objects and issues related to treatment, and to the experiences of clients, staff and others. By considering in turn some of the major dualisms at work in treatment, and their relation to each other, it is possible to draw out many of these circumstances and experiences. For, while our interest is in the intra-action between the concepts operating in methadone treatment and in Western liberal thought, it is also, overwhelmingly, in the material implications of this conceptual intra-action for people and their daily lives.

The dualisms most commonly encountered in the material collected for this book are:

Autonomy	Dependence
Drug free	Drug addict
Masculine	Feminine
Subject	Object
Active	Passive
Discourse	Matter
Reality	Representation
Originality	Repetition
Real	Replacement

As we have seen (and notwithstanding the apparent order implied in the rather too-neat columns employed above), while these always hierarchically valued dualisms operate in powerful, often intensely disciplinary, ways in MMT, they are also fundamentally disrupted by it. The autonomy/dependence binary is perhaps the most obvious example, in that, as we saw in the Introduction and in later chapters, autonomy is a prime value of liberalism, and while methadone treatment allows clients a degree of autonomy from the demands of an illicit drug-using way of life, it simultaneously imposes a regime that is equally, or more, controlling. As we have seen, autonomy is little more than a fantasy for clients, and this is the case for liberal subjects in general. While clients must shift to daily dosing, and to following the directives of staff, staff themselves are by no means autonomous. They must attend to guidelines and procedures, must answer to others. Our observation here is not a criticism – we do not present autonomy as an ideal, realisable or otherwise. Instead, we register its elusiveness, and also its questionable merit. We are not the first to note that autonomy is a curious ideal, denying, as it does, the richness and productivity of relation, the inevitability of connection and contingency. As MMT figures so nicely, there is no way to move into autonomy. Such moves can only take place from one kind of dependence to another. From this point of view, a new question arises: How can we shape and sustain rich, productive forms of dependence?

Equally central to the operations of addiction and drug treatment mapped in this book is the dualism masculine/feminine. As we saw in Chapter 1, this dualism, and its accompanying denigration of the feminine helps shape public discourse on drug use and drug treatment, in particular through the status of metaphor as feminine, and the status of methadone as itself metaphor. These associations co-produce equally denigrating understandings of drug users and treatment clients, understandings that mirror femininity's central paradox: the requirement to gain full legitimacy within Western liberal institutions and thought and the concomitant impossibility of doing so. The operations of gender within understandings of drug use and drug treatment come up again explicitly in Chapter 5, where the asymmetrical treatment of male and female clients is described, and the associations and reflexes behind this differential treatment are explored. In between these two chapters, however, gender runs as an undercurrent through the phenomena discussed. The links between dependence and femininity within Western thought are robust if often implicit, and these inform the related notion, for example, that drug users require guidance from benign but firm paternal figures (the prescriber, the pharmacist).

In thinking through gender, of course, other associated dualisms emerge. As the link between femininity and metaphor is identified, for example, broader links come into view, such as that between femininity and passivity and repetition. All these terms incorporate the notion of dependence. As femininity is defined as dependence against masculinity's autonomy, passivity against masculinity's activity, repetition against masculinity's originality, it is conceived as intrinsically reliant upon masculinity to provide or provoke those elements of originality, of activity, of autonomy. Within treatment, these links perform, as noted above, in terms of a paternalistic relation. Yet this paternalistic relation does not limit itself to those effects described already. Its implications are, of course, further reaching. Respect (in either direction) between providers and clients is difficult to sustain under conditions of paternalism, and some of the least complimentary images of treatment included in this book can be directly related to the question of what happens when a paternalistic approach comes to be materialised in day-to-day treatment. Indeed, in that drug dependence and treatment tend to feminise all clients (male or female – albeit in different ways), this materialisation is not focused solely on women clients. Here we are thinking, for instance, of the fortress-like dispensaries; of the poorly explained, arbitrary-seeming treatment decisions; and of the unilateral curtailment of takeaway 'privileges'. Some instantiations of this link found elsewhere are even more troubling, such as in the US where blind dosing is an accepted practice.

While MMT operates through these intensely political binaries, it also, however, confounds them, or at least, helps us think differently about them. Chapter 1 reminded us that the representation of MMT in the media is neither intrinsically good nor intrinsically bad: it is a mechanism for co-producing ideas of drug use, and the materiality of treatment itself. In this sense, and following Barad, the representation/reality dualism is of limited analytic utility. On a different note, as we saw in Chapter 2, service providers are not clients' polar opposite: they share something important with clients in that they describe enduring frustratingly paternalistic relations, in their case with regulators. Thus, mapping power here must be undertaken carefully so as to recognise these complexities without flattening power relations. Again taking a slightly different tack, as Chapter 4 showed, treatment undeniably limits the freedoms of clients but it also enables the production of a range of new identities, and these come both from above and below. More broadly, methadone treatment does, of course, confound autonomy/dependence, intoxication/sobriety binaries, and in this sense it has been a radical innovation. At the same time, as we have already noted, this disruption of binaries, in particular the latter, does not go unpenalised. It is part of the reason why both MMT itself and its participants remain marginalised and unable to establish social legitimacy. Nevertheless, it would be a mistake to see MMT as merely a materialisation of hegemonic dualisms. It has a disruptive, excessive quality that means that, despite many of the indignities and privations associated with it, it cannot be dismissed as merely repressive.

Indeed, MMT is such a sprawling, contradictory phenomenon that the question that appears at the outset of this conclusion is probably slightly misconceived. We asked, *what kind of problem throws up methadone maintenance treatment as a solution?* The multifarious, contradictory character of treatment would suggest that it is *a series of partially overlapping problems* that has thrown up this solution, rather than a single, clearly articulated one. Perhaps, then, it is possible to say that MMT exists, that, at least in Australia it is growing, some would say thriving, because it responds to a *confusion* of problems centred on heroin and other opiate use. This confusion cannot quite reach univocality on central questions such as the value of abstinence, the reality of autonomy, the legitimacy of individual responsibility, the merits of conceiving drug use as disease, and clients as ill, the extent of the gap between the respectable 'us' and the marginal 'them'. In this confusion, in this 'mess' as Law might put it, lies most of the scope – most of the potential for becoming otherwise – of MMT. This, of course, is no small, no insignificant, claim. What does it mean to describe MMT as confusion or mess, to focus on its contradictions, and, it must be said, on its shortcomings, as we have done at times in this book?

Research: representation: risk

Here, we return to the second method assemblage noted above. Treatment is the first, this book the second. As method assemblage, *Substance and Substitution* is deeply implicated in its object of study. From the development of research questions to the collection of interview data, the choice of themes through which to sort this data, and the privileging of particular issues, topics, perspectives, this research, as with all other research, has been engaged in the production of partial realities. This process of production is wholly political and carries with it those responsibilities attached to any activity that speaks of – enacts – the lives of others. This principle is particularly solemn where that process involves searching criticism and the presentation of potentially disturbing material. As we have noted, MMT has its opponents. In Australia and overseas there are those who would prefer to see it scaled down or abolished, and some of these opponents have ready access to power. Discussions of MMT in the media can be intensely hostile. Public attitudes towards it are largely unknown, but regularly assumed to be negative. Where opposition exists, it is vocal. All this means criticism carries with it a particularly serious responsibility. There are many ways in which research co-produces the realities it studies, and one of these can be in lending weight to opposition to those realities. This is not the aim of this book. As we have emphasised, MMT – complex, imperfect, contradictory as it is – remains a valuable, in some respects (or, at some junctures) compassionate, phenomenon. Our intention is that the work that appears here be used to generate further thought on the paradoxes of treatment, the challenges clients and providers face, and the many ways in which services could be made more respectful, more humane, and thus more effective. Below we revisit the main observations the book makes on possible changes to treatment. These are some of the nuts and bolts of becoming otherwise. Before turning to this, however, it is also important to reiterate that this book is not solely about one kind of treatment. It is about Western liberal societies in general and what this particular form of treatment exposes and enacts of these. Thus, our observations about the nature of the subject, the asymmetrical valuing of masculinity and femininity, the myth of autonomy, the limits of authenticity, can inform our understanding of other aspects of liberal society. In this, the phenomenon of MMT can surely be defined very broadly.

Becoming otherwise

To return, then, to methadone in its specificity, this book makes a range of recommendations for improving the conceptualisation and delivery of treatment. Our first recommendation is broad in scope. It relates to the argument we make in Chapter 1 about the implications of routinely describing MMT as substitution or replacement therapy. Our view is that understandings of methadone as substitute or replacement operate, at best, as a double-edged sword in defining treatment. While there is no doubt that, for new clients, the notion that a drug might succeed in replacing heroin and circumventing withdrawal can be attractive and comforting. However, as our analysis suggests, these terms do not confer legitimacy or status on treatment or its clients, indeed the opposite is the case. All are associated in culture with inauthenticity, and as a result, their value is permanently in question. It might be that, endemic as this language of substitution has become within treatment and within public discourse on methadone, new terms should be found. The argument made in Chapter 5 supports this suggestion. If replacement or substitution carries with it a sense of mere repetition understood as sameness, it may not do justice to treatment as it is lived. There are other ways of conceptualising repetition, for example, as a condition of possibility for change, and, as we have seen, clients sometimes report experiencing treatment repetition in this alternative way.

To consider this question of representation more generally, we must also consider the argument made about the role of media representation in materialising treatment. Press and other media coverage of drug use and drug treatment is inevitable and in some respects ubiquitous. Our suggestion is that those working in MMT acknowledge this, and view it as an opportunity for materialising treatment in new or better ways. Where silence is maintained, we argue, this opportunity to generate change is lost.

From a discussion of the discursive basis of treatment in Chapter 1, we move to an examination of its regulatory basis in Chapter 2. Here, we make some quite different recommendations, for example, we argue that consistently applied treatment standards need to be devised and enforced. This is difficult to achieve as the poor standards of treatment currently in place are at odds with the intentions of many of the people who work in policy, advocacy and delivery. The shortage of pharmacists and doctors willing to be involved in treatment, and the political difficulties of improving care for drug users, mitigate against measures requiring service providers improve their treatment of clients. As we found during our research (and other research concurs), doctors do not like being told what to do, and pharmacists and nurses feel the same. If individual doctors and pharmacists withdraw from the field of pharmacotherapy treatment, this can have drastic consequences for clients in their area. Usually the program relies heavily on each service provider involved. Nevertheless, there is probably no more direct way than this of improving the experience of treatment for clients (and for clinic and pharmacy staff who dislike the poor standards of treatment they witness). It might be that service providers' equally strong preference for clinical support could be more effectively folded into the rationales provided for any such moves to codify acceptable standards of treatment. In both this and the previous recommendation the emphasis is on elaboration and expression rather than silence.

Related to this focus on elaboration and expression in treatment, we argue that risk management principles should be communicated more effectively to clients if they are to remain embedded in treatment. If, for instance, the limitations imposed on takeaway provision are mirrored by limitations imposed on the broader community when strong pain medications are prescribed, then this should be made known. Our data suggest that, at present, methadone clients believe themselves exceptional in terms of the limits placed on access to their medication.

Addressing the practices of individual service providers, while useful, is not the whole answer, of course. As Chapter 4 demonstrates, service providers recognise the needs and capacities of clients, and would like to be able to refer clients to other services where appropriate: housing, employment, counselling and parenting assistance are the most obvious. MMT does not exist in a vacuum, and cannot address all its clients' needs. Issues of interagency partnership and referral are often discussed in the context of meeting the complex needs of drug users, but a more pertinent question is often the existence and accessibility of these services in the first place. As we have argued, the forms that solutions take reflect the efficacy with which problems have been formulated. To generate valuable solutions we must formulate problems insightfully and clearly. Treating MMT as the provision of a drug and little else entails a particularly narrow view of the 'problem' of regular heroin use, and is unlikely to generate the necessary resourcing or, in turn, produce optimal results.

There is, of course, a burgeoning literature on poverty as a 'determinant' of problematic drug use. Our focus has been on the responsibilities of the state to meet the needs of its (present and potential) citizens – nevertheless, it is clear the retreat of the state has the greatest impact on those without resources, and methadone clients are often among these. This point invokes another potent binary with which we have been concerned, that of the opposition between the material and the intimate (between base and superstructure; between the economic and the cultural). Connected very closely with the real/representation binary, this is also concerned with 'material' in a different register from Barad's materiality: that of materialist criticism, especially that concerned with the lives of the socially marginalised. We have operated from a critical perspective on any distinction between the material and the ideal. Poverty and privilege do not 'cause' the practices of everyday life, any more than everyday habits cause poverty, but neither do intimate practices and material resources float free of each other. While rejecting the trend to enumerate the cultural deficits of clients, caused by their poverty or drug use or both, we have nonetheless been concerned throughout to elaborate the enfolding of the material and the intimate.

Such enfolding practices include those noted in Chapter 3, where excesses of waiting and queuing were described, along with alienating treatment such as outdoor dosing. This chapter included the most directly formulated recommendations of all chapters, many of which relate to the conclusions drawn in the others. Is treatment adequately funded? Are enough places available? Are the environments in which treatment is delivered given sufficient attention as to comfort and security? Is urine testing conducted in the most efficient, most humane way? Indeed, is its indispensability regularly reviewed? If, as we have argued, MMT produces the very subjects it seeks to cure, how can it be redesigned to minimise this tendency?

Part of this process of elaboration also involves generating greater awareness of the heterogeneity of clients, and this was in part the aim of Chapter 4. The most visible clients are usually the most marginalised.

The majority of methadone clients do not make demands on an over-stretched system, do not place themselves or their children in danger, and do not require extra surveillance or support. The right of these clients to be 'invisible' within policy and media debates must be protected, at the same time as their existence is acknowledged. Where adequate recognition of the diversity among clients occurs, insufficiently respect-ful practices will neither be conceived nor tolerated.

In the last chapter we examined the operations of gender in materi-alising treatment, and found, among other things, that asymmetrical understandings of men's and women's agency significantly influenced treatment decisions among service providers. Decisions about continu-ing to treat clients or referring them on, decisions about allowing clients' takeaways, decisions about dosing levels: all these are co-produced through gender, though rarely in considered ways. As we argued, the notions of agency informing these decisions are directly linked to con-cepts of repetition and passivity at work in treatment, and all these related concepts (again, those found in the dualisms laid out earlier) impact on male and female clients in different ways. This chapter prompts two quite different recommendations, then. One returns to a point made earlier on questioning the benefits of conceiving treatment as repetition (in particular as sameness), and proposing new ways of thinking treatment that incorporate the possibility of change without elevating it to an ideal. The second is more local: training for service providers needs to consider carefully the ways in which understandings of gender result in male and female clients being treated differently and, in particular, responsibilising women not only for their own acts, but for those of their male associates as well.

In making all these observations and recommendations, we stress that our main emphasis is not on individual (be they client or staff) defi-ciencies and solutions, although of course we have relied on the time and generosity of individuals in sharing their experiences of treatment, and this book has been animated by their accounts. Instead, we call for change that involves a different scale of analysis – the reconceptualisa-tion of key concepts, the rethinking of central relationships, the expan-sion of funding. In keeping with our argument, of course, the changes we propose do not invoke sobriety, autonomy or rationality. In all this critique and construction, however, we take a risk. This is the very real risk we call on others to take: that of representation, and its concomi-tant (yet unruly) materialisations.

Our intention is that amid the many ideas and paradoxes thrown up by this book, our central set of concepts, and the relations between them, repeat, and in that repetition, propose and even signal change. What does MMT *do*? What is the relationship between concepts and matter? What, and who, acts? How can agency be understood within a critical approach to liberal values? Lastly, what is research, what is its action and its responsibilities? This final question is, of course, merely a specific instance of the three questions that came before – concepts, matter, agency. All these questions, these terms, are contingent. Indeed, they are entirely intra-active, or we could say, 'intra-dependent'. Here, of course, we invoke dependence deliberately. As this book has suggested, aversion to dependence is at the centre of addiction's denigration, and MMT's marginalisation. Yet dependence is intrinsic to us all: clients; service providers; those in policy and the media; researchers; and families, friends and acquaintances of those in treatment. All co-constitute, albeit some more directly than others, the phenomena of addiction and treatment, so all are intra-actively responsible for their materialisation.

Notes

Introduction

1. See Persson (2004) on *pharmakon*, specifically in relation to anti-retroviral therapy for HIV.
2. Methadone treatment is also finding increasing acceptance in other locations, especially South East Asia and Eastern Europe, but the systems of delivery there are often very different: restricted, for example, to prison populations. (Irawati et al., 2006; U.S. Department of State, 2006)
3. So named because they are located in the community, not because they are not-for-profit. Community pharmacies are privately owned businesses.
4. This is of course a single example of a much broader field of scholarship: Nancy Fraser's work is exemplary (N. Fraser, 1995; N. Fraser, 1997; Fraser and Gordon, 1997).
5. As is perhaps signalled by the use of terms from baseball ('three strikes') in welfare reform. Baseball is of marginal interest to the Australian population at large.
6. The starting dose of methadone is low, around 30 mg (effective doses are thought to be 60–80 mg on average), and is only increased gradually. In part this is because of the time taken for methadone to equilibrate with tissue reservoirs and accumulate in the body. There are concerns that too high initial doses will lead to overdose. Commencement of treatment is distressing for many clients as they can experience severe withdrawal symptoms until their dose rises to become adequate. Many continue to use heroin during this time (this is both a cause and effect of the starting dose being so low). In NSW there were 134 methadone-related deaths between 1990 and 1995. Drug overdose accounted for 84 of these, 24 of which occurred in the first 7 days of treatment (Sunjic and Zador, 1997).
7. Resource scarcity is evident in other, less effective but more politically popular modes of treatment as well, such as residential rehabilitation. The costs of these treatments are not always borne by the client, as some are with pharmacotherapies. Methadone and buprenorphine are subsidised through the Pharmaceutical Benefits Scheme (PBS), but clients pay around $30 a week for a dispensing fee from pharmacists or clinics. Clients who have no access to a free bulk-billing doctor (who is paid directly by the government through Medicare) also need to pay consultation fees when getting their prescriptions renewed.
8. Aspects of Barad's theory will be familiar from existing science studies work such as actor network theory. Most useful for the argument we wish to make here is her appealing synthesis of aspects of this theory, combined with her innovative use of Butlerian performativity in thinking through the action of matter.
9. Indeed, Haraway's *Modest Witness* (1997) comments on material-semiotic aspects of blood in contexts such as genomics, race and family.

10. This project has been approved by the UNSW Human Research Ethics Committee, and by relevant state and area health service ethics committees.
11. Among the service users interviewed for the Victoria arm of this study were three individuals who were on buprenorphine treatment at the time of interview. All had been in MMT in the past, and were interviewed because some aspects of MMT are closely linked to aspects of buprenorphine treatment.
12. After data collection, each interview was de-identified, cleaned and coded. Each participant was assigned a pseudonym to protect anonymity. The data were then analysed to identify themes.
13. Research Participants:

		n=	Female	Male	Age range
Service Users (total = 50)	NSW metro	20	8	12	27–52
	NSW regional	5	2	3	24–49
	Vic metro	20	12	8	24–47
	Vic regional	5	1	4	31–39
Health care workers (total = 29)	NSW metro	10	4	6	32–55
	NSW regional	5	1	4	45–59
	Vic metro	9	3	6	36–62
	Vic regional	5	2	3	37–54
Policy (total = 8)	NSW	5	2	3	44–61
	Vic	3*	0	3	42–'50-ish'
	TOTAL	87*			

*Two interview participants classified as Health Care Workers (HCW) were also classified as policymakers in the analysis due to their experience in both service delivery and policy development.

1 Substitution, Metaphor and Authenticity

1. Items retrieved via Factiva do not include full page numbers, therefore these will not be supplied with quotations.
2. Figures retrieved from the United States Audit Bureau of Circulations web site (http://www.accessabc.com/), retrieved 6 June 2006.
3. Figures retrieved from the United Kingdom Audit Bureau of Circulations web site (http://www.abc.org.uk), retrieved 6 June 2006.
4. Figures retrieved from the John Fairfax Holdings Publishers' Statements, released 21 April 2006.
5. Helen Keane makes a similar observation in her invaluable book, *What's Wrong with Addiction?* See page 62.
6. Other examples include: Holden, 2005; Kurutz, 2004; Macleod, 2004; Lister, 2004; and O'Neill, 2004.
7. We do not wish to imply that withdrawal symptoms are 'merely' the product of representation, and so of little import or power. Rather, our argument is

informed by scholarship indicating the fragility of *norms of* withdrawal (see for example Keane, 2002).
8. In this vein, Sedgwick (1993) writes persuasively on the powerful dualism central to notions of addiction: that of free will and compulsion.
9. Here we do not assume that such support is usually uncomplicated or unconditional. Many who support the programs at least in Australia see them as a flawed solution to a historically and politically contingent (even produced) problem.

2   Governing Treatment

1. The 1999 documents were in place during our period of data collection, which took place between July 2004 and May 2006. The 2006 documents were obviously in the process of being compiled, drafted and refined during this time.
2. As noted in the Introduction, these are doses which clients take away from the clinic or pharmacy premises and self-administer. They are highly valued by clients as they reduce the number of days on which they have to attend dosing points, and make working, going on holiday and other activities easier.
3. 'What scant data are available indicate that the consumers of diverted methadone are mostly established heroin users. However, there is one group of opioid naïve persons at risk of death from takeaway doses. Children, especially those of parents taking part in a methadone program, have occasionally died as a result of taking methadone [...] methadone was detected postmortem in eight children who died between July 1990 and December 1995 in NSW. In five of these children, methadone was presumed to have contributed to death. In three children, the child had ingested the mother's takeaway dose' (Bell and Zador, 2000). Victoria has a smaller population than NSW and fewer analyses of this type exist, but the situation appears to be similar: in 1997, for example, 'three of the four methadone single-drug deaths [...] were well established in their treatment. The fourth death was a non-registered user who took a friend's methadone' (Bystrzycki and Coleridge, 2000).
4. The NSW definitions of 'access' remain substantially unchanged in the 2006 guidelines.

3   The Chronotope of the Queue

1. At the time our interviews were conducted, regularity of attendance at the dosing point was guided by recommendations made in the New South Wales Methadone Maintenance Treatment Clinical Practice Guidelines (NSW Health, 1999), which limited the recommended number of takeaways to be prescribed to clients. Depending upon the length of time a client had been in treatment, and assessment of other aspects of treatment such as the client's level of continued illicit drug use, between zero and four takeaways per week were prescribed. In some cases, however, the number of takeaways prescribed did exceed the level recommended in the guidelines. After the

interviews were conducted, new guidelines were released (see NSW Health, 2006). These do not allow for an increase in takeaway availability, indeed, in some respects they regulate takeaway access more heavily.

2. The data used in this chapter comprise our New South Wales client data set of twenty-five interviews. Twenty confidential interviews were conducted in the Sydney metropolitan area, and another five in the Hunter region of New South Wales.

3. Australian Institute of Health and Welfare, 2005: 68. The remaining 19 per cent are dosed under a variety of different structures including in prisons, and via combined public/private arrangements.

4. While methadone maintenance treatment is considered a treatment for addiction (where addiction is defined as dependence upon a drug or other substance/practice), it also involves a continuation of addiction in these terms in that clients take regular doses of methadone and experience withdrawal symptoms when doses are missed.

5. This interview was conducted by Nadine Krejci.

6. Notwithstanding this, some fine work which engages with aspects of the risk 'environment' of drug use, and the spatiality of drug use, has also been published in recent years. See for instance, Dovey et al., 2001; Measham, 2004; Moore and Dietze, 2005 and Rhodes et al., 2005. It would be productive, we think, to consider some of the issues raised in this body of work (for example those around haste in injecting) from the point of view of the intra-activity of space and time.

7. It is, of course, possible to argue that the world not only shapes the text, but that the reverse is also true (indeed, Barad, who will be returned to later, argues against representationalism).

8. Belinda Davis's history, *Home Fires Burning: Food, politics, and everyday life in World War I Berlin* (2000), provides an account of the hardship often associated with queuing for essential goods in wartime.

9. We are indebted to Susan McGuckin of the New South Wales Users' and AIDS Association for drawing this distinction to our attention.

10. Moran (2005) observes that bus queues can see violent acts too. He notes that 'The bus queue is a reminder that even the most mundane routines incorporate complex spatial politics and cultural meanings'. Moran's observation highlights the contribution of spatial arrangements (and temporal ones too) to the generation of violence, even, it appears, among those otherwise considered ordinary, respectable members of society. His comments, in other words, suggest that violence, or other behaviour, should not be seen as the product of intrinsic attributes of individuals, but of phenomena produced in intra-action.

4 Treatment Identities

1. There are a small number of cases recorded annually of parents and carers administering methadone to children; also a small number of children drinking methadone that has been improperly stored or sealed is recorded. Three reviewable child deaths in 2005 were related to methadone poisoning (NSW Ombudsman, 2006). Of 10,133 hospitalisations of children aged 0–4 years in

Australia between the years 1999/00 to 2003/04, 313 had taken the class of drugs in which methadone is included (Cripps and Steel, 2006).

5 Repetition and Rupture: The Gender of Agency

1. This estimate was supplied in a personal communication by Dr Alex Wodak, St Vincent's Hospital, New South Wales.
2. See Chapter 3 for a detailed discussion of the implications of Lenson's observation.

Bibliography

Adkins, L. (2001). Risk culture, self-reflexivity and the making of sexual hierarchies. *Body & Society, 7*(1), 35–55.

Adkins, L. (2002). *Revisions: Gender and sexuality in late modernity.* Buckingham: Open University Press.

Agar, M., Bourgois, P., French, J. & Murdoch, O. (2001). Buprenorphine: "Field trials" of a new drug. *Qualitative Health Research, 11*(1), 69–84.

Altman, M. (1990). How not to do things with metaphors we live by. *College English, 52*(5), 495–506.

Altman, D. (1994). *Power and community: Organizational and cultural responses to AIDS.* London and Bristol, PA: Taylor & Francis.

Anderson, J., Perry, J., Blue, C., Browne, A., Henderson, A., Khan, K. B. et al. (2003). "Rewriting" cultural safety within the postcolonial and postnational feminist project: Toward new epistemologies of healing. *Advances in Nursing Science, 26*(3), 196–214.

Ashton, M. & Witton, J. (2004). The power of the welcoming reminder. *Drug and Alcohol Findings, 11,* 4–18.

Australian Council of Social Services. (2006). *ACOSS welfare to work recommendations 2006.* Sydney: Australian Council of Social Services.

Australian Government. (2003). *Road to recovery: Report on the inquiry into substance abuse in Australian communities.* Canberra: Parliament of Australia.

Australian Government. (2006). *Budget 2005–6.* Canberra: Commonwealth of Australia.

Australian Injecting & Illicit Drug Users League. (2006, 18 November 2006). *AIVL home page.* Retrieved 14 December 2006 from http://www.aivl.org.au/default.asp.

Australian Institute of Health and Welfare. (2005). *Alcohol and other drug treatment services in Australia 2003–4: Report on the national minimum data set* (Drug Treatment Series 4). Canberra: AIHW.

Australian Institute of Health and Welfare. (2006a). *Alcohol and other drug treatment services in Australia 2004–05: Report on the national minimum data set* (Drug Treatment Series Number 5). Canberra: AIHW.

Australian Institute of Health and Welfare. (2006b). *Australia's health 2006.* Canberra: AIHW.

Bakhtin, M. (1981). *The dialogic imagination* (Trans. S. Emerson and M. Holquist). Austin and London: University of Texas Press.

Banwell, C. (2003). "Methadone mothers": Converging drug and mothering discourses and identities. *Sites: A journal of social anthropology, 1*(1), 133–160.

Banwell, C. & Bammer, G. (2006). Maternal habits: Narratives of mothering, social position and drug use. *International Journal of Drug Policy, 17,* 504–530.

Barad, K. (1998). Getting real: Technoscientific practices and the materialisation of nature. *differences: a journal of feminist cultural studies, 10*(2), 87–128.

Barad, K. (2001). Re(con)figuring space, time, and matter. In M. Dekoven (Ed.), *Feminist locations: Global and local, theory and practice* (pp. 75–109). New Brunswick, NJ and London: Rutgers University Press.

Barad, K. (2003). Posthumanist performativity: Toward an understanding of how matter comes to matter. *Signs: Journal of women in culture and society, 28*(3), 801–831.

Barnett, P., Rodgers, J. & Bloch, D. (2001). A meta-analysis comparing buprenorphine to methadone for treatment of opiate dependence. *Addiction, 96*(5): 683–690.

Bath, N. (2006). When you can't see the wood for the trees: Drug treatment consumer satisfaction – what does it really tell us? *9th Social Research Conference on HIV, Hepatitis C and Related Diseases, StigmaPleasurePractice.* Sydney.

Beck, U. (1992). *Risk society: Towards a new modernity.* London: Sage.

Beck, U. (2004). Cosmopolitical realism: On the distinction between cosmopolitanism in philosophy and the social sciences. *Global Networks: A Journal of Transnational Affairs, 4*(2), 131–156.

Bell, J. & Zador, D. (2000). A risk-benefit analysis of methadone maintenance treatment. *Drug Safety, 22*(3), 179–190.

Bergson, H. (1955). *An introduction to metaphysics.* New York: Bobbs-Merrill.

Bessant, J. (2002). The politics of official talk about welfare. *Just Policy, 28,* 12–22.

Bird, S. (2004). One left an adoring family, the other fled parental abuse and racism. *Times (London),* 31 January.

Bleich, A., Gelkopf, M., Hayward, R. & Adelson, M. (2001). A naturalistic study on ending blind dosing in a methadone maintenance clinic in Israel. *Drug and Alcohol Dependence, 61*(2), 191–194.

Boeri, M. (2004). "Hell, I'm an addict, but I ain't no junkie": An ethnographic analysis of aging heroin users. *Human Organisation, 63*(2), 236–245.

Bourdieu, P. (1995). Structures, habitus, practice. In J. D. Faubion (Ed.), *Rethinking the subject: An anthology of contemporary European social thought* (pp. 31–45). Boulder, CO: Westview Press.

Bourgois, P. (1995). *In search of respect: Selling crack in el barrio.* Cambridge and New York: Cambridge University Press.

Bourgois, P. (2000). Disciplining addictions: The bio-politics of methadone and heroin in the United States. *Culture, Medicine and Psychiatry, 24*(2), 165–195.

Braithwaite, V., Gatens, M. & Mitchell, D. (2002). If mutual obligation is the answer, what is the question? *Australian Journal of Social Issues, 37*(3), 225–245.

Brodie, J. F. & Redfield, M. (Eds). (2002). *High anxieties: Cultural studies in addiction.* Berkeley: University of California Press.

Broom, D. & Stevens, A. (1990). Doubly deviant: Women using alcohol and other drugs. *International Journal on Drug Policy, 2,* 25–27.

Brown, R. M. (2000). Community health within the context of health reform. *Australian Journal of Primary Health, 6*(1), 85–96.

Brownlie, J. (2001). The "being-risky" child: Governing childhood and sexual risk. *Sociology, 35*(2), 519–537.

Bryant, J., Saxton, M., Madden, A., Bath, N. & Robinson, S. (forthcoming[a]). *The National Treatment Service Users (TSU) Project.* Monograph (no. pending), Sydney: National Centre in HIV Social Research.

Bryant, J., Saxton, M., Madden, A., Bath, N. & Robinson, S. (forthcoming[b]). Consumers' and providers' perspectives about consumer participation in drug treatment services: Is there support to do more? What are the obstacles? Under review with *Drug & Alcohol Review.*

Burroughs, W. (1982). The naked lunch. In J. Calder (Ed.), *A William Burroughs reader* (pp. 25–130). London: Pan.

Butler, J. (1999 [1990]). *Gender trouble: Feminism and the subversion of identity*. New York and London: Routledge.

Bystrzycki, A. & Coleridge, J. (2000). Drug- and poison-related deaths in Victoria during 1997. *Emergency Medicine, 12*, 303–309.

Calsyn, D. A. & Saxon, A. J. (1999). An innovative approach to reducing cannabis use in a subset of methadone maintenance clients. *Drug and Alcohol Dependence, 2*(7), 167–169.

Cass, B. & Brennan, D. (2002). Communities of support or communities of surveillance and enforcement in welfare reform debates. *Australian Journal of Social Issues, 37*(3), 247–262.

Castel, R. (1991). From dangerousness to risk. In G. Burchell, C. Gordon & P. Miller (Eds), *The Foucault effect: Studies in governmentality*. Chicago: University of Chicago Press.

Castles, F. G. (2001). A farewell to Australia's welfare state. *International Journal of Health Services, 31*(3), 537–544.

Charmaz, K. (1997). *Good days, bad days: The self in chronic illness and time*. New Brunswick, NJ: Rutgers University Press.

Chater, D. (2004). Viewing guide: Television. *Times (London)*, 8 June.

Chessell, J. (2004). Argus to take iris scans to market. *Sydney Morning Herald*, 19 March.

Chutuape, M., Silverman, K. & Stitzer, M. (2001). Effects of urine-testing frequency on outcome in a methadone take-home contingency program. *Drug and Alcohol Dependence, 62*(1), 69–76.

Cixous, H. (1976). The Laugh of the Medusa. *Signs, 1*(4), 875–893.

Clarke, A. E., Shim, J. K., Mamo, L., Fosket, J. R. & Fishman, J. R. (2003). Biomedicalization: Technoscientific transformations of health, illness, and US biomedicine. *American Sociological Review, 68*(2), 161–194.

Cook, D. M. & Fine, M. (1995). "Motherwit": Childrearing lessons from African-American mothers of low income. In B. B. Swadner & S. Lubeck (Eds), *Children and families "At promise": Deconstructing the discourse of risk*. Albany, NY: State University of New York Press.

Coomber, R., Morris, C. & Dunn. L. (2000). How the media do drugs: Quality control and the reporting of drug issues in the UK print media. *International Journal of Drug Policy, 11*, 217–225.

Courtwright, D. T. (1997). The prepared mind: Marie Nyswander, methadone maintenance, and the metabolic theory of addiction. *Addiction, 92*(3), 257–265.

Cripps, R. & Steel, D. (2006). *Childhood poisoning in Australia*. Adelaide: AIHW National Injury Surveillance Unit, Research Centre for Injury Studies.

D'Aunno, T. & Pollack, H. A. (2002). Changes in methadone treatment practices: Results from a national panel study, 1988–2000. *JAMA, 288*(7), 850–856.

Davis, B. (2000). *Home fires burning: Food, politics, and everyday life in World War I Berlin*. Chapel Hill and London: University of North Carolina Press.

de Beauvoir, S. (1984 [1949]). *The second sex* (Trans. H. M. Parshley). Harmondsworth: Penguin.

Deleuze, G. (1994 [1968]). *Difference and repetition* (Trans. P. Patton). New York: Columbia University Press.

Denton, B. (2001). *Dealing: Women in the drug economy*. Sydney: UNSW Press.

Department of Health, Scottish Office Department of Health, Welsh Office & Department of Health and Social Services Northern Ireland. (1999). *Drug *misuse and dependence – guidelines on clinical management*. London: The Stationery Office.

Derrida, J. (1974). White mythology: Metaphor in the text of philosophy (Trans. F.C.T. Moore). *New Literary History, 6*(1), 5–74.

Derrida, J. (1993). The rhetoric of drugs. An interview. *differences: A Journal of Feminist Cultural Studies, 5*(1), 1–25.

Deutscher, P. (2006). Repetition facility: Beauvoir on women's time. *Australian Feminist Studies, 21*(51), 327–342.

Deveaux, M. (1994). Feminism and empowerment: A reading of Foucault. *Feminist Studies, 20*(2), 223–247.

Digiusto, E., Shakeshaft, A. P., Ritter, A., Mattick, R. P., White, J., Lintzeris, N., Bell, J., Saunders, J. P. & NEPOD Research Group. (2006). Effects of pharma-cotherapies for opioid dependence on participants' criminal behaviour and expenditure on illicit drugs: An Australian national evaluation (NEPOD). *Australian and New Zealand Journal of Criminology, 39*, 171–189.

Dole, V. & Nyswander, M. (1967). Heroin addiction – a metabolic disease. *Archives of Internal Medicine, 120*, 19–24.

Douglas, M. (1990). Risk as a forensic resource. *Daedalus, 119*(4), 1–16.

Dovey, K., Fitzgerald J. & Choi, Y. (2001). Safety becomes danger: Dilemmas of drug-use in public space. *Health & Place, 7*(4), 319–331.

Drug and Alcohol Services Information System. (2006). *The DASIS report.* Rockville, MD: Office of Applied Studies, Substance Abuse and Mental Health Services Administration.

Drugs and Poisons Regulations Group. (2006). *Policy for Maintenance Pharmacotherapy for Opioid Dependence.* Melbourne: Department of Human Services.

Duden, B. (1993). *Disembodying women: Perspectives on pregnancy and the unborn* (Trans. L. Hoinacki). Cambridge, MA: Cambridge University Press.

During, S. (1993). Introduction. In S. During (Ed.), *The cultural studies reader* (pp. 1–25). London and New York: Routledge.

Elliott A. & Chapman, S. (2000). "Heroin hell their own making": Construction of heroin users in the Australian press 1992–97. *Drug and Alcohol Review, 19*, 191–201.

English, S. (2005). Father stabbed ex-partner to death in front of girls. *Times (London)*, 18 March.

Erian, A. (2005). Eternal sunshine of the addicted mind. *New York Times*, 27 March.

Esping-Andersen, G. (1990). *The three worlds of welfare capitalism.* London: Polity.

Fiellin, D. & Lintzeris, N. (2003). Methadone syrup injection in Australia: A sentinel finding? (editorial). *Addiction, 98*, 385–386.

Fiellin, D. A., Friedland, G. H. & Gourevitch, M. N. (2006). Opioid dependence: Rationale for and efficacy of existing and new treatments. *Clinical Infectious Diseases, 43*(12), S173–S178.

Foucault, M. (1973). *The birth of the clinic: An archaeology of medical perception* (Trans. A. M. Sheridan). London: Tavistock.

Foucault, M. (2003). *"Society must be defended": Lectures at the College de France, 1975–76.* New York: Picador.

Fraser, J. (1997). Methadone clinic culture: The everyday realities of female methadone clients. *Qualitative Health Research, 7*(1), 121–139.

Fraser, N. (1995). What's critical about critical theory? In J. Meehan (Ed.), *Feminists read Habermas: Gendering the subject of discourse.* New York and London: Routledge.

Fraser, N. (1997). *Justice Interruptus: Critical reflections on the 'postsocialist' condition.* New York and London: Routledge.

Fraser, N. (2003). From discipline to flexibilisation? Rereading Foucault in the shadow of globalisation. *Constellations*, *10*(2), 160–171.

Fraser, N. & Gordon, L. (1997). A genealogy of "dependency": Tracing a keyword of the US welfare state. In N. Fraser (Ed.), *Justice interruptus: Critical reflections on the "postsocialist" condition*. New York and London: Routledge.

Fraser, S. (2003). *Cosmetic surgery, gender and culture*. Basingstoke: Palgrave Macmillan.

Fraser, S. (2004). "It's your life!": Injecting drug users, individual responsibility and hepatitis C prevention. *Health: An Interdisciplinary Journal for the Social Study of Health, Illness and Medicine*, *8*(2), 199–221.

Fraser, S. & Moore, D. (in press). Dazzled by unity? Order and chaos in public discourse on illicit drug use. *Social Science & Medicine* (accepted 12 September 2007).

Fraser, S. & Treloar, C. (2006). "Spoiled identity" in hepatitis C infection: The binary logic of despair. *Critical Public Health*, *16*(2), 99–110.

Fraser, S. & valentine, k. (2006). "Making blood flow": Materialising blood in body modification practice and blood-borne virus prevention. *Body & Society*, *12*(1), 97–119.

Friedman, J. & Alicea, M. (2001). *Surviving heroin: Interviews with women in methadone clinics*. Gainesville, FL: University Press of Florida.

Gascon, J. J., Sanchez-Ortuno, M., Llor, B., Skidmore, D. & Saturno, P. J. (2004). Why hypertensive patients do not comply with the treatment: Results from a qualitative study. *Family Practice*, *21*(2), 125–130.

Gibbs, S. (2004). Sniffed out and searched: One man's humiliation. *Sydney Morning Herald*, 2 July.

Gibson, D. R., Flynn, N. M. & McCarthy, J. J. (1999). Effectiveness of methadone treatment in reducing HIV risk behaviour and seroconversion among injecting drug users. *AIDS*, *13*, 1807–1818.

Giddens, A. (1998). Risk society: The context of British politics. In J. Franklin (Ed.), *The politics of risk society*. Cambridge: Polity.

Giddens, A. (2001). Introduction. In A. Giddens (Ed.), *The global third way debate*. Cambridge: Polity.

Gomart, E. (2002). Methadone: Six effects in search of a substance. *Social Studies of Science*, *32*(1), 93–135.

Gomart, E. (2004). Surprised by methadone: In praise of drug substitution treatment in a French clinic. *Body & Society*, *10*(2–3), 85–110.

Gourlay, J., Ricciardelli, L. & Ridge, D. (2005). Users' experiences of heroin and methadone treatment. *Substance Use and Misuse*, *40*(12), 1875–1882.

Great Britain. (2006). Hansard, House of Commons, 18 May, Column 1169w.

Greene, J. Y., Weinberger, M., Jerin, M. J. & Mamlin, J. J. (1982). Compliance with medication regimens among chronically ill inner city patients. *Journal of Community Health*, *7*(3), 183–193.

Grosz, E. (1994). *Volatile bodies: Toward a corporeal feminism*. St Leonards, Allen and Unwin.

Hacking, I. (1983). *Representing and intervening: Introductory topics in the philosophy of natural science*. Cambridge: Cambridge University Press.

Hacking, I. (1995). *Rewriting the soul: Multiple personality and the sciences of memory*. Princeton, NJ: Princeton University Press.

Hacking, I. (2002). *Historical ontology*. Cambridge, MA and London: Harvard University Press.

Hall, W., Ward, J. & Mattick, R. (1998). Introduction. In J. Ward, R. Mattick & W. Hall, (Eds), *Methadone maintenance treatment and other opioid replacement therapies* (pp. 1–14). Amsterdam: Harwood.

Hall, W., Ward, J. & Mattick, R. (1998). The effectiveness of methadone maintenance treatment 1: Heroin use and crime. In J. Ward, R. Mattick, & W. Hall, (Eds), *Methadone maintenance treatment and other opioid replacement therapies* (pp. 17–57). Amsterdam: Harwood.

Haraway, D. (1991a). A cyborg manifesto: Science, technology and socialist feminism in the late twentieth century. In *Simians, cyborgs and women: The reinvention of nature* (pp. 149–181). New York and London: Routledge.

Haraway, D. (1991b). Situated knowledges: The science question in feminism and the privilege of partial perspective. In *Simians, cyborgs and women: The reinvention of nature* (pp. 183–201). New York and London: Routledge.

Haraway, D. (1992). The promises of monsters: A regenerative politics for inappropriate/d others. In L. Grossberg, C. Nelson, & P. Treichler, (Eds), *Cultural studies* (pp. 295–337). New York and London: Routledge.

Harden, J. (2000). Language, discourse and the chronotope: Applying literary theory to the narratives in health care. *Journal of Advanced Nursing, 31*(3), 506–512.

Hartouni, V. (1997). *Cultural conceptions: On reproductive technologies and the remaking of life.* Minneapolis, MN and London: University of Minnesota Press.

Helén, I. (2004). Technics over life: Risk, ethics and the existential condition in high-tech antenatal care. *Economy & Society, 33*(1), 28–51.

Holden, S. (2005). Samurai, drugs, a failed revolution and a sick health system. *New York Times,* 24 September.

Howard, J. & Newman, J. (2000). *Statement in response to final report of the reference group on welfare reform.* Canberra: Department of Family and Community Services.

Hubbard, R. (1995). Genes as causes. In V. Shiva & I. Moser (Eds), *Biopolitics: A feminist and ecological reader on biotechnology* (pp. 38–51). London: Zed Books.

Huyssen, A. (1986). *After the great divide: Modernism, mass culture, postmodernism.* Bloomington, IN and Indianapolis: Indiana University Press.

Irawati, I., Mesquita, F., Winarso, I., Hartawan & Asih, P. (2006). Indonesia sets up prison methadone maintenance treatment. *Addiction, 101*(10), 1525.

Irigaray, L. (1985 [1977]). *This sex which is not one* (Trans. C. Porter). Ithaca, NY: Cornell University Press.

Jacobs, A. (2004). Crystal meth use by gay men threatens to reignite an epidemic. *New York Times,* 12 January.

Janusz, S. (1994). Feminism and metaphor: Friend, foe, or force? *Metaphor & Symbolic Activity, 9*(4), 289–300.

John Fairfax Holdings (2006). *Publishers' statements: Circulation figures for newspapers and the Internet for 6 months to March 2006.* Report released 21 April.

Jones, L. (2003). Life imitates art: The chronotope of the Twin Towers in fact and fiction. *Australian Humanities Review, 29,* 1–8.

Kaufman, L. (2004). Amid Upper East Side wealth, a beggar found open hearts. *New York Times,* 14 February.

Keane, H. (2002). *What's wrong with addiction?* Carlton South: Melbourne University Press.

Keane, H. (2003). Critiques of harm reduction, morality and the promise of human rights. *International Journal of Drug Policy, 14*(3), 227–232.

Keire, M. (1998). Dope fiends and degenerates: The gendering of addiction in the early twentieth century. *Journal of Social History, 31*(4), 809–822.

Kilgannon, C. (2005). Casting methadone as ingredient for a cross-addiction. *New York Times,* 6 October.

Klingemann, H. (2000). "To everything there is a season" – social time and clock time in addiction treatment. *Social Science & Medicine, 51,* 1231–1240.

Koester, S., Anderson, K. & Hoffer, L. (1999). Active heroin injectors' perceptions and use of methadone maintenance treatment: Cynical performance or self-prescribed risk reduction? *Substance Use & Misuse, 34*(14), 2135–2153.

Körner, H. & Treloar, C. (2004). Needle and syringe programs in the local media: "Needle anger" versus "effective education in the community". *International Journal of Drug Policy, 15,* 46–55.

Kurutz, S. (2004). Up in the old hotel. *New York Times,* 13 June.

Latham, M. (2001). The third way: An outline. In A. Giddens (Ed.), *The global third way debate.* Cambridge: Polity.

Law, J. (2004). *After method: Mess in social science research.* London and New York: Routledge.

Le Doeuff, M. (1989). *The philosophical imaginary* (Trans. C. Gordon). Stanford: Stanford University Press.

Lenson, D. (1995). *On drugs.* Minneapolis, MN and London: University of Minnesota Press.

Levitas, R. (1998). *The inclusive society? Social exclusion and new labour.* Basingstoke: Macmillan.

Lewontin, R. (2000). The dream of the human genome. In G. Bender & G. Druckrey (Eds), *Culture on the brink* (pp. 107–128). Seattle: Bay Press.

Lilly, R., Quirk, A., Rhodes, T. & Stimson, G. V. (2000). Sociality in methadone treatment: Understanding methadone treatment and service delivery as a social process. *Drugs: Education, Prevention & Policy, 7*(2), 163–178.

Lister, D. (2005). Pounds 5 cocaine becoming the new drug of choice. *Times (London),* 1 April.

Lister, S. (2004). Seven doctors face GMC over controversial heroin treatment. *Times (London),* 5 October.

Lovejoy, M., Rosenblum, A., Magura, S., Foote, J., Handelsman, L. & Stimmel, B. (1995). Patients' perspective on the process of change in substance abuse treatment. *Journal of Substance Abuse Treatment, 12*(4), 269–282.

Mackenzie, A. (2002). *Transductions: Bodies and machines at speed.* London and New York: Continuum

Macleod, A. (2004). Methadone addicts the new worry, says Goldie. *Times (London),* 2 December.

Maher, L. (1997). *Sexed work: Gender, race and resistance in a Brooklyn drug market.* Oxford and New York: Clarendon Press.

Maher, L. (2002). Don't leave us this way: Ethnography and injecting drug use in the age of AIDS. *The International Journal of Drug Policy, 13*(4), 311–325.

Malins, P., Fitzgerald, J. L. & Threadgold, T. (2006). Spatial "folds": The entwining of bodies, risks and city spaces for women injecting drug users in Melbourne's central business district. *Gender, Place and Culture, 13*(5), 509–527.

Marston, G. & Watts, R. (2004). The problem with neo-conservative social policy: Rethinking the ethics of citizenship and the welfare state. *Just Policy, 33,* 34–45.

May, C. (2001). Pathology, identity and the social construction of alcohol dependence. *Sociology, 35*(2), 385–401.

McArthur, M. (1999). Pushing the drug debate: The media's role in policy reform. *Australian Journal of Social Issues, 34*(2), 149–165.

Measham, F. (2004). Play space: Historical and socio-cultural reflections on drugs, licensed leisure locations, commercialisation and control. *International Journal of Drug Policy, 15*(5–6), pp. 337–345.

Middleton, R. (1996). Over and over: Notes towards a politics of repetition. *Beitrag zur Konferenz Grounding Music.* Retrieved 12 February 2007 from http://www2.hu-berlin.de/fpm/texte/middle.htm.

Miller, D. (2006). The politics of metaphor. *Theory, Culture & Society, 23*(2–3), 63–65.

Mitchell, T., Dyer, K. & Peay, E. (2006). Patient and physician characteristics in relation to clinical decision making in methadone maintenance treatment. *Substance Use & Misuse, 41*(3), 393–404.

Moore, D. (1990). Anthropological reflections on youth drug use research in Australia: What we don't know and how we should find out. *Drug and Alcohol Review, 9*(4), 333–342.

Moore, D. (1992). Deconstructing "dependence": An ethnographic critique of an influential concept. *Contemporary Drug Problems, 19*(3), 459–490.

Moore, D. (2004). Governing street-based injecting drug users: A critique of heroin overdose prevention in Australia. *Social Science & Medicine, 59*(7), 1547–1557.

Moore, D. & Dietze, P. (2005). Enabling environments and the reduction of drug-related harm: Re-framing Australian policy and practice. *Drug and Alcohol Review, 24*(3), 75–284.

Moore, D. & Fraser, S. (2006). Putting at risk what we know: Reflecting on the drug-using subject in harm reduction and its political implications. *Social Science & Medicine, 62,* 3035–3047.

Moore, Dawn (2004). Drugalities: The generative capabilities of criminalized "drugs". *International Journal of Drug Policy, 15*(5–6), 419–426.

Moran, J. (2005). *Reading the everyday.* London and New York: Routledge.

Mugford, S. K. & O'Malley, P. (1991). Heroin policy and deficit models. *Crime, Law and Social Change, 15*(1), 19–36.

Murphy, S. & Irwin, J. (1992). "Living with the dirty secret": Problems of disclosure for methadone maintenance clients. *Journal of Psychoactive Drugs, 24*(3), 257–264.

Mykhalovskiy, E., McCoy, L. & Bresalier, M. (2004). Compliance/adherence, HIV, and the critique of medical power. *Social Theory & Health, 2*(4), 315–340.

N.A. (2004). Heroin dealer pensioner hid drug in his stick. *Times (London),* 16 October.

National Centre in HIV Epidemiology and Clinical Research. (2006a). *Australian NSP survey national data report 2001–2005.* Sydney: National Centre in HIV Epidemiology and Clinical Research, University of New South Wales.

National Centre in HIV Epidemiology and Clinical Research. (2006b). *HIV/AIDS, viral hepatitis and sexually transmissible infections in Australia annual surveillance report 2006.* Sydney: National Centre in HIV Epidemiology and Clinical Research, University of New South Wales.

Neale, J. (1998). Drug users' views of prescribed methadone. *Drugs: Education, prevention and policy, 5*(1), 33–45.

Neale, J. (1999). Understanding drug-using clients' views of substitute prescribing. *British Journal of Social Work, 29*, 127–145.

Nelkin, D. & Lindee, S. (1995). *The DNA mystique: The gene as cultural icon.* New York: W. H. Freeman.

Newbury, C. (2000). Patrons, clients, and empire: The subordination of indigenous hierarchies in Asia and Africa. *Journal of World History, 11*(2), 227–263.

NSW Health. (1999). *NSW methadone maintenance treatment clinical practice guidelines.* Sydney: NSW Health Department.

NSW Health. (2006). *NSW opioid treatment program: Clinical guidelines for methadone and buprenorphine treatment of opioid dependence.* Sydney: Mental Health and Drug & Alcohol Office, NSW Department of Health.

NSW Ombudsman. (2006). *Report of reviewable deaths in 2005 volume 2: Child deaths.* Sydney: NSW Ombudsman.

O'Connor, A. (2004). New ways to loosen addiction's grip. *New York Times,* 3 August.

O'Neill, D. (2000). Victoria: Rolling back – or reinventing – the Kennett revolution? *Australian Journal of Public Administration, 59*(4), 109–115.

O'Neill, S. (2004). Rapist's victim died alone with pills by her side. *Times (London),* 25 August.

Ogden, J. (1995). Psychosocial theory and the creation of the risky self. *Social Science & Medicine, 40*(3), 409–415.

Olsen, P. & Champlin, D. (1998). Ending corporate welfare as we know it: An institutional analysis of the dual structure of welfare. *Journal of Economic Issues, 22*(3), 1998.

Orcutt, J. & Turner, B. (1993). Shocking numbers and graphic accounts: Quantified images of drug problems in the print media. *Social Problems, 40*(2), 190–206.

Otten, C. (1986). Introduction. In C. Otten (Ed.), *A lycanthropy reader: Werewolves in Western culture* (pp. 1–17). Syracuse, NY: Syracuse University Press.

Oxford English Dictionary. (1989). Addiction. *OED Online.* Oxford University Press. 11 January 2007. http://dictionary.oed.com/cgi/entry/50002459?single=1&query_type=word& queryword=addiction&first=1&max_to_show=10.

Oxford English Dictionary. (1989). Guide. *OED Online.* Oxford University Press. 26 March 2007. http://dictionary.oed.com/cgi/entry/50100042?query_type=word&queryword=guide&first=1&max_to_show=10&sort_type=alpha&result_place=2&search_id=tbyl-kMnpns-13074&hilite=50100042.

Pani, P., Pirastu, R., Ricci, A. & Gessa, G. (1996). Prohibition of take-home dosages: Negative consequences on methadone maintenance treatment. *Drug and Alcohol Dependence, 41*, 81–84.

Parton, N. (1998). Risk, advanced liberalism and child welfare: The need to rediscover uncertainty and ambiguity. *British Journal of Social Work, 28*, 5–27.

Patton, C. (1990). *Inventing AIDS.* New York: Routledge.

Peel, M. (2003). *The lowest rung: Voices of Australian poverty.* Cambridge, New York, Port Melbourne, Madrid, Cape Town: Cambridge University Press.

Pelly, M. (2004). When treatment is scarier than jail. *Sydney Morning Herald,* 26 February.

Persson, Asha (2003). Incorporating pharmakon: HIV, medicine and body shape change. *Body & Society, 10*(4), 45–67.

Persson, A. (2004). Incorporating Pharmakon: HIV, medicine and body shape change. *Body & Society, 10*, 45–67.

Petersen, A. (1997). Risk, governance and the new public health. In A. Petersen & R. Bunton (Eds), *Foucault, health and medicine* (pp. 189–206). London and New York: Routledge.

Quint, J., Edin, K., Buck, M. L., Fink, B., Padilla, Y. C., Simmons-Hewitt, O. et al. (1999). *Big cities and welfare reform: Early implementation and ethnographic findings from the project on devolution and urban change*: Manpower Demonstration Research Corporation. Retrieved 25 January 2007 from http://www.wkkf.org/Pubs/Devolution/Big_Cities_and_Welfare_Reform_Urban_Changes_00331_02740.pdf.

Quirion, B. (2003). From rehabilitation to risk management: The goals of methadone programs in Canada. *International Journal of Drug Policy, 14*(3), 247–255.

Race, K. (2003). The death of the dance party. *Australian Humanities Review, 30*. Retrieved 12 February 2007 from http://www.lib.latrobe.edu.au/AHR/archive/Issue-October-2003/race.html.

Reed, L. (1967). I'm waiting for the man. On *The Velvet Underground & Nico* [record album]. Verve-Polygram.

Reference Group on Welfare Reform. (2000). *Final report: Participation support for a more equitable society*. Canberra: Department of Family and Community Services.

Reith, G. (1999). In search of lost time: Recall, projection and the phenomenology of addiction. *Time and society, 8*(1), 99–117.

Reynolds, R. (2002). *From camp to queer: Remaking the Australian homosexual*. Carlton South: Melbourne University Press.

Rhoades, H., Creson, D., Elik, R., Schmitz, J. & Grabowski, J. (1998). Methadone dose and visit frequency. *American Journal of Public Health, 88*(1), 34–39.

Rhodes, T., Singer, M., Bourgois, P., Friedman, S. R. & Strathdee, S. A. (2005). The social structural production of HIV risk among injecting drug users. *Social Science and Medicine, 61*(5), pp. 1026–1044.

Ricoeur, P. (1978). *The rule of metaphor*. London: Routledge and Kegan Paul.

Roberts, C. (2006). "What can I do to help myself?" Somatic individuality and contemporary hormonal bodies. *Science Studies, 19*, 54–76.

Roberts, C., valentine, k. & Fraser, S. (forthcoming). Rationalities and non-rationalities in clinical encounters: Methadone maintenance treatment and hormone replacement therapy.

Rødner, S. (2005). "I am not a drug abuser, I am a drug user": A discourse analysis of 44 drug users' construction of identity. *Addiction Research and Theory, 13*(4), 333–346.

Rofes, E. (1998). *Dry bones breathe: Gay men creating post-AIDS identities and cultures*. New York: Haworth Press.

Room, R. (2003). The cultural framing of addiction. *Janus Head, 6*(2), 221–234.

Rosaldo, R. (1989). *Culture and truth: The remaking of social analysis*. Boston, MA: Beacon Press.

Rose, N. (1996). *Inventing our selves: Psychology, power, and personhood*. Cambridge and New York: Cambridge University Press.

Rose, N. (2001a). The neurological self and its anomalies [electronic version]. In R. Ericson (Ed.), *Risk and morality*. Toronto: University of Toronto Press. http://www.lse.ac.uk/collections/sociology/pdf/Rose-TheNeurochemicalSelfandItsAnomaliesOct01.pdf

Rose, N. (2001b). The politics of life itself. *Theory Culture & Society, 18*(6), 1–30.

Rose, N. & Novas, C. (2005). Biological citizenship [electronic version]. In A. Ong & S. Collier (Eds), *Global assemblages: Technology, politics and ethics as anthropological problems.* Malden, MA: Blackwell. http://www.lse.ac.uk/collections/sociology/pdf/RoseandNovasBiologicalCitizenship2002.pdf

Rosenbaum, M. (1985). A matter of style: Variation among methadone clinics in the control of clients. *Contemporary Drug Problems, 12*(3), 375–399.

Rouse, J. (2004). Barad's feminist naturalism. *Hypatia, 19*(1), 142–161.

Rowe, J. (2002). Heroin epidemic! Drugs and moral panic in the western suburbs of Melbourne 1995–6. *Just Policy, 27*, 38–45.

Russell, B. (2000). Rebuilding Victoria after Kennett. *Dissent, 1*, 54–57.

Savage, S., Joranson, D., Covington, E., Schnoll, S., Heit, H., & Gilson A. (2003). Definitions related to the medical use of opioids: Evolution towards universal agreement. *Journal of Pain and Symptom Management, 26*(1): 655–667.

Scalmer, S. (2006). Searching for the aspirationals. *overland, 180*, 5–9.

Scott, D. (2006). Sowing the seeds of innovation in child protection, *10th Australasian Child Abuse and Neglect Conference.* Wellington, New Zealand.

Sedgwick, E. (1993). Epidemics of the will. In E. Sedgwick, *Tendencies* (pp. 130–142). Durham, NC: Duke University Press.

Sedgwick, E. K. (1992). Epidemics of the Will. In J. Crary & S. Kwinter (Eds), *Incorporations.* New York: Zone.

Seitz, J. (1991). Composition's misunderstanding of metaphor. *College Composition and Communication, 42*(3): 288–298.

Shand, F. L. & Mattick, R. (2002). *Clients of treatment service agencies: May 2001 census findings.* Canberra: Commonwealth Department of Health and Ageing.

Sitzia, J. & Wood, N. (1997). Patient satisfaction: A review of issues and concepts. *Social Science & Medicine, 45*(12), 1829–1843.

Smith, N. (1992). Contours of a spatialised politics: Homeless vehicles and the production of geographical scale. *Social Text, 33*, 54–81.

Southgate, E. & Hopwood, M. (1999). *The drug use and gay men (DUGM) project issue papers 1–5.* Sydney: National Centre in HIV Social Research, University of New South Wales.

Squier, S. (2004). *Liminal lives: Imagining the human at the frontiers of biomedicine.* Durham, NC: Duke University Press.

Stancliff, S., Elana Myers, J., Steiner, S. & Drucker, E. (2002). Beliefs about methadone in an inner-city methadone clinic. *Journal of Urban Health, 79*(4), 571–578.

Stanton, P., Young, S. & Willis, E. (2003). Financial restraint, budget cuts and outsourcing: Impact of the new public management of health care in Victoria. *Contemporary Nurse, 2003*(14), 2.

Stengers, I. & Ralet, O. (1997). Drugs: ethical choice or moral consensus. In I. Stengers (Ed.), *Power and invention: situating science* (pp. 215–231). Minneapolis, MN: University of Minnesota Press.

Sunjic, S. & Zador, D. (1997). Methadone-related deaths in New South Wales. *Medical Journal of Australia, 167*(3), 174.

Teo, P. (2000). Racism in the news: A critical discourse analysis of news reporting in two Australian newspapers. *Discourse and Society, 11*(1), 7–49.

Thorpe, D. & Bilson, A. (1998). From protection to concern: Child protection careers without apologies. *Children & Society, 12*, 373–386.

Tong, J. (2004). Finally, tasting success in battling a tenacious foe. *New York Times*, 16 January.

Treloar, C. & Fraser, S. (2007). Public opinion on NSPs: Avoiding assumptions for policy and practice. *Drug and Alcohol Review, 26*, 355–361.

Treloar, C., Fraser, S. & valentine, k. (2007). Valuing methadone take-away doses: The contribution of service user perspectives to policy and practice. *Drugs: Education, prevention and policy, 14*(1), 61–74.

Treloar, C. & Körner, H. (2005). NSPs and the media: A case study of balanced and accurate reporting? (letter). *Australian and New Zealand Journal of Public Health, 29*(5), 489–490.

Turner, B. (1992). *Regulating bodies: Essays in medical sociology.* New York: Routledge.

UNAIDS. (2007). *United States of America.* Retrieved 7 February 2007 from http://www.unaids.org/en/Regions_Countries/Countries/united_states_of_america.asp.

U.S. Department of State. (2006). *International narcotics control strategy report.* Washington, DC: Bureau for International Narcotics and Law Enforcement Affairs.

Valverde, M. (1998). *Diseases of the will: Alcohol and the dilemmas of freedom.* Cambridge, Melbourne and New York: Cambridge University Press.

van Dyke, L. (2003). Milking the system. *overland, 170*, 110–116.

Vice, S. (1997). *Introducing Bakhtin.* Manchester and New York: Manchester University Press.

Waldby, C. (1986). *Mothering and addiction: Women with children in methadone programs* (monograph series no. 4). Canberra: Australian Government Publishing Service.

Waldby, C. (1996). *AIDS and the body politic: Biomedicine and sexual difference.* London: Routledge.

Ward, J., Mattick, R., & Hall, W. (1998). *Methadone maintenance treatment and other opioid replacement therapies.* Amsterdam: Harwood.

Warren, C. (2005). My addiction to addicts; First Person. *Times (London)*, 7 February.

Watney, S. (1994). *Practices of freedom: Selected writings on HIV/AIDS.* Durham, NC: Duke University Press.

Willems, D. (1998). Inhaling drugs and making worlds: A proliferation of lungs and asthmas. In M. Berg & A. Mol (Eds), *Differences in medicine* (pp. 105–118). Durham, NC, and London: Duke University Press.

Wodak, A. (2002). Methadone and heroin prescription: Babies and bath water. *Substance Use & Misuse, 37*(4), 523–531.

Wodak, A. & Cooney, A. (2006). Do needle syringe programs reduce HIV infection among injecting drug users: A comprehensive review of the international evidence. *Substance Use & Misuse, 41*, 777–813.

Wright, A. L. & Morgan, W. J. (1990). On the creation of "problem" patients. *Social Science &Medicine, 30*(9), 951–959.

Index